Transformative Learn Creative Life Writing

Arising from a research project conducted over two years, *Transformative Learning through Creative Life Writing* examines the effects of fictional autobiography on adult learners' sense of self. Starting from a teaching and learning perspective, Hunt draws together ideas from psychodynamic psychotherapy, literary and learning theory, and work in the cognitive and neurosciences of the self and consciousness, to argue that creative life writing undertaken in a supportive learning environment, alongside opportunities for critical reflection, has the power to transform the way people think and learn. It does this by opening them up to a more embodied self-experience, which increases their awareness of the source of their thinking in bodily feeling and enables them to develop a more reflexive approach to learning.

Hunt locates this work within recent developments in the influential field of transformative learning. She also identifies it as a form of therapeutic education arguing, contrary to those who say that this approach leads to a diminished sense of self, that it can help people to develop a stronger sense of agency, whether for writing or learning or relations with others. Topics covered include:

- creative writing as a tool for personal and professional development
- the transformative benefits and challenges of creative writing as a therapeutic activity
- the relationships between literary structures and the processes of thinking and feeling
- the role of cognitive-emotional learning in adult education
- collaborative learning and the role of the group.

This book will interest teachers in adult, further and higher education who wish to use creative life writing as a tool for learning, as well as health care professionals seeking art-based techniques for use in their practice. It will also prove useful to academics interested in the relationship between education and psychotherapy, and in the theory and practice of transformative learning. Additionally, it will appeal to writers seeking a deeper understanding of the creative process.

Celia Hunt is Emeritus Reader in Continuing Education (Creative Writing) at the University of Sussex, where she founded the pioneering MA Creative Writing and Personal Development. She was awarded a National Teaching Fellowship by the Higher Education Academy in 2004.

Transformative Learning through Creative Life Writing

Exploring the self in the learning process

Celia Hunt

LONDON AND NEW YORK

First published 2013
by Routledge
2 Park Square, Milton Park, Abingdon, Oxon OX14 4RN

Simultaneously published in the USA and Canada
by Routledge
711 Third Avenue, New York, NY 10017

Routledge is an imprint of the Taylor & Francis Group, an informa business

© 2013 C. Hunt

The right of the editor C. Hunt to be identified as the author of the editorial material, and of the contributing author Christine Cohen Park for her individual appendix chapter, has been asserted in accordance with sections 77 and 78 of the Copyright, Designs and Patents Act 1988.

All rights reserved. No part of this book may be reprinted or reproduced or utilised in any form or by any electronic, mechanical, or other means, now known or hereafter invented, including photocopying and recording, or in any information storage or retrieval system, without permission in writing from the publishers.

Trademark notice: Product or corporate names may be trademarks or registered trademarks, and are used only for identification and explanation without intent to infringe.

British Library Cataloguing in Publication Data
A catalogue record for this book is available from the British Library

Library of Congress Cataloging in Publication Data
Hunt, Celia.
Transformative learning through creative life writing:exploring the self in the learning process / Celia Hunt.
    pages cm
Includes bibliographical references.
1. Creative writing – Study and teaching. 2. Transformative learning.
3. Self in literature. I. Title.
PE1404.H85 2013
808'.042071 – dc23   2013000631

ISBN: 978-0-415-57843-1 (hbk)
ISBN: 978-0-415-57842-4 (pbk)
ISBN: 978-0-203-81813-8 (ebk)

Typeset in Galliard
by Cenveo Publisher Services

Printed and bound in Great Britain by
TJ International Ltd, Padstow, Cornwall

redemption in part lies ... in awakening ourselves to the spatiality of our being and tuning ourselves to its demands and possibilities.
Maxine Sheets-Johnstone, '*Can* the body ransom us?'
The Corporeal Turn, 2009

For Bernard Paris,
dear friend and mentor,
with love and thanks

Contents

	Introduction	ix
1	Creative life writing for personal and professional development	1

PART I
Stories of transformative change — 13

2	Expanding the psyche through the learning process	15
3	Finding a stance as a writer: Simon's story	29
4	Reconnecting with the felt body for writing and learning: Maria's story	40
5	Re-conceptualising the self in time: Susanna's story	50

PART II
Understanding mechanisms of change in transformative learning — 61

| 6 | Reflexivity and the psyche as a dynamic system | 65 |
| 7 | Vicissitudes of the dynamic psyche and their consequences for learning and creativity | 79 |

PART III
Facilitating transformative change through creative life writing — 97

| 8 | Developing reflexivity through creative life writing | 103 |

Contents

  9 Reflexivity and group process   119

10 Reflection and reflexivity   132

PART IV
Implications for adult learning   147

11 Challenges of transformative learning through
      creative life writing   151

12 Is transformative learning a form of
      therapeutic education?   164

      Conclusion   172

      Appendix by Christine Cohen Park: The
           Cohen Park Exercises   175

      References   178

      Index   188

Introduction

This book and the research on which it is based have occupied me for the past eight years. During that time the programme of study that is the book's subject – the Postgraduate Diploma, subsequently MA in Creative Writing and Personal Development at Sussex University – has been discontinued in the wake of the Labour government's decision not to continue subsidising people wishing to study in higher education at a level equivalent to, or lower than, the qualifications they already hold, and the resulting dissolution of adult education departments at British universities. This was a considerable blow for an area of work – the use of creative writing as a developmental and therapeutic tool – that was just establishing itself in higher education, and very distressing for the students who were taking the programme at the time and for the tutors who had been teaching it for many years. It was also a considerable blow for me personally, came late to the academic world and spent most of my time there developing this work. My retirement in 2010 to coincide with the discontinuation of the programme left me deeply disappointed, but it made the writing of this book doubly important as a record of a powerful learning experience for many people. I hope that it will provide an insight into an approach to learning that draws on psychodynamic psychotherapy, and will encourage others to take this work forward.

From the start of my involvement in academic research I have been fascinated by the effects on students of engaging in what I originally called 'fictional autobiography' and am now calling 'creative life writing'. I define this as creative writing that uses fictional and poetic techniques to capture self-experience, including physical and emotional experience, personal memories, and present and past relations with others (Hunt, 2010a). My interest in this was stimulated initially by the benefits I myself experienced from using fictional and poetic techniques to encapsulate my thinking and feeling in psychotherapy in the late 1980s. When in 1991 I started teaching creative writing at Sussex, I found that many of my students benefited in a similar way from fictionalising themselves and significant people in their lives; this happening serendipitously rather than as a result of the aims of the course. In 1994 I embarked on research into these benefits, looking at the experience of students taking my creative writing course 'Autobiography and Imagination', the first term of a one year Certificate in Creative Writing offered by the then Centre for Continuing Education (CCE). I concluded from that study that starting to write by fictionalising self-experience not only helped students to find a better working relationship between the creative and critical faculties in their writing process, but also had the potential for enhancing the flexibility of the psyche more generally, and that therefore this approach could be useful in a therapeutic context (Hunt, 2000).

In 1996, at the CCE's suggestion, I set up the postgraduate programme in creative writing and personal development (CWPD),[1] with an explicit focus on the use of creative life writing as a developmental and therapeutic tool. As with the Certificate course, from very early on in the life of the CWPD programme[2] significant numbers of students were telling me that they had undergone major changes as a result of their studies. For some people this involved what they referred to as a 'breakthrough' (their word) in their ability to write or study, against a background of blocks to, or difficulties with, learning or writing, with the result that they now felt able to take themselves seriously as writers or to consider embarking on a doctorate. For others it involved a 'life-changing' (again, their words) shift, such as being able to make the decision to leave or take a lengthy break from professional careers, in order to find more meaningful employment or life situations. Some people also found themselves making the decision to leave long-term relationships, often something they had previously felt they needed to do, but on which they had been unable to act. Whilst these are clearly different kinds of changes, the common factor underlying them is an increase in the ability to act on one's own behalf, in other words an increased sense of agency.

At the same time as I was hearing these stories, I was becoming increasingly aware of the challenges of the programme both to students and to tutors. Undergoing such major life changes meant that students often felt exposed and fragile during their studies, and the tutor team was having to learn sometimes very painful lessons about what it could and could not do safely in this challenging learning environment. My research into the effects of the Certificate course had helped me to gain some understanding of how and why creative life writing could enhance students' sense of agency, but now that I was running a programme of study specifically focused on the developmental potential of this kind of writing, I needed to understand more deeply how the programme as a whole worked to facilitate these changes, so that the learning environment could be structured and managed to best effect.

The opportunity to undertake further research arose in 2004 when I was awarded a National Teaching Fellowship by the Higher Education Academy, with £50,000 to undertake a project of my choice. This enabled me to set in train a new project focused on gaining a deeper understanding of the nature of the changes in students' sense of self as a result of the programme, the elements of the programme that facilitated these changes, and the challenges it posed for students and tutors, with the aim not just of informing our own teaching but of making this knowledge more broadly available to the adult learning community.

This book presents the results of that research. It builds on my previous research into students' experience of the Certificate course (Hunt, 2000), but in light of critiques of that book I have broadened my primary focus on the dynamics of individual psychology to look more broadly at the teaching and learning context, thus making it more of a psycho-social project. Seeing also that, since I published my previous research, I have been immersing myself in the cognitive neuroscience of the self and consciousness, my approach here could be more accurately described as bio-psycho-social (Froggett and Richards, 2002). Such a cross-disciplinary approach might seem ambitious. However, seeing that my main concern is the self, it was impossible not to engage with this important new work, and I was encouraged by other psychodynamically based researchers who were treading the bio-psycho-social path. Alan Shuttleworth (2002), for example, describes how the findings of neuroscience forced him to 'stretch' his thinking about his child psychotherapy practice beyond his psycho-social grounding in object relations theory. I like his metaphor of stretching thinking; it implies transgressing the boundaries of one's own discipline to get a different perspective on the phenomena one is seeking to understand, which is precisely what I have been doing. It has been a difficult challenge but one that has enriched my thinking enormously.

So what constitutes my bio-psycho-social approach? It is probably true to say that my approach has always been psycho-social, although I did not think of it that way. I came to social research with a strong background in the psychodynamic thinking of Karen Horney (1885–1952), a leading representative of the 'interpersonal' school. Ironically, seeing that one of the critiques of my work is that it has focused too much on individual psychology and neglected the broader social and cultural context, interpersonal theorists such as Horney have often been disparaged (by Freudians and object relations theorists) as 'culturalist' or 'sociological' (Greenberg and Mitchell, 1983: 80). In fact, whilst Horney certainly went through a 'cultural phase' when she moved from Germany to America in the 1930s, her 'mature' theory (Paris, 1994) embraces intrapsychic as well as interpersonal mechanisms. Both of these have been important for my own thinking; for example the way that, as Horney puts it, personality problems often develop in response to difficult childhood environments or challenging life experience in adolescence or adulthood, but are compounded by psychic vicious circles.

Horney's theory continues to be at the heart of my thinking, although I also draw on object relations theory,[3] including the work of Marion Milner and Christopher Bollas on the creative process, and that of Donald Winnicott and Wilfrid Bion on 'holding' and 'containment' as applied to the learning environment. The work of Peter Fonagy, who develops Bowlby's attachment theory, has helped me to extend my thinking about the developmental role of feeling and emotion, and how problems in this area can inhibit learning throughout life. However, to borrow Shuttleworth's helpful taxonomy, all these might be thought of as the 'intimately psycho-social' dimension of my approach, which previously dominated to the exclusion of the 'micro- and macro-social' (Shuttleworth, 2002: 207–8). In this new research, then, the main stretching of my thinking is towards the micro-social in the form of a deeper exploration of the contribution to students' changes of the broader learning environment of the CWPD programme, in particular the effects of the collaborative, experiential group work that was at the heart of our approach. Work in social realism by Gordon Brown, amongst others, has been helpful here. In thinking more broadly about the nature of the learning taking place in the CWPD programme, I draw extensively on a large body of learning theory and practice originating in the USA known as 'transformative learning', which resonates strongly with the approach we developed at Sussex. As the title of this book indicates, transformative learning has become my primary way of thinking about the CWPD programme. I have also expanded my thinking to embrace a macro-social dimension, responding to the critique of 'therapeutic education' by Kathryn Ecclestone and Dennis Hayes, who argue that it infantilises learners and compromises the intellectual pursuit of knowledge.

As to the 'bio' component of my bio-psycho-social approach, my thinking has been strongly influenced by the work of neuroscientist Antonio Damasio, amongst others, on the central role of bodily feeling and emotion in our sense of self and the operation of reason. Iain McGilchrist's work on the relationship between the brain's hemispheres has also been fundamental, as has dynamic systems theory, which I have come to via Andrew Tershakovec's pioneering attempt to place Karen Horney's thinking in a dynamic systems framework. I have also found helpful the coming together of neuroscience, phenomenology, and embodied cognition in the work of Mark Johnson, Shaun Gallagher, and Dan Zahavi.

So there are many different strands to my bio-psycho-social approach – the intimately psycho-social, the micro- and macro-social, and the biological – and whilst I have made a point of separating them out here, in the discussions that follow they are not so easily distinguished; rather they provide, I hope, a more rounded and multi-levelled understanding of the changes students have experienced as a consequence of engaging in creative life writing in a personal development context.

The research project

The research was carried out within what I have come to think of as an embodied critical realist paradigm, drawing both on the social theory of critical realism (Sayer, 2000) and on the cognitive theory of embodied realism (Lakoff and Johnson, 1999). Whilst these ontological theories originate in different traditions, there are some strong similarities between them (Nellhaus, 2004). Both assume that there is a world independent of our understanding of it, of which we can have stable knowledge. Both also see that knowledge as mediated by the concepts and theories we use to make sense of the world, but for critical realism these concepts and theories arise out of social discourses, whilst for embodied realism they arise first and foremost out of the human body's on-going interaction with the environment. However, critical realist theorising has recently shifted towards embodiment, with reality being conceptualised as 'stratified', i.e. consisting of a series of layers including the socio-cultural, the psychological, and the biological (Bhaskar and Danermark, 2006). This has enabled me to stretch critical realism's fundamental concern with the relationship between social structure and individual agency to embrace the psychological and biological realms as well. I have similarly stretched critical realism's key concept of emergence, which indicates the way that 'particular combinations of things, processes and practices in social life frequently give rise to new emergent properties' (Carter and New, 2004: 7), to include the psychological and the biological. Both of these are key ontological themes in the findings of my research.

There is also a strong similarity in the epistemological thinking of critical and embodied realism. Critical realism argues that, whilst our theories will always be fallible, through our research we will progressively develop better interpretations of reality that are not so much true in any absolute sense as 'practically adequate' (Sayer, 2000: 40); that is, adequate to explain the way the world works in practice. Embodied realism also looks for 'converging evidence' (Lakoff and Johnson, 1999: 89) of how the world works, for example by bringing into relation the findings from first-person phenomenological research and cognitive neuroscience (Gallagher and Zahavi, 2008). Thus an embodied critical realism with a stratified ontology fits well with my bio-psycho-social conceptual framework and my quest to understand not only psychic mechanisms involved in individual change but also mechanisms at work in the learning environment out of which that change emerges.

My preference for a form of realism stems from my long-term conviction, based on my own experience and my immersion in Karen Horney's ideas, that there is something innately real about the experience of self and that it is possible to feel more or less real; this is contrary to the dominant constructivist and poststructuralist view that the self is purely an effect of language. Horney's idea that there is a 'real self' at the heart of the psyche, which is the basis for the development of values and a sense of agency (Horney, 1951), is admittedly unclear – it sometimes sounds like an entity and sometimes like a bodily-felt process. But in light of the new thinking about self and consciousness in the cognitive and neurosciences, where the self is being understood as first and foremost an innate, bodily-felt process and only secondarily as a product of language, Horney's ideas take on new meaning (see Chapter 6).

Within the broad paradigm of embodied critical realism, I have used an eclectic methodology. I have explored my research questions both intensively and extensively, on the critical realist view that 'Extensive research shows us mainly how extensive certain phenomena and patterns are in a population, while intensive research is primarily concerned with what makes things happen in specific cases' (Sayer, 2000: 21). The extensive dimension of the research involved generating retrospective material via a questionnaire from students who took the CWPD programme in its various forms between 1996 and 2002 (56 respondents). I refer to these as Group 1. The intensive dimension involved generating material contemporaneously via questionnaires and interviews from 15 students taking the two-year part-time Master's during 2004–06. I refer to these as Group 2. I was also able to draw on all the work for assessment from this latter group, including their creative writing. Both groups were diverse in age and background (see Chapter 1), but predominantly female. The intensive dimension also included an interview with three tutors of the programme: Christine Cohen Park, Cheryl Moskowitz, and Sarah Salway.

The interviews were interactive (Sayer, 2000: 21), meaning an approach in which the interviewer does not attempt to minimise her presence, on the critical realist assumption that the research context is an open, or quasi-closed (see Part III), system that cannot be isolated. For example, I shared my own personal experience when appropriate, and the students and I sometimes engaged in collaborative interpretation of their experience, so that the interviews became a 'transitional space' for change (Merrill and West, 2009). This is consonant with a psychodynamic approach that encourages people to engage more closely with thoughts and feelings that may be hidden from the conscious mind (Leiper and Maltby, 2004: 13). It needs to be seen in the context of a personal development programme where students were consciously seeking insight into themselves, with many seeing the research as an additional opportunity for this. Obviously, then, the research changed somewhat the learning experience under investigation – more so for some participants than for others, according to my findings – by creating another level of reflection and another layer of support or 'holding' (see Part III). However, seeing that the kinds of changes visible amongst Group 2 students are also visible amongst significant numbers of Group 1 students who had minimal contact with the research, I would argue that the learning process is essentially similar for both groups, although enhanced by the research for some Group 2 students. This is not to suggest that all students who took the programme experienced the same effects as those under discussion here.

Material from Group 1 was categorised cross-sectionally through free, tree, and conceptual levels of coding (Bazeley, 2007). This categorisation provided a template for processing material from Group 2, which was analysed separately for each student and then cross-sectionally across all the material from this group. In-depth case studies were developed from the material of three students from this group to illustrate the experience of change in the context of different conditions: different combinations of courses, different reasons for studying, and different bio-psycho-social factors at work. As there were no students in Group 2 for whom the experience of the CWPD programme was not ultimately beneficial, I have drawn on the experience of several Group 1 students for exploring negative instances (see Chapter 11). All names have been changed.

My analysis of the data was informed by interpretative phenomenology (IPA). Phenomenology explores the lived experience of individual human beings, putting the emphasis on what experience feels like to those individuals (Todres, 2007), whilst the interpretative or hermeneutic dimension enables the researcher to reflect on the experience of a number of different individuals, attempting to understand commonalities and differences and to conceptualise them. IPA has been particularly useful in enabling me to explore students' experience of their learning and thinking processes not only through their literal descriptions of them, whether spoken or written, but also through what can be inferred about these processes from the metaphors and symbols that occur spontaneously in their speaking and writing (Smith *et al.*, 2009) and in their creative life writing. In embodied realism, metaphor is seen as not just as a feature of literary language, but as a central mode of cognition at work in language generally (Lakoff and Johnson, 1980). Analysis of these metaphors can, therefore, help to understand structures of thinking and feeling that are less conscious. Seeing that, in a critical realist context, the researcher is not only interested in what participants tell her, but also in what she can learn about mechanisms that might lie beneath conscious experience, an approach that sets out to elicit and explore less conscious material makes sense. However, it does raise questions about the ethics of exploring and interpreting participants' deeply personal experience (Hollway and Jefferson, 2000). In pursuing this approach I have endeavoured from the outset to make clear the personal nature of the research through the research protocol, and in writing up the material I have worked closely with those Group 2 students who opted to see drafts of chapters in progress (almost all of them, in fact). The research was approved by the University's research ethics committee.

Structure of the book

Chapter 1 introduces the Creative Writing and Personal Development programme, its structure and courses, and gives details of key writing exercises and pedagogical techniques referred to in later chapters. I also relate here how I came to see the programme within the general framework of transformative learning and the consequences of this for the research. Part I focuses on students' experience of change as a result of the CWPD programme, with Chapter 2 providing an overview of what I am calling the expansion of the psyche, where the term 'psyche' denotes the complex of mind, including conscious and unconscious processes, and sense of self. This is followed by three individual case studies focusing on different kinds of learning about the self: sense of self as writer (Chapter 3), sense of self as learner (Chapter 4), and the sense of self in time in chronic illness (Chapter 5).

Part II seeks to understand the nature of these changes through a bio-psycho-social exploration of the dynamic system of the psyche (Chapter 6) and of its vicissitudes and their consequences for learning and creativity (Chapter 7). The concept of 'reflexivity' is at the heart of my concerns here and Chapter 6 discusses it at length. As a starting point for the reader, reflexivity can be thought of as a mechanism of consciousness that enables knowledge of the world and of oneself to be acquired through a relaxed kind of intentionality and at a low level of consciousness rather than through more conscious and directed thinking. I see the work of the CWPD programme as providing a range of opportunities for 'practising' reflexivity.

In Part III I discuss the three most significant elements in the learning environment that can be seen to work together to enhance students' reflexivity. These include the creative life writing exercises (Chapter 8), the student-led and tutor-led experiential groups (Chapter 9), and critical reflection on experience through course diaries, learning journals, and end-of-course essays and papers, with the aid of conceptual material from course readings (Chapter 10). I explore these three elements through a critical realist conceptualisation of the learning environment as 'laminar' or layered, suggesting that individual agency emerges from the CWPD learning environment when the different layers work together to challenge students and the learning groups to be more open and in process whilst simultaneously creating 'holding' for this to happen.

Part IV explores the implications of the research for adult learning. Chapter 11 looks at the challenges, both for students and for tutors, of a programme of study in which the learner's sense of self is the main focus of learning. I argue here that, in spite of the intrinsic difficulties of this approach to teaching and learning, the learning environment can be rendered safe-enough, although the work needs greater resources than more standard approaches to learning. In Chapter 12 I explore the similarities and differences between the CWPD programme and psychotherapy and suggest that if transformative learning involves a fundamental change in the functioning of the psyche, then it might reasonably be seen as a form of therapeutic education.

Acknowledgements

This book would not have been written without the contribution of a large number of people. First and foremost I am indebted to the students who took part in the research, particularly the 15 students whose progress through the MA I followed with questionnaires and interviews between 2004 and 2006. Most of them have read chapters in progress and I have much appreciated their thoughtful comments, as well as their tolerance of the length of time the research has taken to come to fruition. Sincere thanks are also due to the three tutors of the programme who participated in the project. Christine Cohen Park is a fiction writer, with extensive experience of working with creative writing and personal development at universities in Britain and Canada. Cheryl Moskowitz is a poet, fiction writer, and dramatist, who has been using creative writing developmentally in a wide variety of settings in education and healthcare for many years. Sarah Salway is a fiction writer, with long experience of teaching creative writing in higher education. I have much valued their wisdom in exploring the research questions and their thoughtful comments on chapters in progress.

Another person whose contribution must be acknowledged is Sarah Jackson, who assisted me with the research during the first six months, organising and collating the data, and undertaking a preliminary categorisation in collaboration with me. I could not have begun the project without her and benefitted enormously from the deep thinking she brought to the task. I am equally indebted to Jeannie Wright and Les Todres, who recommended the book proposal, and to those who commented on chapters in progress, including colleagues Phyllis Creme, Jack Danielian, and Linden West, and members of the Creative Writing Research Group at Sussex. My ideas for this book were very much enhanced by the two papers Linden and I wrote together during the period of the research (Hunt and West, 2006, 2009). They were also enhanced by working with Pauline Cooper, Sarah Jackson, Michael Maltby, and Sophie Nicholls during their own researches. Sophie's thesis has particularly influenced my thinking.

The research would not have been undertaken at all without the generous financial support of the Higher Education Academy and the British Academy, and the backing of the then Centre for Continuing Education at Sussex University. Acknowledgement is also due to Sage publications for permission to reprint material from Lyle Yorks and Elizabeth Kasl, 'I know more than I can say: a taxonomy for using expressive ways of knowing to foster transformative learning', *Journal of Transformative Education* 2006, 4: 43–64.

More personally, I want to thank my husband Randolph for tolerating my long sojourn in the 'book burrow'. Hopefully we will get to see a little more of each other now the book is finished. The book is dedicated to my dear friend and fellow Horneyan Bernard Paris, Emeritus Professor of English at Gainesville University, Florida, who has kept me company through the years I have been developing my ideas and taught me how to find clarity in my thinking and writing. I am deeply grateful to him for all his support. Needless to say, none of the above-named is responsible for the views contained here.

Notes

1 I define personal development as any process of beneficial self-reflective change an individual undergoes as a result of life experience or of a specific activity such as education, therapy, or the arts (cf. Hunt and Sampson, 1998: 200).
2 I use 'CWPD programme' when referring to the Postgraduate Diploma and MA together, but also refer separately to the Diploma and the MA.
3 Object relations theory seeks to understand the way people and experiences are internalised into the psyche and the role they play there as psychic 'objects'.

Chapter 1

Creative life writing for personal and professional development

As I said, the CWPD programme emerged in 1996 out of my experience of teaching an autobiographically based undergraduate creative writing course and the suggestion that this could be developed into a professional postgraduate programme with an explicit focus on using creative writing developmentally. But there was a wider context. Concurrently with my teaching I was working as Literature Officer at the South East Arts Board, one of the then regional arts outposts of The Arts Council of England, where a large part of my remit was to set up writing projects in the community. This involved employing published writers to run writing groups or to work with individuals in education or health and social care, partly with the aim of helping people develop their writing skills and partly to provide them with an opportunity for gentle self-reflection. Through meeting these writers I became aware of the increasing number of people wishing to facilitate 'developmental creative writing' (Nicholls, 2006) and the dearth of formal training or study opportunities for it. Around this time the National Poetry Society set up a discussion group for those of us interested in this work, and this group eventually evolved into *Lapidus*, the networking organisation representing the diverse field of creative writing and reading for health and wellbeing (www.lapidus.org.uk). One of the people I met through the discussion group was Fiona Sampson, who at that time was writer-in-residence for the Isle of Wight Health Authority, the first long-term healthcare residency in the UK. It was to Fiona that I turned when asked to set up the Postgraduate Diploma at Sussex, and together we developed a structure for it.

The programme's first format was a one-year part-time Postgraduate Diploma, with three one-term courses: an experiential, practice-based course, followed by a theory course, and culminating in a research project. The rationale for this was that in order to be able to facilitate developmental writing with others, future practitioners needed not only experience of doing their own developmental writing, but also a solid theoretical grounding. Further, engaging in research, whether qualitative or text-based, would extend their understanding of the relationship between theory and practice and help to build a body of evidence for the developmental and therapeutic effects of creative writing. The initial tutor team consisted of myself as convener, Fiona, and some of the other people I had met through my work at South East Arts or the Poetry Society's discussion group, including Cheryl Moskowitz and Graham Hartill. From the outset the programme attracted a wide range of people, mostly women, a mixture of health and social care professionals, teachers, and people from the business world seeking additional practical skills; established and aspiring writers seeking to deepen their writing or overcome writing blocks; and people seeking to develop their creativity or to find deeper self-understanding or more meaningful employment opportunities. This latter category often included people in transition between jobs or countries, or between work and retirement. The programme operated in its one-year Diploma format for five years.

In 2001 Christine Cohen Park joined the tutor team, having just returned to Britain after 10 years working with writing in healthcare at universities in Vancouver. She suggested that people wishing to acquire professional skills to undertake work with creative writing in developmental and therapeutic contexts needed opportunities to learn from experienced practitioners about the practicalities of working in different contexts, and to have an opportunity to facilitate an actual developmental writing group. Neither of these possibilities was available at the time within the Diploma. This suggestion coincided with a move at Sussex to increase the credits of Postgraduate Diplomas and led us to extend the programme to 16 months (four terms), with the addition of two new 'professional development' courses: *Contexts for Practice* and *Writing and Groups* which Christine devised. This, however, necessitated dropping the research project. Subsequently, in 2002, the Diploma was further developed into a two-year part-time Master's programme with the addition of two terms of independent study, in which students had the option of undertaking a research project or preparing a portfolio of creative writing with critical introduction. Two further one-term courses – *Writing Practice* and *Projects: Practical and Theoretical* – were also subsequently introduced as options for students not wishing to take the professional development courses.

With these options in place, the programme offered two distinct strands: one for people wishing to develop their own creative writing within a personal development context, and the other for people wishing in addition to acquire skills for use in professional contexts such as education and health and social care. All students took the three core components – the practice course, the theory course, and the two terms of independent study – together with two option courses of their choice. In 2005 a full-time option was made available in addition to the part-time. This necessitated a further restructuring of the programme, so that instead of the two terms of independent study taking place at the end of the programme, these were now split, with the first at the end of Year 1 and the second at the end of Year 2. The programme continued in this form until its discontinuation in 2010.

For most of the 14 years of its existence the CWPD programme was unique in Britain and was always heavily subscribed, with some 60 students attending at its height. As teaching took place all day on Saturdays – once a fortnight for part-timers and once a week for full-timers – people living at a distance from Sussex were able to attend in addition to those living locally. For example, people commuted from as far afield as Glasgow, Aberystwyth, Belfast, Cornwall, Cumbria, Rutland, and even Holland. This was in part facilitated by the University's proximity to Gatwick airport. When the full-time programme began to gather pace, people from the USA, Canada, India, and Thailand came to study with us. In view of the programme's popularity and manifest success, it has been heartening to see other universities in the UK setting up related programmes,[1] so that the approach pioneered at Sussex is not entirely lost.

Structure of the programme at the time of the research project

When the research took place (2004–06), the programme was a part-time, two-year (six-term) Master's, with the independent study component occupying the last two terms, as follows:

Course 1 (core) – *writing for personal development*

Students engaged in creative life writing exercises and shared the results in small student-led groups. Alongside this they read and discussed a small number of creative and critical readings that introduced them to psychodynamic understandings of the creative process and literary writers' accounts of it. Students kept a course diary for recording their experience of the course, drafting writing exercises, and making notes on their reading, both during the class (15 minutes were devoted to this each session) and between classes. Students' learning was assessed through a 5000 word essay reflecting on what they had learned about their writing process and themselves from the experience of the course and the creative writing they had done, 3000 words of which they were expected to append. The creative writing was not formally assessed (see Chapter 11).

Course 2 (core) – *creative writing and the self*

This was the main theory course designed to extend and deepen students' learning from Course 1. The critical readings focused on psychodynamic, neuroscientific, cultural, and linguistic understandings of subjectivity, the ideas arising being explored also through a range of literary texts and specially designed creative writing exercises. Assessment was via a 5000 word critical paper in which students were expected to demonstrate their grasp of one or more conceptual frameworks for understanding the developmental or therapeutic effects of creative writing. The small student-led groups for sharing creative writing continued as in Course 1. In addition there were student-led groups each session for discussion of the critical readings.

Course 3 (option 1) – *writing and groups*

This course explored both experientially and through textual study the way groups work, with reference to the particularities of writing groups. In the mornings students participated in a tutor-led developmental creative writing group, engaging in a series of writing exercises specially devised by Christine Cohen Park (see Appendix). The afternoons took the form of a tutor-led seminar discussion of students' experience of the morning in the context of a range of texts on the theory and fundamentals of group process and practice. Through being both participants and observers, students had the opportunity of reflecting on the life of the group and of identifying the distinct stages of its growth. Students kept a learning journal for reflecting on their experience of the course. They also developed their creative writing through peer and tutor feedback. For assessment they submitted a portfolio of work consisting of a 4000 word essay reflecting on their learning and the process and learning of the group, in relation to the dynamics and facilitation of writing groups; 3000 words of creative writing produced in response to the exercises (not formally assessed); and notes on facilitating a writing group.

Course 3 (option 2) – *writing practice*

Students prepared 6000 words of creative writing for assessment, accompanied by a 2000 word critical introduction reflecting on the writing and/or personal development issues arising from it. They could focus on long or short fiction, autobiography, or poetry. Published examples of literary forms were read and discussed, according to students' writing priorities, and students shared their creative writing in progress, receiving feedback from the tutor and student group. Critical and self-reflective approaches to the creative writing were also discussed, to prepare for the critical introduction.

Course 4 (option 1) – *contexts for practice: healthcare, therapy and education*

This course had two distinct components. In the mornings, writer–practitioners with experience of working in health and social care, therapy, and education were invited to share their knowledge of the practicalities and challenges of working with particular client or student groups and to introduce students to writing exercises they had found useful. In the afternoons, students took turns to lead a writing group consisting of a small number of their peers and, when not leading, received feedback on a small creative writing project in progress (3000 words), whether a chapter from a novel, one or more short stories, or a collection of linked poems. Assessment was by a 3000 word critical paper either reflecting on issues arising in one or more contexts where creative writing was being used developmentally or therapeutically, or outlining a series of workshops designed for a particular context; and the creative writing project, this time assessed by literary criteria.

Course 4 (option 2) – *projects: practical and theoretical*

Students carried out small qualitative or text-based research projects on a topic of their choice within the broad field of developmental creative writing. Whilst this was largely an independent study course with supervision, students met as a group at regular intervals to study research methods and share work in progress. Assessment was by an 8000–10,000 word dissertation.

Independent study (core) (2 terms)

Students had three choices. (a) A portfolio of creative writing with critical introduction (20,000 words), the critical part occupying 5000–15,000 words. The creative work could take the form of long or short fiction, autobiography, poetry, or a dramatic script, and was assessed on its literary merits. The critical introduction could reflect on the development of the writing, or personal development experienced through the writing, or discuss a literary genre or technique or structure used in the creative writing, or a combination of these. (b) A personal development project (20,000 word dissertation), that is, a critically self-reflective piece of work containing up to 6000 words of creative writing. The creative writing was not assessed on its literary merits but on the way the writer had reflected on and critically evaluated the process of producing the creative writing and the effect of this on his or her personal development. (c) A research project (20,000 word dissertation), either exploring, via primary or secondary literature, a topic or theme arising from or relevant to the field of developmental creative writing, or the experience of a group, or one or more individuals in education, therapy, or health and social care where creative writing was being used for personal development. A maximum of 2000 words of creative writing, whether the researcher's own, written as part of the project, or that of research participants, could be included in the body of the dissertation, but was not separately assessed.

Key writing exercises in course 1 – *writing for personal development*

Over the life of the programme the tutor team developed a wide range of creative writing exercises for personal development and also drew on those developed by others. At the time the research took place, the main exercises in Course 1 were as follows:

Web of words – devised by Graham Hartill

This is a group bonding exercise. Students individually brainstorm the theme of 'beginnings', then share with the group the words and phrases they have unearthed, whilst the tutor collects them on the board. Each person then chooses one of these as a focus for freewriting (see below), from which they craft a short piece of writing to share. Whilst students are doing this, the tutor draws on the collected words and phrases to create different versions of a 'chorus' for use in the final stage. The web is created by each person reading out their writing or an extract from it, with the tutor interspersing each piece with a line or two of the chorus. Students are asked just to read their piece without introduction or apology, so as not to disturb the web's creation (Hartill, 1998: 47–62).

Freewriting – devised by Peter Elbow

This involves writing without stopping for a given period (e.g. five minutes) and without paying attention to spelling, grammar, or punctuation. The aim is to let language flow in a freely associative way. A development from this – 'open-ended writing' – uses several periods of freewriting, pausing after each one to locate significant words or phrases that have emerged, one of which is then used as the starting point for the next period of freewriting. The exercise culminates in a final, more leisurely writing stage that involves extracting something from the last (or, if preferred, an earlier) freewrite and developing it into a short finished piece for sharing (Elbow, 1998: 13–19; 58).

Creating a poem out of words or sayings from childhood – devised by Cheryl Moskowitz

This exercise involves students in recalling and listening to everyday words or sayings that were significant to them in childhood, and then using them to create a rhythmic and/or rhyming poem. Cheryl's instructions for creating the poem are 'to identify a rhythm that appeals to you. This may come from everyday life, such as the rhythm of the train in which you travel to work, or from a poem you particularly like, such as a standard five-foot line (iambic pentameter), or from a remembered activity in childhood, such as swinging on a swing, a clapping game or skipping rope. Live with it for a day simply as a rhythm, playing it in your head from time to time, moving your body in time with it; only when you are fully familiar with it – when you have felt your way into it – start to add some words to the rhythm and develop it into a poem' (Hunt and Sampson, 2006: 38–9).

Imagining your future self – devised by Cheryl Moskowitz

Cheryl's instructions for this exercise are 'to project yourself forward in time, whatever feels like a comfortable distance. It could be 5, 10, 20, or even 30 years. Into that projection imagine a person who will be a significant figure in your life at this time. This should be someone you have not yet met and do not yet know about. It could, for example, be an as yet unborn child, a partner or lover you have yet to meet, a benefactor, a friend, a boss, a daughter-in-law or son-in-law, or an unknown relation who unexpectedly comes into your life. Your task is then to write a narrative, from whatever perspective feels right, which includes your future self in relation to this significant other' (Moskowitz, 2009).

Self as source – devised by Cheryl Moskowitz

This involves identifying a polarity in oneself around a dominant identity, for example 'good mother' and 'bad mother', or 'diligent student' and 'lazy student'. Characters are then created out of these two poles, first by finding metaphors for each of them and then 'fleshing them out' using a collage of cut-outs from magazines. These two self-characters are then brought into relation in a story where they exchange something of mutual value (Moskowitz, 1998: 35–46).

Imagining the reader – devised by Celia Hunt

This is a guided visualisation in three stages. It requires participants to imagine that they are able to go away for a year on their own to write. They can go anywhere in the world, and they must choose and describe the location and the room they have rented, and say how they are going to arrange the room, etc. They then settle into their room to write and, whilst they are writing, they are directed to become aware of who is present for them in the moment of writing. In the next stage this imagined reader enters the room in the writer's absence and reads the writing that the writer has done. This section is written from the imagined reader's point of view. In the final stage, the writer returns to find the reader in the room, and the task now is to write down what these two characters say to each other (see Hunt and Sampson 2006: 90–3).

In addition to the above, there was an exercise that involved participants in evoking a significant place in their lives through long, descriptive sentences, following the example of Marcel Proust (devised by Christina Dunhill). In many of these exercises there was an emphasis on writing about the past in the present tense, and on writing about the self by using first, second, and third person. (For key writing exercises in Course 3 – *Writing and Groups* – see Christine Cohen Park's Appendix.)

Finding an identity for the CWPD programme

From the start of the CWPD programme one of the challenges was to make sense of the programme in academic and professional terms. Because I entered the academic world as a creative writing teacher I conceived of the programme as a variant on the craft-focused creative writing Master's fast evolving across the academic world at that time. However, there were significant differences. Whilst many students of our programme were indeed developing their creative writing skills and some achieving publication, there was comparatively little focus on developing the craft. In addition, many people taking the programme were undergoing the kinds of changes more readily associated with psychotherapy than with academic learning, but the programme was not a form of therapy in the generally recognised sense. Again, when in 2001 we introduced the two professional development courses, the programme provided the only university-based training in the UK for people wanting to facilitate creative writing in therapeutic and developmental contexts, yet students did not graduate with a formal accreditation for undertaking this work.[2] So the programme was a strange hybrid straddling different kinds of personal and professional development and in some students' experience fell between several different stools.

This rather unwieldy hybrid was an inevitable consequence perhaps of developing something completely new, with tutors coming from different backgrounds and with a range of different priorities. We did consider the possibility of re-structuring the programme primarily for people wishing to acquire skills for working in the community (this was a significant recruiting factor), providing them with an opportunity of undertaking a placement with an appropriate organisation and working towards accreditation by a body such as the British Association for Counselling and Psychotherapy. But that would have meant losing the significant numbers of people studying with us who were primarily interested in developing their creative writing in a personal development context or in exploring themselves through creative writing, the strand of the work that was at the heart of the programme from the outset. So we remained with the broad-based structure and, in spite of the anomalies, it did work well for many people, as I will be showing.

During the research project my cogitations about the identity of the programme took a rather different turn. Having more time to think and read, I began to see that there were, of course, other approaches to teaching and learning with similarities to our work. Peter Abbs's (1974) approach to using autobiography in the training of teachers was, in fact, one of the most significant influences on my own intellectual development, through the MA Language, the Arts and Education at Sussex that I took in the 1990s. Again, the work of Duet – The Development of University English Teaching Project founded in 1979 by John Broadbent and others, now sadly no longer in existence – combined creative techniques and psychodynamic thinking for exploring ideas in the humanities (Knights, 1992: 11–12). Indeed Ben Knights, who was closely involved with Duet, was one of our first External Examiners. Essentially both these approaches to teaching and learning were about using the arts as tools for reflection, which was precisely what we were doing with creative life writing.

But there was an essential difference in that these approaches did not, as far as I knew, give rise to the deep change in sense of self that I saw taking place in the CWPD programme.

However, further reading in the educational field revealed descriptions of learning much closer to this aspect of our work. These, mainly located in the USA and Canada, went under the name of 'transformative learning'. They were not mainly concerned with developing the arts, although some did make use of the arts; nor were they aimed at helping people acquire profession-specific skills, although some of this work was taking place in a professional development context. Rather, the focus was on facilitating a kind of learning that gave rise to a deep transformation in participants' 'frames of reference' for engaging with the world, which sounded rather similar to what was happening to students of the CWPD programme. In fact I had come across some of this work years earlier by its founder, Jack Mezirow, but had not found it conducive because his central idea of what facilitated change – critical reflection – was too consciously rational, and ignored the role of feeling and emotion in the learning process, which was centrally important in our work at Sussex. Now I discovered that there was much new work in the transformative learning field, but with greater emphasis on the role of feeling and emotion. I was particularly struck by John Dirkx's use of metaphor and imagery in a Jungian conceptual framework in his professional development work with adults, which enabled people not just to enhance their practical skills but also to reflect on the self. He called this 'self-work' or 'soul-work' (Dirkx, 1997). I also found helpful Lyle Yorks's and Elizabeth Kasl's approach to using drama to engage adult learners' cognition and emotions simultaneously in a collaborative learning environment. They called this 'holistic' learning (Yorks and Kasl, 2002), a term that resonated deeply with the conceptual frameworks we had been developing in the work at Sussex. Thus I began to see our work as a kind of transformative learning, in which students were engaging not just for their own personal development but also to acquire the skills to work professionally with others. This provided a way of bringing the personal and the professional dimensions of the programme together conceptually. The location of Dirkx and others in depth psychology also offered a way of bringing together the academic and therapeutic dimensions of CWPD.

A key part of the research, then, has been to relate my findings to the theory and practice of transformative learning. Whilst there is much in this rich and fascinating body of work that resonates with my thinking, as I have immersed myself in it more thoroughly I have found that in certain fundamental respects I am at odds with it, having come to it after years of working with other conceptual frameworks. The main difficulty I have is with its dominant ontological grounding in constructivism:

> As far as any particular individual is concerned, the nature of a thing or event consists of the meaning that that individual gives to it. This does not negate

the existence of a world external to us but only asserts that what we make of that world is entirely a function of our past personal experiences.

(Mezirow, 1991: loc. 47)

On this view, whilst each person constructs his or her own reality, in the first instance this usually means adopting the dominant constructions of their familial, social, and cultural environments. Making personal meaning involves liberating oneself from these dominant 'frames of references' and developing meanings that are 'more true or justified' (Mezirow, 2000: 8). However, this fundamentally relativist position does not account for how 'more true or justified' knowledge can be obtained. Epistemologically, 'we have no criteria for judging between different mental constructions and therefore the mental constructions of each [person] are of equal value' (Brown, 2009: 12). This is not to suggest that our knowledge is not in any way constructed, but leaving out of consideration a reality that can be accessed, even if imperfectly, leaves us adrift in a world of constructs that we cannot evaluate with any objectivity.

Another problem of this paradigm is that, whilst developing 'a more confident, assured sense of personal efficacy, of having a self – or selves – more capable of becoming critically reflective of one's habitual and sometimes cherished assumptions' is a central feature of the process of change in transformative learning (Mezirow, 2000: 25), like everything else in human experience the self is seen as a construct rather than involving anything innate, hence the focus on schemas, scripts, narratives, and discourses (McLeod, 1997: 82). As a result, in-depth discussions of the self in transformative learning theory have been largely confined to the Jungian strand (Boyd and Myers, 1988; Cranton, 2000; Dirkx, 2012). Seeing that Jung's is a realist – indeed, one could argue, an embodied critical realist – theory that posits innate structures in the psyche, such as the archetypes and the collective unconscious, and the ability to access them indirectly via images and symbols (Samuels, 1985: 10), it is difficult to see how this is compatible with a constructivist ontology.

In spite of this there is pressure within the field for a unified theory within an overarching constructivist framework (Cranton and Taylor, 2012: 8), which paradoxically may be why transformative learning theory is, according to some of its leading members, in danger of stagnating (ibid.: 10–12). One of the ways of preventing stagnation is to develop new thinking outside of the dominant paradigm. As Michel Alhadeff-Jones points out:

> For transformative educators, challenging assumptions is at the core of what we promote among learners – despite the fact that we seldom consider questioning the legitimacy of the paradigms that frame our own educational practice and research.
>
> (Alhadeff-Jones, 2012: 178)

I note that thinking outside of the dominant paradigm has already begun in Alhadeff-Jones's own work (2012), which brings a dynamic systems approach to bear on transformative learning, and in that of Mathison and Tosey (2008; 2009), which re-locates it in embodied cognition. In addition, E. W. Taylor (2001) looks towards the neurosciences for an alternative understanding of transformative learning, and Gunnlaugson (2007) applies ideas from consciousness studies. All of these are related to my own approach. Hopefully my bio-psycho-social perspective within an embodied critical realist paradigm will contribute to what Gunnlaugson calls the 'second wave' of transformative learning theory.

Notes

1 For example, the Metanoia Institute, Bristol, accredited by Middlesex University, offers an MSc in Creative Writing for Therapeutic Purposes, based on the Sussex model.
2 There is as yet no formally accredited profession of therapeutic or developmental writing facilitator, but individuals with appropriate qualifications and experience can apply to be accredited by bodies such as the British Association for Counselling and Psychotherapy. The National Association of Poetry Therapists in the USA also trains and accredits poetry therapists in the UK.

Part I
Stories of transformative change

Chapter 2

Expanding the psyche[1] through the learning process

What does transformative learning look like, then, in the experience of students of the CWPD programme? The most striking feature of the material from Group 1 is the experience of opening-up to a less cognitively-driven, more spontaneous, and bodily-felt approach to learning or writing. One respondent notes a shift away from 'a narrow attitude towards learning … as an intellectual and academic exercise' towards a more 'fragile process of exploring and finding one's self/voice in writing … a subtle, quiet process at times [whose] rewards are not be found in grades or marks'. This shift away from 'narrow' thinking is highlighted by another respondent: 'I now have a much broader perception of education and my learning is continually updated by my surroundings and circumstances'. This implies a greater openness to contingency for learning, which is echoed by another respondent who learns the value of loosening cognitive control: 'a type of passivity [as a learner] is empowering and not impotent'. This is implied too in another comment: 'I know more than I think I do'. These responses indicate an increased sense of inner space for thinking, a willingness to relax cognitive control and be open to a kind of learning that comes through bodily-felt and emotional experience rather than just through conscious reason. It involves a greater bodily awareness of, or ability to reflect feelingly on, one's own learning processes.

This sense of greater openness and ability to 'think feelingly' is echoed in respondents' comments about changes in their writing process. Again there is an opening-up to the necessary contingency of creativity and a greater understanding of writing as a process that needs space and trust: 'I learned to write through my blocks, to use freewriting to loosen my pen and to move on and process rather than pre-emptively censoring and scrubbing ideas'. There is increased openness to the bodily or emotional nature of the writing process: 'I developed a kind of "ear" for what I wanted to say', one person says; and another that 'most of my writing is about expressing some feeling or mood, even if I don't think it is going to be'. Another finds herself needing to write beyond the 'brick-like coastline' of 'words/self/other' and to enter more fully into the felt nature of writing by 'watercolour[ing] my expressions somehow'. Here familiar but apparently rigid ('brick-like') conceptualisations are challenged to give way to a more diffuse self-experience in the writing process.

With this loosening of control comes, for some people, a greater flexibility in the writing process. One says: 'What I called "free" before wasn't really and I now recognise different levels of "free"'. Another notices that relinquishing control in the early stages of writing through 'listening to my own voice as I write', paradoxically gives her 'more control over the way [the piece] finally reads'. This is echoed by others. One has developed: 'The ability now to "go with the flow" and then stand back and appraise my writing critically'. This increased ability to be one's own critic or arbiter of whether the writing is good or bad is a significant theme, as is the understanding of blocks to, or difficulties with, the writing process and the ability to 'deal gently with them'. For these respondents a more flexible but simultaneously more robust relationship with their writing has come into being.

For many respondents the shift towards a more spontaneous and bodily-felt self-experience brings new and more authentic conceptualisations of themselves as learners or writers. One expresses this as opening-up to a more complex learning self: 'I began to understand that I am both a creative and an analytical thinker and that it is possible to find ways of integrating these two potentially conflicting aspects of my self'. For another the opening-up is to a more authentic and agentic sense of self as a learner beyond existing self-concepts: 'I realised that I desperately wanted to prove that I am as academically high-achieving as I believe my father always wanted me to be and that it is impossible for me to do this'. But finding this more authentic sense of self is also quite challenging. It involves engaging with 'dark and dangerous territory' within herself, which is sometimes 'enlightening and inspiring' but can also be 'shocking and scary ... working *against* the creative impulse' (see Chapter 11).

Loosening cognitive control

A similar but much more detailed picture of this shift to a more spontaneous, flexible, and bodily-felt but sometimes less comfortable experience of learning and being is provided by Group 2 students' material. An increase in cognitive flexibility is visible in many students' ability to tolerate a more spontaneous, relaxed, and intuitive writing or learning process. Here is Tess talking about the writing of her *Independent Study* dissertation at the end of Year 2:

> the way in which I've written this has been much more intuitive than how I've written things before and I've just let go a lot more. And now I've just sort of, even though I've done a lot of research, it's almost like I've kind of stuffed my head full of research and then just kind of let it cook in my head somehow and then just go and ... I did lots of freewriting, I'd sit down and just let it all come out and it would come out in the most strange ways sometimes ... .

Her metaphor of writing as cooking implies sufficient confidence to set the process in motion and then distance herself from it – to let it go, as she puts it – and to trust that she will be able to work with whatever results, even if it is not what she expects. There is no sense here that letting go means abdicating responsibility for the process: whilst she has loosened her tight control over it, she is still generally in charge. This is against a background of imposing strict control on her writing at the start of the programme.

Rhiannon, a practised science writer, highlights a similar experience at the end of Year 1:

> I am less attached to my writing, it holds less emotional relevance. At the beginning of the academic year I would pore over every word, edit profusely, and feel very emotionally attached to the written work. I am now managing to write more fluently, with far less editing, which leaves potential for my written output to increase.

Again, loosening control and gaining distance on the writing are key features. The reference to decreased emotional relevance of the writing indicates that control was serving an important function (see below). Former marketing executive Jill also uses the metaphor of cooking to describe her less controlling approach to learning:

> I'm increasingly amazed by how much learning is like cooking. I take a pinch from a newspaper article, 250 g of discussions with a friend, a shake of writing exercises and mix them up in my journal, dredge them with old ideas and a sprinkling of new insights and voilá ... I've produced a product. Never saw it like that before.

Here again it is the newfound freedom of the process that is striking, freedom to select and combine the ingredients spontaneously, as well as the obvious confidence that such a process requires. For Claire, a non-fiction writer, loosening control leads to a similar spontaneity for writing and learning. In Year 2 she notices herself getting:

> very excited by the routes that learning takes you – one path leading to another, surprises and synchronicities. I'm finding that I'm taking up lots of opportunities to learn, especially about writing. I'm seeing plays I wouldn't usually, buying music and books I wouldn't usually and generally stretching. Even striking up conversations with strangers, listening to how they speak and the way they use language. I feel a little like a magpie at the moment, dipping into and taking my pick of just about everything, trying to synthesise.... It feels scatty and blurred at times but it does suit me ... .

The metaphor of the magpie captures very well this new, more spontaneous experience: she is allowing her mind to roam around and choose whatever pleases it, even though this feels a little unnerving at times.

Developing cognitive flexibility means for some people being able to take more risks with writing. Harriet, a strong academic writer who has struggled to give her creative side more space, finds herself deciding:

> to do the minimum essay [for Independent Study] and tak[ing] the risk of putting more of the writing in, I suppose. I think two years ago I wouldn't have done that. I would have assumed that I couldn't risk that much on [creative] writing. So it's given me a different way of, yes another mode of thinking I suppose... .

Stella, a manager in the care sector, who begins the MA feeling very unconfident about engaging in creative writing, feels similarly strong enough by Year 2 to throw caution to the wind and experiment with a new genre for her *Writing Practice* project: '[The course] encouraged me to say what the hell, I'll write a play as that's what I want to do, even if it turns out not to be that good!' Her reference to a piece of work not being as good as she would like needs to be seen in the context of her previous feelings of inadequacy as a learner that she says stem from her 'struggle with a cold, unaffectionate mother, whose love was conditional on my academic success'. Loosening the compulsion to live up to high academic or literary expectations, real or imagined, is a significant theme for Group 2 students generally and often appears as a realisation that they are allowed to get things wrong. Claudia, a single mother of three returning to study after a gap, learns that: 'I'm allowed to make mistakes. I'm allowed to change my mind. I don't suffer from that crushing shame or that need to be right like I used to'. Letting go of the need to get things right is also part of Ruth's learning:

> I learnt that going wrong is part of going right! There were times when I thought I would never get beyond the second chapter, and I wrote and rewrote lots of versions. Eventually the right answer comes along, but I had to learn that writing isn't necessarily a linear process where one word comes after another, and to trust that process of keeping going when you really feel like throwing in the towel.

Claire, who identifies the main factor in starting to overcome her blocks to creative writing as 'learning to let go of what might be right or wrong, good or bad, and just write', elsewhere captures this metaphorically as guarding against 'black and white thinking styles'. She goes on to say that practising this: 'can help to develop flexibility of thought which can in turn, I would argue, lead to healing or at least a healing effect across any number of aspects of life. This is new learning for me'. When I press for clarity about this 'healing effect' in her life, she illustrates it by reference to her looser, less controlling approach in her relationship with her troubled sister, whose destructive behaviour towards her has been a lifelong problem:

> I think it's to do with sort of problem solving, and if I think about the ... whole issue with my sister. Initially all of my energy was into how can I solve this, how can this be ended and how, you know, how can I make this better? And it took me two years to realise that actually there wasn't anything that I could do and I had to ... then *not try* basically, because everything I tried was fruitless and exhausting and all of those very negative things and draining, took away from pretty much everything in my life so I ... I then had to see ... it was like just sort of an opening-up of just thinking well actually maybe me completely backing off is the most creative thing I can do in this situation ... that probably was my biggest lesson in realising that ... you know I had to be looser in my thinking.

Claire recognises that this shift to 'looser' thinking is grounded in a less rigid conceptualisation of truth, which allows her to entertain different ways of seeing things. Miranda, who has spent much of her life caring for her mentally ill mother, also begins to understand truth differently. She has been 'inhibited in my writing [about my relationship with my mother] by the idea that my truth could be wrong' when compared with that of other family members. But she learns that:

> the process of writing is an almost magical combination of at once focusing on words and their arrangement and yet releasing the content to become exactly what it feels right that it should be. It's much easier when one gives up on being true to the original truth.

The shift here is characterised by learning to rely for writing her story on what *feels right to her* rather than on some externally validated version of events. It implies risking a more authentically felt self-expression. And indeed this seems to be at the heart of these students' experience: greater confidence to respond to spontaneous, authentically felt self-experience. Thinking is more fluid and intuitive; there is greater trust in the psyche's own organic life; there is playfulness, fun, a more comfortable – although sometimes more challenging – engagement with bodily feeling.

Blocks to self-expression

Loosening cognitive control begs the question of why control was necessary in the first place. When I unpack the way control presents itself at the start of students' studies, I find widespread fears of authentic self-expression and exposure to scrutiny, whether by oneself or others. Whilst Miranda is a 'natural storyteller', she has 'yet to find my own voice *as a writer* and feel that there is something I have yet to know in order to write a longer piece, a story or a novel'. This is not just a question of learning the craft, she says, but 'of having something I want to write about that is very personal'. That she fears placing this 'very personal something' on the page becomes visible some months later when she notes 'a tendency that I have to panic when exposed to scrutiny and so to dry up creatively'.

Ruth has long been aware of 'a small internal voice tapping me on the shoulder, asking to speak' but has shied away from 'fac[ing] the possible content of my in-house orator'. She has 'a great affinity with words', which has stood her in good stead academically, but when she tries to write creatively, she finds that 'it's difficult to avoid [my own] truth and sometimes I'm not inclined to address matters'. Stacey, just moving out of full-time mothering, also fears self-exposure whilst at the same time: 'I would love to be able to access the inner voice I hear laughing at my life!' For Megan the fear is of potential readers:

> I don't seem to be able to free myself up enough to write what I really want to write. I am so aware of people being able to – or think they are able to – know too much about me if I let myself go![2]

There are other indications that creative writing poses a threat that sets up a conflict with the desire to do it. Tess will 'do anything to avoid [getting started with her writing] e.g. cleaning, shopping, talking on the phone'. Jill comes to the MA because she has run into problems putting her autobiographical material into a book she is writing on women's experience of the menopause. She wonders whether this is because she fears revealing her 'murky past' or because she has 'not developed the right voice yet' or because of 'the lack of identity you suffer during the [menopausal] years'.

Cognitive control is necessary here to keep uncomfortable self-experience out of sight. This is often achieved by adherence to dominant identities. At the start of the MA Rhiannon is comfortable with her identity of practised science writer, but engages in creative writing against huge resistance. She shows tacit awareness that science writing is possible for her because it does not involve engaging with the subjective when she notes that 'my [science] writing has had very firm objective (as opposed to subjective) boundaries'. Claire is also tacitly aware at the outset that her strong professional identity as non-fiction writer provides her with safe, controlled boundaries that keep emotional issues at a distance. Whilst she feels comfortable with the self she presents in her non-fiction writing, the creative writing she has done 'doesn't seem to be by me', she says, 'I don't recognise it', then adds, 'Maybe that's because I don't want to own it'. This indicates that her creative writing expresses something that is uncomfortably at odds with the way she thinks about herself. Lucy also indicates that accepting her desire to write involves taking her out of the comfort of her familiar business identity:

> Categorising myself as someone who writes more than ... e-mails, reports, conference papers and shopping lists feels presumptuous and awkward. For me, the label 'writer', or even 'apprentice writer', presupposes ... that I have something worth saying and worth reading.

This is in the context of her 'lack of self-belief' that she can become a 'creative artist', having dropped out of her Fine Arts undergraduate degree. It hints at idealised expectations of what it means to write or create and the possibility of self-punishment if she fails to live up to her expectations, which becomes clear later when she says: 'I am very self-critical and even if I'd got 100% on each essay would not be satisfied'. Claudia is also hampered in her attempts to fictionalise her autobiographical material by 'my inner critic being in full flow telling me I am not clever enough or good enough to do whatever it is', which undermines her confidence. Ruth feels similarly undermined after Course 1 because her creative writing has not lived up to her expectations: 'it's not Shakespeare and that bothers me! Not that I want to be Shakespeare, but I don't want to write *badly* either. I think of most of it as mediocre'. There is no acknowledgement here that developing the writing will take time; it has to be excellent straightaway. Tess catches sight of her inner critic through the imagined reader exercise:

> A dark presence, some kind of teacher, not sure if it's male or female, seems to oscillate between the two, rather stern. I want them to leave the room or change their colours – literally to 'lighten up'. They want excellence.

There are two main themes, then, in students' fear of exposure in their creative writing. First, the possibility that it will unearth aspects of themselves that might disrupt existing self-conceptualisations and, second, the difficulty of facing up to where they *actually* are with their writing or learning rather than what they imagine they *should* be able to achieve. In the first, cognitive control defends the psychic status quo; in the second, it defends the psyche against inner attack when excellence is not achieved. In both instances cognitive control impairs cognitive flexibility and restricts the possibilities for creativity. This explains Rhiannon's reference above to her writing now holding 'less emotional relevance': she no longer needs to defend herself so rigidly (see Chapter 7).

Expressing repressed emotions

When psychic control is loosened, as it is to varying degrees for all Group 2 students over the two years of the programme, repressed emotions come readily to the surface. Claire experiences emotional distress as soon as she starts to write about herself in Course 1, although at first this is not visibly connected to the central issue that eventually emerges: her anger at her troubled sister. Once revealed, this becomes 'all-consuming ... finding its way as an issue into almost every page of my journal, every conversation with fellow students and every piece of creative writing'. Being able to express her anger at her sister indirectly gives her a much-needed outlet, as she has 'been advised [that expressing it directly] is not useful'. But it also challenges her lifelong strategy of being the good, stable child. Because of the 'huge instability' of her sibling, she has to be the one who is 'honest and true and you have to stick to your word and follow things through'. This 'solid framework' of self-control – her 'strict parent' self, as she later calls it – has become 'quite rigid' and created 'very high expectations for myself'.

Harriet, who was already emerging from a 20-year creative block at the start of the MA, begins in Course 1 to confront her anger at her mother for instilling in her the view 'that writing was a dangerous, male activity, incompatible with being a "good" wife and mother', which she now believes was at the root of her block. Being able to confront this is 'a new development for me. I'm dealing for the first time directly with my mother, and associating her with my emotional and creative blocks'. This happens through poetry, as it does also for Stella who starts to express 'my unresolved anger with my mother' for making her feel a failure academically. In fact, Stella releases huge anger during the two years of the MA, not only at her mother, but also at her husband, from whom she separates during her studies: 'I feel driven to the depths of anger that I never knew I had', she says in the final interview. Expressing her anger involves coming to terms with a less likeable side of herself: rather than the good mother/professional carer roles she has occupied all her life, which 'validated' her, she now recognises that she has to let them go and face up to her 'vulnerability' if she is to find the space she desires for self-expression.

Jill similarly confronts 'an increasing anger I have been feeling towards my father since his death', because of his high academic expectations and his re-marrying so soon after her mother's death, that, he had hinted, was caused by Jill's birth. Like Claire, she became the 'good' sibling in response to a difficult sister and has never felt comfortable with anger:

> My sister ... and my father used to row a lot and my self-imposed role was one of mediator. I would throttle back my emotions for the greater good of peace. As I grew up I became more and more frightened of anger and angry people and yet also fascinated by them.

Tess's anger, which she also begins to notice in her poetry in Course 1, is associated, she realises, with 'the sense of loneliness and anxiety' she experienced at being sent to boarding school, as well as the punishments and humiliation she suffered there for not being 'a naturally tidy or ordered child'. Unable to complain to her parents because *they* did not have such a privileged education, she learned to put on a 'brave face' that eventually 'became a permanent way of coping' with her fear and anger: 'I have often felt that I impose a strict order on external things as a means of coping with a kind of internal "disorder" which I sometimes feel'.

Whilst for most people anger emerges very early on in the programme, for others it becomes available only towards the end. Through exploring her family history for *Independent Study* Miranda has discovered her father's infidelity, which makes her very angry: 'I spend so much of my time being angry', she says. Yet she doesn't like it: 'anger is such a horrible emotion to experience'. But she recognises that:

in order to proceed with the fiction writing I have to accept that I have a right to write and I think in order to do that you have to accept that your anger is somehow legitimate and that your truth is perfectly legitimate.

And in any case, she would 'sooner be angry than desperately sad', which means that she wants to move away from her dominant emotion of sadness previously masked in her relations with others by a humorous persona:

I just do this funny person, I do it quite well, but ... if you want to change your writing and write in anger you're going to be exposing another person who might not be so nice. So ... my trick for getting on with people is to be sort of accessible, quite funny, sometimes to let yourself be put down a tiny bit and say that's OK, but it's not really.

For some students sadness or loss is the companion to anger. Miranda begins to confront the pain of her mother's mental illness when she was a child: 'I never mourned the loss of my mother. I did not perceive her descent into madness as such at the time, though the reality was like a death'. But there is also pain at the loss of the many years of her life when she could not take control of her own life, and learning and creativity were difficult:

I'd existed, beyond a certain point in my childhood, in a sort of stunned fog, shocked by what was taking place around me. There are many places in my past that I still don't even like to visit, doors that when open reveal sad rooms, musky with regret, empty of furniture. I stumbled through my teenage years, in an accidental sort of non-trajectory that lasted, sad to say, well into my twenties.

Confronting repressed grief is a major undertaking for Ruth, which begins for her in Course 1 against huge resistance: 'I was clearly very cross at having to open up to myself'. But the grief, she discovers, is not only for her former partner, with whom she is obsessed even though she is now in a new relationship, but also for her father, who died when she was at university without her family telling her he was ill:

writing the line [in a freewriting exercise] *'If I was to say what was really on my mind it would be to say that I miss my love'*, I could no longer hold back the force of a huge emotional outpour. Although I was well aware that the two and a half years I had spent as the partner of someone in the chronic stages of alcoholism had deeply affected me, I was still impressed by how the writing of a very simple honest sentence could evoke such a massive resurgence of overwhelming feelings connected to my history, not only with my ex-boyfriend, but also with others, such as my late father.

Engaging with these two painful relationships and the rage and grief associated with them occupies Ruth for much of her two years on the MA and eventually leads her into counselling as an extra means of support.

For some students emotional expression is less direct. Lucy encounters loss as a recurring theme in her creative writing, with absent males particularly dominant. Whilst there is an obvious connection with the fact that her father died when she was 9, she does not explore this head-on:

> I noticed early on that everything I wrote about was about losing something, and once I'd noticed it, it stopped being an issue and I didn't really think about it again. So probably it was something that I could have explored further but I think I got to a point with it and thought, I don't know if I deliberately thought, but somehow it ended up not being the thing that I pursued ...

This is not necessarily avoidance. Whilst she is aware that on a programme like the MA 'you're kind of on the lookout for ... some personal development issue to pursue and dig into and [the death of my father] feels like a really obvious one', when she reflects on her feelings about this, she realises that:

> I never had a dream about having a father who looked after me and things because he was always ill, so when he died it wasn't a big deal for me. I never had those dreams and I think that's very different to my brothers and sisters, and I think that could be maybe what I want to write about, because I think what I'm curious about is the fact that I'm not curious about him, it's like a double negative or something ... .

She does suspect though that 'underneath there's other stuff which I keep skirting around and avoiding', and indeed later it is her distressing tendency to lose her identity in relationships with men that becomes the main focus of her writing, and how to feel comfortable with being a childless woman at 40. Rather than engaging directly with the loss of her father, then, Lucy's indirect approach to her dominant emotional themes, using science fiction as a frame, allows her to engage with the *consequences* for her present sense of identity of this loss, which she seems to experience implicitly rather than explicitly.

Liberating lost parts of the personality

A striking development for many of the students is that expressing repressed emotions liberates parts of the personality associated with them, which often emerge in the guise of unruly childish 'sub-personalities' (Rowan, 1990) (see Chapter 8). Claudia experiences the emergence of the unruly 'rebel' self she was at her Catholic school, where she was often excluded. She describes herself at that time as 'very very bright intellectually ... [wanting] ... to question things, particularly religion', which did not go down well with the nuns. She has the sort of mind, she says, that 'find[s] strange connections' between things and 'embroider[s] the truth and elaborat[es] stories', which she came to believe were 'character defects' that got her 'in trouble a lot'. Because this part of her personality had to be repressed, her confidence went with it, and she now understands her use of alcohol and cigarettes as a way of keeping herself under control. Learning fictional techniques for conveying her experience is hugely liberating, because it validates her natural ways of thinking: 'the idea that I could take my experience *and* fictionalise it, colouring in the bits in between, it was just like a new lease of life'. By the end of Year 1 she had written 40,000 words of an autobiographical novel and sent it off to an agent, practised being a rebel again in the 'Writing and Groups' course where she challenged the tutor (see Chapter 9), and contributed confidently to a discussion at a public literary event.

Stacey also experiences the re-emergence of a 'rebellious' or 'transgressive' part of herself that is associated in her memory with 'a terrible school' she attended as a teenager where she was 'branded stupid':

> I just was very rebellious and I came from ... there was just me and my sister and my mum, and all the time I was being told that I was a problem because I was from a one-parent family ... and it just reinforced the rebellious side of my nature really.

When her children were young, she had to put up 'a bit of a front', be 'a really conventional person', but now that they are older: 'I don't really have to conform, I don't have to go to parents' evenings and be that person. And so I do feel that I can probably come back to myself a bit more.' Coming back to herself involves revisiting uncomfortable incidents from childhood and adolescence that have left her with a sense of guilt. But writing them down and sharing them functions as a kind of purging: 'Through my writing I have rid myself of acts of aggression and defilement that I had carried unwittingly as my own'. This enables her to delve into an area of her psyche marked 'restricted access' and to use less comfortable material more spontaneously in her writing.

For many of the students the emergence of repressed emotions and hidden parts of the personality makes the psyche more risky and difficult to manage. Stacey finds that sometimes writing feels like 'a kind of madness' that is 'scary as well as uncomfortable', and she uses the metaphor of vomiting to capture it: 'Just as when you are ill you keep a bucket beside the bed, I keep my journal and pen at the ready for I never know what will come bubbling up to the surface in the depth of the night'.

Rhiannon who is forced, by doing the creative writing and reflective essay in Course 1, to abandon her 'passive [scientific] voice' and 'perfectionistic' learning and writing methods in favour of finding out what *she* thinks, discovers that the part of herself that contains her 'stagnant creativity' is 'still very childish'. Wilful and potentially unruly, it floods her with exciting ideas that she then finds difficult to develop into a coherent piece of academic work. Tess's angry, unruly side is similarly challenging. In the 'Self as Source' exercise it emerges as a crazed redhead threatening to throw herself off the local suspension bridge unless her lover leaves his wife and disabled child. The emergence of Claudia's repressed child self sends her into a manic high:

> there were times when I did feel almost infallible that yes I *can* [complete the MA in spite of having no money] and you know if I really want something I can go out there, I can write a novel, I can paraglide …

But this 'ecstatic' state does not last; it is too chaotic and she takes 'a nose dive' emotionally. This is exacerbated by learning from the agent that her novel is not sufficiently developed for publication, which damages her confidence in her writing. Expressing repressed emotions and releasing lost parts of the personality, then, disrupts the previous configuration of the psyche kept in place by cognitive control, opens it up to greater complexity and the possibility of increased creativity, but renders is more difficult to manage.

Learning to manage the expanded psyche

In spite of the challenges many Group 2 students begin to learn how to manage their riskier, more unpredictable psyche over the course of the MA, which brings increased agency. Claire finds that releasing her anger opens up the possibility of tolerating inconsistency: of having empathy for her sister's illness whilst also feeling legitimate anger at her destructiveness. This allows her to think more flexibly, to 'define my limits and convey those to others'. This has 'at times … caused me some distress but there is a strengthening sense of my confidence in my ability to ride with the uncertainty that is created by me finally taking a stand and stating my position'. Being stronger in human relations enables her to be 'easier on myself' and to relinquish her high expectations in favour of a 'gentler understanding of the processes we go through in our lives and of the meaning we make for ourselves'.

Tess also experiences 'a greater sense of agency and purpose in my life'. She now understands the process of change as not just a linear movement 'from the centre out towards enlightenment' but a spiral involving 'moving inwards … towards the centre, backwards into the past and sometimes downwards into a darker place of isolation and pain'. Working with this more emotionally felt and challenging sense of self helps her to understand 'what holds me back, not only from writing but from succeeding in other areas of my life'.

Whilst Claudia's changes have also been difficult to manage: 'just getting to know myself, you know, as this person and in this world and re-establishing all my relationships … finding new boundaries …', she finishes the MA feeling that she 'learned to sort of connect with my creativity'. She also feels more connected up with herself generally:

> I was thinking about how I was [when I did my first degree], there was the public me and there was the private me and nobody saw the private me, not even my husband, I was another [Claudia] for him. Now I think I'm much more aligned, what you see here is very much who I am at home and who I am on my own, very much who I take out into the world.

Rhiannon begins to find 'middle ground' in her management of the rediscovered, unruly dimension of herself, neither too controlling nor too lax (see Chapter 8). Gradually learning to do this, she finds that she is able for the first time to make a plan for her academic writing. She can now 'see her thinking', she says, revealing through the visual metaphor a sense of increased space for the imagination. This more open, more reflexive sense of self brings her a deeper understanding of her subtle difficulties with learning: 'I am more open to the dynamics of the learning situation and aware that the learning process is much more than the mere acquisition of facts. It is an on-going process involving much self-questioning and self-regeneration'. She has also 'undergone some radical alterations in my personal life that have produced a sense of self that is newly emerging but on a much stronger, realistic footing than before'.

For some people inner conflicts are still visibly at work. Having expressed and processed a great deal of anger and loosened her tendency to be the carer, Stella feels 'much more confident … and much clearer about what I want and don't want to do, and will and won't do'. But 'I'm still sort of convincing myself', she adds, 'because … I still need that kind of vindication from outside and I'm not getting it'. 'Vindication?', I query. 'Sorry not vindication, validation' she replies. It's interesting that she says 'vindicate' here rather than 'validate'. Clearly at a less conscious level she still has to justify her need to have more time for herself, to defend against inner accusations of selfishness. Stacey experiences something similar:

> I can take more risks now, I've brought my children up, … and yes I think last time I was maybe talking about how I could be more myself … but I *was* myself when I was looking after them all day as well, just now I can journey into myself a little bit more … explore myself a bit. It's a selfish thing I suppose whereas [Celia: selfish?] well I'm spending time on myself rather than on them I suppose.

Whilst, then, there has been movement out of dominant self-concepts into a freer and more creative psychic space, for some people this is inevitably still tentative and sometimes uncomfortable.

Understanding the trajectory of change

So there is a trajectory in many Group 2 students' experience of change, from repressed emotions and parts of self often kept under control by dominant self-concepts or idealised images (Horney, 1951) (see Chapter 7), through opening-up to a broader range of emotional expression and parts of the personality, culminating in a more flexible, bodily-felt and agentic self-experience. This in turn facilitates a more spontaneous understanding of learning and writing processes, as well as relationships with others. The expanded, more complex psyche is more challenging, but there is much evidence that by the end of the two years students are beginning to find ways of containing and managing it. Whilst all Group 2 students experience this trajectory, there are of course differences. Some students' difficulties with learning or writing are more easily addressed than others (see Chapter 11). Some have already done a fair amount of work on themselves before they start the programme. Some engage in a direct encounter with their emotional problems, whilst others work at them more obliquely through the creative life writing. Students also demonstrate different degrees of insight into the processes involved in change, although all of them show a significant movement towards a more bodily-felt engagement with their writing and learning processes.

Whilst the material generated from Group 1 students is less detailed, as I have shown there is evidence that significant numbers of them experience a similar shift to a more open, complex, reflexive and bodily-felt self-experience that in many instances facilitates increased flexibility in writing and learning processes and in life more generally, but is sometimes less comfortable than that experienced previously. However, Group 1 material demonstrates a greater frequency of negative experience of the programme, particularly in the early years (see Chapter 11). I now proceed to look in detail at how change takes place across the two years of the MA in the experience of three students from Group 2.

Notes

1 I use the term 'psyche' to denote the complex of mind, including both conscious and unconscious mental processes, and sense of self (see Chapter 6).
2 Megan felt more comfortable placing her material on the page once she learned about the implied author in fictional autobiography (see Chapter 8), which indicates that her fears were partly a consequence of not having this knowledge. However, she also discovers fears of placing on the page what she calls the dark side of herself, so there is more involved here than just the need for technique.

Chapter 3

Finding a stance as a writer
Simon's story

I have chosen Simon's story as my first case study because he was the only male in Group 2 and I wanted to consider gender differences in the experience of change (although, as it turned out, there were no significant gender differences visible).[1] He was also one of only three students who took the personal rather than the professional development route through the programme (see Chapter 1) and I wanted to compare the impact of the different routes (see Chapter 11). His story demonstrates the shift from a troublesome imbalance between freedom and control in the creative process to a more flexible but simultaneously grounded and agentic stance for writing. Importantly this includes the emergence of challenging emotions in the creative writing and of an unruly part of the personality Simon calls his creative 'writer self', with which he begins to collaborate.

Problems in the writing process

Simon is almost 70 when he starts the MA. He has been trying to write novels in his spare time and identifies two main problems: that of choosing 'the correct words [to] convey the image in my mind clearly without overwriting',[2] and repeatedly getting bored with his writing projects. The latter is particularly troublesome: 'Having started and written part of a story, I have a full image in my mind of how it should continue and end. I find the effort of continuing further less interesting than starting on a new idea'. What he likes best about writing is the excitement and novelty of finding out what is going to happen next: 'I've got a grasshopper mind', he says. Yet he'd also like to complete a novel and submit it to an agent or publisher, but: 'I'm not sure what I have to do after I've written something and finished it to go through it and work it out'. This, he says, is because of his lack of knowledge of the crafting and structuring process. He also finds it difficult to judge his own writing and is confused by the very different reactions of different readers.

At first sight, then, Simon's problems with his writing appear to be a lack of knowledge of the craft, which any creative writing course, or studying 'how-to' books at home, might remedy. But Simon has chosen a personal development context for addressing these problems and this is not by chance:

> I was more frustrated as a writer than I realised [... which ...] I was only expressing subconsciously by joining the programme for a start, you know, and telling myself that I was doing it for entirely different reasons, from the need to write, you know, and I chose this programme with all the psychological stuff which I despise.

Simon has undertaken other arts courses, hoping that they will be 'life-enhancing and mind-expanding experiences', but has always been disappointed. So what exactly is he seeking? Looking beyond the craft element of Simon's writing problems, one could say that there is a conflict in his creative process between freedom and control: either he can give his writing total freedom, letting himself be seduced by the appeal of action with characters that are, in his words, 'reactive' at the surface level, which does not ultimately lead to a rounded story, or he can impose total control on the story by 'pursuing a direct, pre-planned line' that leads to boredom and abandoning the project for a new one. Neither of these approaches produces a workable novel, so the writing lapses: 'I fail through lack of persistence'. Between the total freedom and total control of Simon's writing process, there is insufficient middle ground, and the metaphor 'grasshopper mind', with its connotation of leaping from one vantage point to another, captures this exactly. It creates a picture of thinking stuck in an either/or, resulting in writing that he finds frustratingly superficial. By joining the MA Simon is not only seeking to develop the craft of writing, but also, even if not fully consciously, a way of expanding and enhancing his cognitive processes.

Opening up space for the imagination through fictional dialogues

This latter begins to happen already in Course 1 (*Writing for Personal Development*). In response to the 'Self as Source' exercise (see Chapter 1) Simon creates two self-characters: Anselm, an explorer returning from the Arctic, who is angry and narcissistic, centrally concerned with bolstering his expansive persona; and Cyril, an airport official with 'a deep need to be liked', whose job is to deal with problem people like Anselm. Simon reports that this exercise 'caused a terrific input, a blast of energy – writing, writing, writing'. The two characters emerged 'alive and vibrant' and by the end of the term he had written 50,000 words of a novel around them: 'It feels as if I have been unable *not* to write. This was not so much an unblocking of writer's block as a removal of writer's boredom. The characters now engage me'. Identifying and drawing on aspects of his personality as a source for writing means that not only do his characters have more psychological depth and are therefore intrinsically more interesting to him, but at a deeper level there is also potential for the characters' engagement through the story to create an inner dialogue between different aspects of his personality.

Another kind of self-dialogue is triggered by the 'imagined reader' exercise. Simon finds this 'unexpectedly difficult', because he cannot conjure up an imagined reader: 'there was no one there. I was writing for someone that I denied'. Confronted with this difficult insight, he is 'unable to read ... out aloud' what he has written:

> Well, it took me by surprise, I mean it was a class exercise, write in ten minutes, you know [the tutor] gave us the various circumstances, and I thought: 'oh that's terrific', and I wrote this stuff down and thought it was a hoot, you see, this guy, and then when I came to read it out I couldn't, I broke down in tears. I mean that's just extraordinary [see Chapter 12].

However, he does manage to create an imagined reader when he writes up the exercise at home: a ghost who visits the writer's room when the writer is away. In this first person piece ('Ghost Writer') the ghost describes the room as a bare, impoverished space. When he reads the manuscript lying on the table, he discovers that it is 'meaningless scrawl' interspersed with pictures torn from magazines. Nevertheless the ghost-reader wants to meet the writer and settles down to wait for his return. It is a very long wait; the room progressively deteriorates, the window loses its glass and the wind carries off the pages of the manuscript. When the writer eventually appears, he is old and worn: 'his face grey, lined and sagging, his body stooped and halt, supported by a heavy wooden stick'. Clearly he has been through a harsh experience, yet he is unable to tell the ghost anything about it:

> 'Where have you been?' I said [the ghost is narrator].
> 'Out', he said.
> 'Where did you go?' I said.
> 'Nowhere', he said.
> 'What have you been doing?' I said.
> 'Nothing', he said.

It is striking that the writer here cannot talk about where he has been and what he has done. One explanation is that what he has experienced is just too terrible; another that, as with his writing, he has simply been wandering around in confusion. Either way, there is no meaningful dialogue between the writer and the reader. Yet a tentative relationship is established between these two textual selves in the writing process, even if only at the metaphorical level. As the ghost-reader follows the writer out of the room, he thinks that: 'Maybe there was enough of time left for us'.

Structuring the space for the imagination

Simon's emotional opening-up to a more challenging and dialogic psyche triggered by the writing exercises is significantly supported by the relationship he develops with his Course 1 reading group (see Chapter 1). This is not without its challenges however: 'faced with the prospect of reading to a group of strangers, I froze. I think that at that early stage I was unwilling to make any real commitment of myself in public'. Yet once he begins to trust them, he is able to drop his mask and to feel more comfortable about sharing his personal writing. He describes these fellow group members as 'generous' and 'constructive' and feels that they provide 'a secure base within which to lower barriers and write more self-revealingly'. Later groups are less significant, but being in small groups suits him. In fact, his view is that 'without the groups the thing wouldn't have worked ... they are the essential basis on which the whole thing runs'.

Equally significant in framing and containing Simon's more challenging and dynamic psyche is his study of theory. In Course 1 he finds particularly appealing Chatman's (1978) schema of textual 'agents' in a narrative – narrator, implied author, implied reader – that provides him with a conceptual framework for thinking about the different 'selves' and others in his writing. In Course 2 (*Creative Writing and the Self*) he uses a combination of autobiographical and theoretical writings, including Bakhtin on the 'multi-voicedness' of the novel (1984) and Bruner on the cultural shaping of life narratives (1990), to enable him to 'erect a three dimensional mental framework or scaffolding on which the narratives, events, metaphors and biographical fictions of my life can be spread out and examined'. In Course 4 (*Projects: Practical and Theoretical*) he draws together Neisser's cognitive psychological schema for understanding different perceptual senses of self (1988) and Damasio's neurophysiological model of conscious and non-conscious selves (2000), to formulate his own self-schema. This brings him 'a deeper understanding of the structure and basis of a view of the self which is of practical use to me'. Later he develops this into a metaphor of the self as a rope made up of a multitude of strands twisted together and constantly undergoing change although giving an outward impression of uniformity.

This re-conceptualising of the self and the writing process through theory and practice comes to fruition in Simon's final dissertation for *Independent Study*, where he explores how he has come to understand that he has an unconscious or subconscious 'writer', which he refers to as 'it' and that is the source, or resource, from which his writing springs. He distinguishes between this unconscious or subconscious 'writer' and his more conscious 'author' self, and understands his writing process as involving constant negotiation between them. Essentially this requires loosening his tendency to control the story, allowing his material to emerge spontaneously out of his 'writer', and then crafting the material into its final form. However, he acknowledges that he is still trying too hard to direct the process, sometimes causing his 'writer' to 'sulk' or refuse to write, such as when he decides that the end of the novel featuring Anselm and Cyril should take place in Antarctica. Whilst he manages to write this ending: 'It now sits, okay in itself, but not yet attached to the main story. It has seemed unlikely that my *writer* will allow it to join in and that instead, another different, darker end will happen'.

Challenges of opening the space for the imagination

Simon's reference to a 'darker end' is significant, as he has discovered that his 'writer' is as unpredictable as a normally 'good natured and hard-working [elephant that] can turn nasty and become fatally dangerous from one moment to the next'. He is nervous of this potential for the spontaneous emergence of dark material, which may explain the unspeakability of the writer's experience in the 'imagined reader' exercise. He notices that 'things go best between us' if he feeds his 'writer' some information and then writes whilst partly distracted, by eating a meal for example. Some of his strongest and most formed writing has emerged spontaneously in this way, including a very violent section of the novel, in which a female character is brutally raped and murdered. Its emergence, however, causes Simon to feel 'revulsion' and 'resentment' at his 'writer' and was 'such a shock to me that I did not write any more for several weeks'.

Opening a dialogue with his 'writer' or 'subconscious source of creative writing' helps Simon to understand better the main problem he identifies at the start of the MA: how to choose 'the correct words [to] convey the image in my mind clearly without overwriting'. Whilst he still emphasises his role as director of his writing process, there is evidence that he is beginning to understand it as 'felt and bodily' (Nicholls, 2006): referring to the 'magical knack' some authors have of transforming writing 'from mere recording to lively informing', he says that 'I can sometimes taste its flavour at the back of my throat'. This metaphor for the feeling of writing indicates a new-found trust in the embodied nature of the creative process that enables him to give it its freedom whilst also managing it. This is captured in the metaphor Simon uses at the end of the MA for his sense of self as a writer, which is very different from the one in 'Ghost Writer': 'I feel now as a self or writing self or learning self as if I might feel as a rancher, standing on the veranda of my ranch house, surveying the wide open prairie of my ability to exist as a learning writer'. Here the writer-self is able to articulate his experience of being a writer and can describe his psychic terrain. That he is characterised as a rancher implies ownership of the space for the imagination and a stronger sense of agency: from the solid and comfortable vantage point of the veranda of his ranch house he is not afraid to confront the potential dangers and challenges of the wild and unpredictable prairie of unconscious processes. But ownership and agency do not imply absolute control; rather there is managed cooperation between the different psychic forces in the writing process. That Simon applies the metaphor not just to his sense of self as a writer, but to his sense of self more generally, indicates that the psychic shift has been systemic, as he later confirms: 'A whole new satisfactory side of my self has been revealed'.

However, his problem of getting bored with a novel in progress is not completely gone. Deciding to finish it still brings 'a shallower and less surprising and interesting content to the writing', but he feels more able to 'direct the path of my writing towards (at least) an ending and that the end product still surprises and interests me'. He does this 'partly by agreeing with myself that the rest of the story will be told in subsequent volumes', but partly also 'by concentrating on the detail at the surface level of what I'm writing and letting my sub-conscious direct the main thrust of the story, even though I've told it where to go'. These reflections indicate Simon's increased collaboration between his creating 'writer-self' and his managing 'author-self', and increased trust that any dark material emerging unexpectedly can be coped with.

Fragmentation of the personality and conflicts in the creative process

Material in Simon's Course 2 paper helps to understand the conflict between freedom and control in his creative process. We learn that psychically he feels very fragmented, which he ascribes to his early life. Both his parents were driven to raise themselves out of impoverished backgrounds. His father ventured into the City to work for 'an upmarket stockbroker', and when his parents married they lived in a new, semi-detached house in a 'leafy suburb'. But when glaucoma left his father blind and without his 'high-status job', his mother's 'disappointment and bitterness' rendered home life 'miserable', as she continued to push for a better life for the family through constant relocations. She managed to get Simon a grant into public school that:

> disconnected me from my family; I felt apart and different, not least because my mother treated me so. For her I had become, I think, a 'symbol', a focal point around which she could build a restructured life narrative that reinforced her progress (climb) into the higher (upper, better) social strata on which her life's ambition was based.

A year after leaving school, Simon found himself, again 'more or less by accident', in the armed forces in the Malayan jungle, having to develop another persona in order to integrate into 'a completely different milieu with completely new or alien social mores and social background'. He describes his life during the 50 years following the war as 'a series of shows or incidents or happenings or adopted metaphors'. Like a cartoon character in the Daily Express, he 'pulled a hoop over his head and was instantly transported into a new adventure'. He has lived 'a continual series of different, often completely disconnected, overlapping, long or short life narratives'. This constant shift of identity meant that he did not form 'any deep roots' and, when he married, his wife became 'the central shaft around which all the other events and narratives in my life have whirled and wheeled'. Now he is a 'much loved husband, father and grandfather', which is 'delightful but feels strange. I have to adapt and adjust my speech and behaviour to fit the mould and keep the narrative going'.

Simon's implicit metaphor for self here of what could be called a quick-change artist implies a sense of inauthenticity at the surface level, with more authentic aspects of himself kept at bay. This connects with what he tells me about his schooling. Simon refers several times to being blocked at school and hating learning, except in art. Because he did not take Latin, he managed to spend one whole day a week in the art room, where he was given complete freedom by the art teacher, an 'innovative sort of man'. All his learning came from this teacher, whilst 'the rest of it was forced in in the sort of traditional way', which he hated. He says he 'got over that' later and managed to develop a career and support his wife and family. But it may be that getting over it required keeping out of sight the child-self who simply wanted to play, so that the adult-self could get on with the more mundane business of earning a living, and that the resulting tension between them continues to manifest itself, particularly in creative work where the child-self's playfulness has more legitimate scope for expression. In the final interview I suggest tentatively to Simon that being given freedom all day in the art room to play without interference was formative and had disadvantages as well as advantages. Whilst he was learning to access his spontaneous creativity, he was not learning how to manage it and to bring a product to fruition. He found this idea 'very true and I mean, looking back, that is a key element; if you want to talk about the self, that is a key element in myself, now that you point it out. Always.'

Creating a dialogue between parts of the personality through narrative techniques

In psychodynamic thinking, parts of the personality that are odds with external circumstances or dominant ways of thinking about oneself tend to get split off and labelled as 'bad'. Rather than getting rid of them though, this just makes them frustrated and angry – the playful child becomes the murderous 'wild child' – necessitating increased psychic control that can have adverse consequences for creative freedom. Simon often refers to having a less 'nice' side that he describes as 'impatient, pushy, grumpy, tactless, bossy and probably arrogant', but being aware of these characteristics makes it 'easier for me to control them'. Amongst students on the MA he tries 'to be nice', although underneath he 'knows' that really he is not; he's a 'cranky old man'. His dominant way of being with people is to use humour to moderate his darker side – another key element in his make-up, he says – and this is to the fore when he creates fictional characters:

he tries 'to see a good side in most of [them] and ... to let them all have some good times and ... become involved in something humorous'. So in the novel he begins in Course 1, his darker side is present in the guise of the angry, narcissistic explorer Anselm, but the humorous narrative tone renders him endearing rather than bad and therefore protects writer and readers from the full force of the darkness.

As the MA progresses, however, the humour in Simon's writing gives way to a more visceral representation of his darker side. In Course 3 (*Writing Practice*) he writes a story ('Murder') about Ian Ferris, who murders first the man who killed his daughter, and then, his grief not being assuaged, other people he thinks are murderers, although he has no evidence for this. This self-based character ('The murderer was partly me') commits heinous acts, and yet Simon feels sympathy for him and manages to express this by conscious use of double-voiced narrative techniques he is learning. Here is Ferris going fishing after the first murder:

> At the big, old, pollarded willow he stopped. A gnarled and twisted mouth and nostrils streamed blood down the bark, screaming silently. He took the fishing rod out of the trolley, assembled it, threaded the line, attached the float and hook and flicked it out into the lake; no blood from the bait, it was already dead. He stood looking out into the lake and into himself. *No remorse, that's definite; no guilt, so is that. So, where am I now? The man is dead, excellent, but what about me?*

In this extract we learn about Ferris's actions and his tortured inner world both from the outside through third person narration and from the inside through direct thoughts (italics), and free indirect style (underlined). This latter incorporates the thoughts or tone of voice of the character without using speech tags (e.g. 'he said'), thus rendering it 'double-voiced' (see Hunt, 2010a). Opening Ferris up in this way and showing that 'his internal nature is increasingly separate from his external behaviour' allows Simon to feel 'intense sympathy for a person who has lost a much loved child to random violence' whilst simultaneously being repelled by his actions. Learning to create self-characters who are not wholly 'nice' but whom Simon can nevertheless empathise with, or at least tolerate, without the defence of humour, gives him, I would suggest, a middle ground for working more comfortably with the different sides of his personality, which allows more of his psyche to be spontaneously available to him as a writer.

Working with metaphors and images of fluidity and process

Similar benefits accrue from his study and use of metaphor. In 'Murder', Simon makes a conscious attempt to deepen the writing 'by using inference, metaphor and extended metaphor' for Ferris's acts and state of mind. For example, he tries 'to develop the use of water as a metaphor for Ferris' life as it changes'. Water is indeed ever present in Ferris's story, from the 'dank, sour smell of mud and rotting reeds' of the lake that envelops him as he walks to his fishing spot at the story's start, to the 'cool womb' of the sea at the story's end, where he goes diving and ultimately commits suicide. In the final scene, Ferris's immersion in the underwater world creates a powerful metaphor for space and letting go into the body. Just like the ferris wheel, Ferris is stuck in a vicious circle, turning repeatedly in the same groove, driven by his unquenchable anger and inability to grieve. No amount of violent acts assuages his tormented state of mind, but once he is beneath the sea:

> [I]t was like an instant rebirth. Gone was the flaying heat. The blinding, head-aching glare vanished, the stench of diesel, hot rubber and hot bodies, was cut off. In its place was a cool womb where he was weightless in a blue-green space full of flitting, flashing colours like his dreams. He rolled effortlessly, seeing first the glittery surface and then the coral reef below with its shoals of technicolour fish. His troubles faded and he felt at last the release for which he had been searching. *So this is where it is, this is where I had to go all along* ....

Rolling like a seal, totally at home in his new environment, he relinquishes his anger and murderous thoughts, and, before he drowns, he is able at last to grieve for his murdered daughter. Whilst Simon is consciously using metaphors here to capture his character's state of mind, these metaphors also have personal relevance. The character's act of letting go of his entrapment in thought patterns, his distancing from them into a more fluid space, increased physical and psychological movement and expansion into a bodily-felt sense of self, all echo the shift from thinking to feeling, from monologue to dialogue, that characterises Simon's own development.

Something similar happens in a piece called 'Pencil' that Simon writes for *Independent Study*. Here, too, water is a metaphor for fluidity, although this time the letting go is more containing than annihilating. The story is set on a planet with a 'vast sun' and two moons. Every time the planet completes a 'full circuit' of the sun and lies 'in linear conjunction' between the two moons, the combined gravitational pull of these celestial bodies causes the waters to inundate the land. The clans that inhabit the land know that once every generation their villages will be flooded and they will have to make their way to the safety of the City On The Rock if they are to survive.

The City lies at the heart of a network of pencil-straight paths, thin raised lines that radiate out across the land in all directions. As the inundation begins the villagers set off on the long trek along these raised paths that keep them just above the level of the rising water 'lying in pools and meres, seeping from morass and moor, trickling always south'. The three day walk sees many casualties, as those who cannot keep up sink to the ground and are swallowed up by the encroaching waters. Those who survive and reach the City are fed and housed for the night, but in the morning they must face the 'ceremony of re-selection', where they are randomly divided into new clans by the City authorities. The re-formed clans head back along the paths that rise up again 'from the morass of the water-covered land'. They arrive to find villages washed away, 'but the materials for a new village lay to hand for those that would use them'. So life begins anew, but in the knowledge that the 'iron compact' with the City that governs their lives will compel them, in a generation's time, to set off once again for the unknown.

This story contains an extended metaphor for reflexivity: the balance between freedom and control, stability and fluidity, movement rather than fixity that lies at the heart of the creative process and of 'creative living' (Rose, 1978) (see Chapter 7). The image of the City at the centre of a network of paths that radiates out in all directions evokes the ferris wheel of 'Murder', but where Ferris's 'wheel' is stuck in perpetual motion from which only death can offer release, the cycle in 'Pencil' is a sustaining framework. Admittedly it is a harsh compact, in terms of both the physical losses along the way and the emotional losses of the re-selection ceremony, but it is there to keep the villages robust, and therefore represents freedom within the constraints. This image also echoes the stability and fluidity in the implicit compact between Simon's rancher-writer and the prairie-unconscious. These spontaneous metaphors for process and fluidity in Simon's writing in the second half of his studies contrast strikingly with his earlier metaphors of closedness and fixity (the lack of dialogue between writer and reader in 'Ghost Writer') and fragmentation ('grasshopper mind' and quick-change artist). Their presence indicates that Simon's creative processes have loosened up considerably over the two years and that he now has an understanding of writing and of the self as embodied processes that have to be trusted.

'Pencil' is one of Simon's 'Dictionary Pieces' written in response to single words chosen at random from the dictionary. These he sees as a kind of play where:

> I don't have to be the rancher ... I'm allowed to write whatever I want to write and stop it when I want to stop it, and I don't have to put any structure into it or anything and if it does end up with a structure that's great.

This supports what I have said about Simon's shift to a more flexible relationship with himself as a writer: he is providing an opportunity for his 'unruly' child-self to play, just like the benevolent art teacher of his childhood. But he understands that writing is not just about spontaneity; it also requires 'learning the skills of construction and repeated practice in order to achieve a more informed spontaneity'. So there is greater cooperation between his different 'selves' in the writing process, and this is crucial: without it, he says: 'nothing will ever get done'.

Simon's development, then, can be characterised as a shift from a sense of fragmentation, with tensions between different parts of himself, towards a greater cognitive flexibility and the ability to utilise a greater range of emotional material for writing, with all the risks and challenges that involves. This implies both an opening-up of the psyche to a more challenging 'inner terrain' and a greater confidence that that terrain can be managed.

Notes

1 A study with a larger contingent of men would no doubt be more useful in this regard.
2 All unascribed quotations in the case studies are from the students' questionnaires, interviews, and work for assessment.

Chapter 4

Reconnecting with the felt body for writing and learning

Maria's story

I have chosen Maria's story because it illustrates very well the reconnection with bodily feeling through creative life writing and the reconceptualising of writing and learning as fundamentally embodied processes. As for many Group 2 students, Maria's opening-up involves closer engagement with what she calls her 'child-self' and, like Simon, she develops an internal dialogue with her newly-found 'writer-self'. Maria experiences the opening-up as very challenging, and suffers depression during the early part of the MA. Her story shows how she begins to manage her expanded sense of self in part through developing containing self-images in her creative life writing.

Splitting and its consequences for learning

Maria is in her early 50s when she joins the MA, of French-speaking Belgian origin, and a healthcare worker. She has been attending creative writing courses for 10 years, which has helped her to gain confidence in her writing. Through the MA she hopes to develop greater fluency and structure in her writing and to 'feel more confident of having a voice'. She feels that understanding her own writing process better will help her personal growth and, for professional purposes, she wants to learn about the therapeutic effects of creative writing.

Maria's main problem is the high level of anxiety she experiences when trying to bring her creative work to completion; indeed it is a troublesome feature of her learning as a whole, sometimes obscuring her capacity to 'absorb and remember' and causing blocks. The fear of being judged academically is particularly strong. These problems have their origins, she believes, in her childhood, where her repressive Catholic upbringing led her to repress her spontaneity, and her 'ambivalent mother' left her feeling 'unheld' (Winnicott, 1960) (see Part III) and deprived of spontaneous love and support. Her creativity and confidence in herself plummeted dramatically during her convent schooling, and not completing her undergraduate degree compounded her sense of academic inadequacy.

Leaving her country of origin was necessary, Maria says, for the sake of her mental health, but it has left her with a deep sense of loss and guilt, and the term 'exile' occurs frequently. When she writes, she does not always know whether to use French or English, and this makes her feel like 'a hybrid, living in the borderland', 'to-ing and fro-ing' across the split in her identity that is 'never going to heal'. Maria's trajectory through the MA, like Simon's, involves becoming more familiar with the different parts of her fragmented personality, bringing them into dialogue with each other, and ultimately finding a way of 'holding' them for herself.

Transgressing the familiar boundaries of self-identity

It is the second session of Course 1, focusing on rhyme, rhythm, and sound in poetry, that begins the opening-up process for Maria. She responds playfully to the task of identifying and listening to the sounds of childhood words: 'I started hearing the sound of words, names of Flemish girls and places. Then memories, images would link with the sound. The more I gave in, lines wrote themselves ...a mixture of memories, inventions, metaphors'. The poem that emerges is a mixture of English, Flemish, and French:

> **I Learned a New Language**
> When I was very little
> I learned a new language
> *'Annemieke', 'Greta'*
> *'Marieka', 'Godelieve'.*
>
> These are the names
> of the girls I went to school with
> in the village of Dilbeek
> *'Kindeke, kapoentje, meisje'*
> I remember the names in Flemish.
> They wore gold earrings
> hoops in their skirts.
>
> My mother says hoops
> and earrings are for peasant girls
> so I can't have any.
>
> My folks are Walloons.
> I don't understand
> why they don't like the Flemish
> who pray to the 'Moeder'.

> I have two tongues.
> It doesn't help.
> My mother cannot hear me.

The poem indicates that otherness and difference are already uncomfortable features of Maria's childhood, even before the move to another culture that compounds her sense of being 'other'. In fact, the idea of *otherness* becomes a central motif for Maria throughout the MA. Later in the above poem it appears as *Ostrelande* (meaning 'Land of the Other'), a fictional town invented by a Belgian poet. It is a place where 'a Flemish Bluebeard, murders young girls'. As the poem is largely from the child's point of view, the emergence of this dark material surprises Maria, but 'being able to conjure this new aspect of the child helps in making me feel more whole. It gives another perspective to the [aspects] my shy, dreamy, withdrawn, lonely child would have chosen to embrace'. The idea of an Other Land where there can be 'tension between opposites, light and dark, child and parent, mother and father' marks Maria's conscious shift away from the good/bad dichotomy of her childhood environment into fairy-tale and surrealism, where the borders between the real and the imagined, the acceptable and the disapproved, can be blurred. It is a means of 'transgressing' her usual way of thinking.

A similar transgressive process takes place in the writing of 'Mother-Food', inspired by a visit to Brussels. Here again sounds of words evoke rich, sensual memories: 'Sneaking in[to] the kitchen, gobbling up half-finished packets of *waffles, galettes, chocolate pralines* ... the smell of rabbit marinated in red wine, black pudding...'. She remembers buying a bag of aniseed sweets without permission and her mother punishing her by not allowing her to eat the 'mouth-watering dessert of raspberries and cream' with the rest of the family at supper time; instead being 'sent to the larder, to stare at undesirable groceries: haricots, dried prunes, tins of orange marmalade'. Yet there were also 'magical days', helping her mother with the baking:

> I can see how the egg yolk mixes with melted butter, brown sugar, then transmutes into a new substance. 'Make sure you flatten the lumps', she says. I am left to stir the mixture for a while, as she sprinkles flour into the brown earthenware bowl...After the golden substance is poured into a tray and left to bake in the oven comes the exquisite moment of licking the bowl. After that you felt warm inside, tantalising aromas of cinnamon and gateau lingering on for the rest of the day.

Focusing on these rich sights and tastes and smells from her childhood enables Maria to step out of time, like Proust (see Chapter 8), and bring the past into the present. Whilst these are ambivalent memories, they allow her to evoke her homeland, *Le Pays de Cocagne*, a 'land of plenty', where food 'holds the promise of *jouissance*' – sensuality, bliss – 'the kind of delicious pleasure bestowed upon us when we give ourselves wholeheartedly to the feast of life'. The writing is itself a feast; it gives her permission to indulge her own sensuality, 'to reinstate a sense of self made from the experiences of growing up as a girl into a sensuous female body'. This helps to counter the sense of deprivation and repression stemming from her childhood. However, opening up to this repressed material and reflecting on it for the end-of-course paper confronts Maria 'with many parts of my psyche' that she finds difficult to manage. The reading groups are not suitable for helping her with this, she says, and she falls into the depression that has long been a feature of her life (see Chapter 12). Yet she does find support from the theory studied in Course 2.

Reconceptualising the self as a process

Julia Kristeva's idea of subjectivity as constantly in process between the Semiotic chora, the bodily-felt, maternal holding environment in which she believes the child is immersed in the early stages of life, and the Symbolic, the realm of language and separation, is a revelation to Maria (Kristeva, 1984). It gives her a new conceptual framework for understanding the splits between her different identities, as her French identity is connected with a sensual, bodily-felt sense of self with which she has lost touch. Kristeva's idea of the chora as a 'melancholic space', because of the inevitable loss, in the Symbolic, of the close relation with the mother, also speaks to Maria's experience of depression which she begins to see as a 'necessary affliction' involved in opening up to a deeper creativity and psychological change. Connecting with ideas in her native language is hugely beneficial in bridging the 'big rift' between her French and English identities; that Kristeva was, like her, an exile, 'crossing cultures' between her native Bulgaria and adopted France, also brings a sense of personal and intellectual companionship. Not surprising then that Maria chooses to write about Kristeva's ideas in her critical paper for Course 2.

After reading Kristeva, Maria says: 'I found myself writing more freely, and I felt I would need to engage in some physical practice, like dance or yoga, in order to continue to free my writing'. What we see happening here is Maria's opening-up to a clearer sense of her own fragmentation and the need for movement and dialogue between the different parts of her personality, but at the same time she is developing a conceptual framework that 'holds' these different parts together.

Grounding theory in experience

Course 3 (*Writing and Groups*) provides Maria with 'experiential grounding' for her theoretical explorations of Kristeva's chora. Unlike the previous two courses, this all-female group with its 'gentleness' and 'feminine quality' feels like the 'maternal holding environment' she needs, both mirroring her back to herself in all her different guises and 'holding' her (see Part III). This in turn helps her to 'hold' herself in the chaotic process of learning. She recalls how alone and unheld she felt when studying for her undergraduate degree, but here 'the centre does hold after all, I can somehow trust the process'.

With this stronger sense of containment (Bion, 1962) (see Part III), both internally and externally, Maria is able to start writing a piece of creative work 'from a fragmented sense of self'. Written in response to the first *Writing and Groups* exercise 'This is Who I Am' (see Appendix), it is structured in short, themed paragraphs representing different self-fragments, but the overall effect is of a dream, shifting back and forth between past and present tense, first and third-person narration, fantasy and reality. At the start there is silence and stasis: 'I lay there for centuries, waiting surrounded by darkness. No words to speak it, forever incubating the unborn'. Then suddenly there is colour and movement. Red predominates: the petals of giant poppies 'outside my window ..., like the wings of the butterfly reflecting light', 'crimson ... geraniums in terracotta pots' on a sunburnt Mediterranean hillside. Then there are other bodily sensations: 'the acrid aroma of the lavandin', and the loss of felt boundaries in lovemaking.

In the final fragment the narrator is observing a gypsy fortune teller sitting on the steps of her ancient wagon: 'her earrings dangle creating sparks all around her sunburnt face ... she is alert and calm, her feet steady, her jet black hair held by a crimson ribbon undulates around her shoulders ... [she] is painting her lips bright red'. This colourful, transgressive woman evokes thoughts of freedom, of the kind of roaming life enjoyed by 'Mongolian yurt dwellers'. But when the narrator gingerly circles the wagon and is surprised by its owner, she takes fright and runs away, lest this gypsy other, with her disruptive potential, 'take a piece of my soul'. Yet it is too late: 'She is already inside of me'.

This striking piece of writing moves back and forth uninhibitedly between the fictive and the real. It continues the work Maria began in Course 1 of opening-up to a more fluid self-experience that involves a deeper sensuality and transgresses her usual conceptual boundaries. The image of Mongolian yurt dwellers is particularly striking, with its connotations of movement across wide open spaces beyond the constraints of settled living, but the fear of the gypsy 'other' bears witness to the challenges involved. Maria notes in her journal that writing this piece feels like 'becoming invaded by something threatening'; yet the fragments are 'ordered into a cohesive piece'. Potentially disruptive Semiotic material is contained by the structured, Symbolic space of the writing, making it possible to begin to find form for the unspeakable 'other' in herself, her lost 'continental self'. By sharing the piece with the group, she 're-enacts [this perilous process of opening up] symbolically', allowing this challenging 'other woman' in herself to be seen and mirrored back to her in the safe-enough space of trusted others: 'This expands my sense of self and takes me out of the internal space of no-self I experienced in the past through lack of adequate mirrors'. Internalising the group as a positive object in whose presence she can write gives Maria a sense of inner presence that contains the other in herself sufficiently to be able to write when alone. She learns from this that not being able to write was the result of not being able to be alone in the space of writing, not being able to hold her own fragmented inner world, and that this applies to her experience of learning generally.

Fragments of poetic prose as containers for selves and others

Whilst, for some people, the creative writing component of Course 4, *Contexts for Practice*, is an opportunity for preparing a piece of honed creative writing, Maria uses it for exploring further her personal development. Over the summer vacation she has put into practice her insight that, in order to develop her writing, she needs to engage in some kind of physical activity, as the writing she selects for her portfolio is full of dancing. Dancing reconnects her to the feel of her body, with which she is now, as it were, in dialogue:

> I had forgotten what it felt like: the dancing body in motion gently flowing, arms creating curves, hands pushing against soft air, swaying in sync with the branches of the apple tree dancing in the courtyard. How could I ignore your subtle knowledge and love for falls, roles, skips and jumps across the wooden dance floor. Now I feel deep stillness as I lay [sic] with face and belly against the earth.

She has also been using her encounters with the visual and literary arts as a stimulus for free associational writing. A chance meeting with an art student at a gallery leads to her involvement in the creation of a series of photographic self-portraits, for which she must dress up and move her body in front of the camera. At first she finds this inhibiting: 'the cold eye of the camera' renders her 'frozen, exposed, vulnerable, stripped bare', so that she cannot find an authentic sense of self in this context. Then, almost giving up:

> Suddenly she came, first in my mind's eye, then in my body. I moved around, dressed her, gave in to her. There she is visible, taking up space on the gallery wall. I see an ageless woman dressed in black. She is sitting with a very straight back on a wooden chair. She is staring at the sea holding a giant conquer [conch?] shell against her heart.

This is a stark but positive image: the agelessness implies endurance and the upright sitting position evokes inner strength, whilst the shell evokes the sound of the sea with its wide open but risky spaces firmly held. This new image of herself '[breaks] through the layers of grief I artfully gathered around my body to protect myself'. After that 'everything flowed': desire emerges 'wearing a see-through black muslin robe', and then the exotic, sensuous gypsy, inspired now by Frida Kahlo's multi-selved portraits, 'wearing my deep blue skirt, feather red earrings and an orange shawl'.

Other artistic encounters continue this process of opening-up to a new, more bodily felt self. In another piece Maria finds herself inhabiting surrealistically the aimless, listless heroine of the novel she is reading. She rambles around the seaside town where she has lived for several years, indulging in 'giant chou buns and coffee éclairs', taking in for the first time the seedy underworld of this place: 'the school of drinking at the edge of the pier … pavements covered in seagull shit', and gathering impressions for writing. She has chance encounters, goes on a 'date from hell'. It sucks her in, this risky, compelling life lived in a novel: 'everything connects with everything, everything is happening really fast'.

As Maria writes about this experience, something new begins to happen. Her 'writer-self', this sensuous, wayward self who is beginning to have a life of her own, seems to be separate from her narrator-self. Whilst the narrator-self is clearly somewhat wary of this writer-self, 'her link to the underwater depths', she knows it is inevitable that 'soon I will return' to this risky, chaotic, creative experience. It is becoming a necessary part of the narrator's sense of who she is and in acknowledging it she feels that 'she has almost found a new equilibrium'. The term equilibrium implies that these two senses of self are not fragments split off from each other, like Maria's English- and French-speaking identities, rather they are complementary parts of the self encountered in the writing process. As we have seen in the example of Simon above, this shift from a sense of fragmentation between different parts of self to a sense of inner dialogue is a foundational moment in the development of a more grounded yet simultaneously more open and flexible stance as a writer, a stance which, in Maria's case, seems to carry over into life more generally.

Narrating the self

Whilst in Course 4 Maria was using her creative writing as a vehicle for personal development, for *Independent Study* she takes up the challenge of structuring her experience into a completed literary product. Her continuing theoretical explorations are helpful here. To Kristeva's conceptualisation of writing as necessarily involving opening-up to a difficult psychic space is added Hélène Cixous's notion of writing as a metaphorical death: the relinquishing of identity and creating space for the other in oneself. Maria finds support for these ideas in Surrealism, with its emphasis, in the process of artistic creation, on the free associative accessing of words and images as a means of subverting fixed self-structures. These ideas help to frame and contain the new project, 'Emily's Gift', as does the device Maria previously discovered of using prose fragments as containers for self and significant others. Her metaphor for the project of 'weaving a tapestry' captures effectively the binding together of disparate material within a framed space.

'Emily's Gift' draws its stimulus from a series of photographs taken by Maria's artist daughter of a house on the Belgian coast that originally belonged to her maternal grandfather, but was inhabited during her childhood by her aunt.

This house, to which Maria returns frequently, has over the years of her 'exile' become a 'shelter for memory', a symbol of her transient connection with her country of origin. She has agreed to write a text about her relationship with the house to accompany the photos in the book her daughter is preparing, but feels blocked. How she overcomes this writing block is the theme of 'Emily's Gift'.

The fragments that make up 'Emily's Gift' are written in the present tense, using a form of third person narration – limited omniscience, with an element of free indirect style (see Chapter 3) – that allows the fictionalised perspectives of members of the family, or Maria herself in the guise of 'Emily', to be embodied and speaking presences in the text, whilst also allowing Maria as framework narrator to structure and contain the whole. The first voice to emerge is Maria's aunt, here called 'Rose', a published writer of novels and short stories and a significant person in Maria's early life. Rose has recently died and we encounter her as a 'spirit bird' from the afterlife hovering over the Channel between Belgium and England. From here she is looking back at the house by the sea, regretting that she did not have time to write another novel, but also watching her niece, Emily, in her apartment in England 'waiting for the words carried by the North Sea wind' to help her write her piece to accompany her daughter's photos.

Several sections further on we switch into Emily's consciousness and learn that, whilst she was estranged from her aunt, she feels they are 'linked by some invisible thread that binds memories and words into the fabric of lines and stories'. She regrets 'the resentment she had felt towards her aunt ... in her later years', because of her 'refusal to engage with Emily's life and struggles'. She also regrets not showing more appreciation of Rose's first novel when she read it as a teenager: 'She had found the plot old-fashioned and was unable to comprehend why ... the heroine chooses to abandon her fiancé in order to devote herself to the contemplative life of the convent'.

On bad days looking at the photos of the house and struggling to write her memories makes Emily depressed. Then waking one morning she feels 'the unborn text like a garment, a second skin weaving itself around her ... [it] had a life of its own, endlessly creating colourful patterns. Before that vision her hands had felt bound'. Having bound hands evokes the unhappy experience at the convent of learning to knit and her mother having to unpick her poor efforts; then how she 'shrank under layers and layers of [her mother's] knitted socks, gloves, bags, blankets', a sort of love substitute, and how she tried so hard to be 'a good girl' for her mother. Her natural spontaneity and sensuality, she feels, were swamped by experiences like these. And then suddenly she understands the reason why she cannot write: it is because writing evokes an Emily of whom the nuns and her mother would disapprove:

> writing made her feel more sexy, gave her an edge, made her eyes sparkle. She could even remember how she had felt when she first learned to read and write. It was in Madame Jeanne's class. She experienced this intense jubilation whilst unravelling the mysterious connections between letters, sounds, words.

To write the text, she decides, she will have to reclaim 'her place of power in the family tree. She would have to follow her aunt Rose's footsteps by becoming a writer herself'.

Catching sight of her aunt's first novel in one of the photos, Emily 'feels compelled to read [it] with fresh eyes ... to find the secret hidden within the plot'. She senses that there is another Rose 'artfully hidden behind the veil of a holy woman' and that finding her is important for her own struggle to write. Immersing herself in the deliciously sensuous language of Rose's novel, Emily is transported back into the sensations of her childhood: 'coarse sand against bare feet, wet shivering body soaking the summer heat of the sun, ... the smell of melting tar on the way back from the beach'. She begins to understand that despite the fact that Rose inhabited the same repressive Catholic environment as herself, 'Rose somehow managed to save herself with her ability to harness the power of words and create poetry with their sounds'. Underneath 'Rose's false persona: the helpless, weak, capricious female' are not only 'her intelligence and brilliance', but the sensual woman who, Emily now remembers, filled her room with 'perfumes and rouge lipsticks ... silk flared skirts, mohair jumpers ... high-heeled shoes'. Emily realises that:

> For all those years [she] had been asking the wrong question: why does [the heroine of the novel] go to the convent? Instead ... she needed to ask: whom did the [novel] serve? Her answer: the writing served pleasure. Rose was enjoying herself and wanted to hide this from us ... her story was telling readers to love life and celebrate earthly sensations, to love poetry and transient feelings.

Emily now understands that by giving the novel an ending that conformed to the ethos of her Catholic environment her aunt was distracting the casual reader from dwelling on her own sensuality spilling out into the text. Emily is exhilarated by this discovery: it is okay to be a sensual woman and sensuality is in any case essential for writing.

Employing Rose's sensuous approach to writing, Emily finds that: 'Words flow more easily as if helped by Rose's pen and she can let the house fill her'. Recalling the felt memory of her mother she is able '...to taste her, smell her, remember her body so often absent, colour it blue, feed it orange, touch it like silk'. She remembers how the French word for sea, *la mer*, was always associated with her mother: 'She would repeat it to herself like a spell: *nous irons à la mer, à la mer!* It was the most succulent word she knew'. Then similarly sensuous memories of her grandmother emerge, her daughter and her father, the nuns and Uncle Raymond, who confusingly was both her godfather and a priest. Focusing on these felt memories, Emily draws important self-experiences 'back inside her own flesh', reclaiming some of the good things she has forgotten. She also finds a method for overcoming her writing block so that she can start writing the text for her daughter's book.

The last fragment concerns Emily's final visit to the house in the company of her daughter and mother for the purposes of the photographic project. The current owner, Rose's son, is selling the house to a distant cousin, so this might literally be their final visit. But Emily and her daughter have 'captured the soul of the family home' in the book that will soon be published, so it will never be completely lost. Back home after the trip, Emily dozes and in that half-dreaming state 'an ageless tall woman dressed in white' appears, whom Emily recognises as a Mexican storyteller, a *curandera*: 'she is sweeping a yard, circling with her whole body, erasing traces … of the dead…Gathering momentum, spinning, the woman in the vision is making space for stories'. Emily feels that she has always known this dancing woman who 'seems to exist beyond time and space'. In fact she is a part of Emily herself who now realises that 'she must keep writing stories so the departed may live'. Coming full circle, Emily is taking over Rose's mantle as the family storyteller, and just as the perspective of 'spirit bird' Rose at the outset binds together the different locales of Emily's life, so Emily now as storyteller similarly transcends everyday time and space, creating a new, potentially containing perspective for her fragmented life. This contrasts strikingly with Maria's earlier conceptualisation of herself as 'to-ing and fro-ing' between her split 'selves'.

The bodily-felt self as container

Reflecting on the writing of 'Emily's Gift', Maria says: 'The project led me to allow for seemingly disparate, split slices of my life to be brought together into a fictionalised whole held together by my Self'. The capitalising of self here seems significant. It implies a more holistic experience of self, which contains both the writing project and the fragments of her life and identity. She continues: 'The more I became able to claim authorship on the material, the more I felt an enhanced sense of Self as a writer'. This indicates that this new sense of self is in part a sense of agency arising out of the increased ability to write. Later she says: 'It is the tension between myself as writer, traveller, exile, and the Self whose roots extend beyond frontiers and time zones that allowed for the creative gesture needed for the making of my text'. Here the holistic sense of self is in productive dialogue with all the different facets of identity.

What becomes clear in Maria's attempts to make sense of her experience is that the more she is able to give coherent shape to her self-on-the-page, the more she feels grounded in a holistic sense of self, and this in turn enhances her ability to write. This virtuous circle of writing and what could be called 'selfing' brings Maria an increased sense of agency as a learner, so that by the end of the MA she is able to 'own my intelligence and [have] confidence in my abilities'. Rather than feeling irretrievably split between different selves, with a yawning abyss of 'no-self' between, she is more present to herself at her centre, better able to tolerate her anxieties, and consequently more trusting of, and open to, the changes that learning and creativity involve.

Chapter 5

Re-conceptualising the self in time

Susanna's story

Susanna's story has certain key differences from those of other Group 2 students. Here it is not (ostensibly) childhood experience that gives rise to psychic inertia but the trauma of loss and illness in the more recent past. Susanna has lost a sense of ongoingness through time and her experience of the MA is characterised by gradual opening-up to greater psychic movement between past, present, and future, experienced particularly, as in the case of Maria, through reconnecting with bodily feeling. This opening-up also brings understanding of learning as felt and bodily.

Loss, illness, and the freezing of identity

Susanna comes to the MA following a decade of life changes and losses, including 'the deaths of a daughter, a partner and a parent; geographical relocation from [Africa] to England; an unplanned career change and a [chronic illness] diagnosis'. She is undergoing psychotherapy but is 'unable to talk about [these events], even within the therapy room'. Her creative writing has also stalled. Drawing, however, has begun to help her find 'expression … outside the therapy room', and participation in a support community is helping her counter the loneliness of her illness. She joins the MA primarily to update her qualifications, and to gain confidence with her creative writing, which she describes as '[lacking] breadth and depth … pieces often remain[ing] undeveloped and becoming "lost"'. She also hopes to get a little personal development along the way.

Susanna's main sense of herself at the outset is of stuckness, partly in her backward-looking focus on the losses she has suffered and even more so in her identity as a chronically ill person. She describes the diagnosis as having 'fixed' her in the past and a sense of regret: 'one … gets thrown back on to the life that has been and what you could have done and should have done and what you'll never achieve anymore'. The medical labelling of 'every blood sample that is taken from me as "Bio-hazard"', compounds the sense of loss: of her health and of the possibility of future intimate relationships. Her self-narrative has ceased to move fluidly between past, present, and future: the present is barely tolerable, the future potentially non-existent, leaving the traumatic past as the overwhelming preoccupation.

It feels very important for Susanna to disclose her diagnosis, so that it can be validated within the context of her studies. She has already found helpful having a voice in her support community and she feels strongly – compulsively – that she similarly needs to have a voice on the MA in her new guise. But she is very uncomfortable about disclosure. There is another inhibiting self-concept at work too. The return to learning after such a long gap she finds very challenging. She is interested in everything, and during the first two terms feels compelled to read all the books on the reading list, putting a great deal of pressure on herself. The model of learning she has inherited from previous education is strongly cognitive and driven by a competitive struggle for achievement.

Reanimating the psyche

Opening-up begins for Susanna already in Course 1, with her reading group playing a central role here. The four members 'bonded very well ... and developed a strong trust' that enables them to develop an intense personal relationship. Particularly important for Susanna is the discovery that one group member is a volunteer for the support organisation she belongs to. This brings reassurance that she can safely disclose her illness identity if she decides to.

The trust Susanna develops in her reading group is fundamental to her changes at the outset, but the creative life writing also plays a significant role, generating space and movement in her psyche. In her response to the 'web of words' exercise on the theme of beginnings, Susanna anticipates that, in starting a new writing life and experiencing the calm landscape of the 'rolling Sussex Downs', she will leave behind the chaos of her present life: 'This banging noise of routine living and fitting things in'; this 'stumbling and staggering [along] paths overgrown with thorns and heavy with bushes and leaves that whip my face'. Waking in the night to the 'long darkness' and the 'hammering' of the rain, she looks forward to the calmer, dreamlike state she hopes her writing will bring, 'an elegant dance of prose', words shaped 'into a ballet'. But her mind refuses to cooperate, the words in her head fighting with each other. She strains to hear the symphony, even a lone flute that will charm the snake – which evokes her elusive creativity – but instead:

> a cymbal crashes and swiftly following, the bass of a drum overthrows it, the high hat screams; the bass tormented, thrashes out its anger and a heavy beat develops. Is it thunder or the drum? The music brings me to my feet but my steps are clumsy and I fall on one knee, grazing it as I scrape across the rough dirt to get back on my feet. Then the beat takes hold – my feet scuffling, stamping, dust flying as a frenzied rhythm develops. I dance a wild dance of exorcism. I have no choice but to move with it, it moves through me and the

letters and the thoughts fight for mind space and then get lost not caring, caught in the whirlwind. There are feathers flying, chickens scatter across the dirt, a child steps back for safety. Then the drum pace drops and the dust scatters over my feet as they slow to the fading rhythm. Eyelids heavy with dance, still no glimmer of dawn. A steady, heavy rainfall. I look for my pen to calm the chaos within.

Here, the desire to achieve a calm state for writing is thwarted by the more pressing need to express the rage at the present. And dance becomes the metaphor for self-expression; it is a wild thing, threatening disruption and the safety of onlookers. The locale evokes the Africa Susanna has loved and lost. Only when the rage has run its course is there any chance of the calm she seeks.

Given Susanna's sense of fixity, the movement and the strong presence of bodily feeling and emotion here, are striking. The fixity clearly has a role: to keep the pain and rage at bay. But the combination of metaphor and present tense in this piece allow her to delve beneath the defended surface, to bring the past symbolically into the present, and to give expression to the pain and rage. Reflecting on this exercise, Susanna writes that 'beginnings' mean 'leaving things behind and that in that departure I might become more diffuse and less focused'. These bodily metaphors anticipate the opening-up to a less fixed sense of self that is already a possibility as a result of this first exercise. They are very different from her earlier ones: fixity, disclosure. Whilst 'disclose' implies bringing into the light something already formed, and control on the part of the discloser, becoming 'more diffuse' and 'less focused' implies loosening control and entering into a process of gentle dismantling. What makes it possible to let go in this way, so soon within this new context, is the nature of the 'web of words' exercise, the way it 'pulled us together through our words', with the tutor as an essential part of the holding environment.

The word 'snake', that emerges in 'Beginnings', becomes the focus of Susanna's next poem. In 'Beginnings' its arrival is unexpected. It is connected with the struggle to write, a creative urge that needs awakening, but it could also represent the excess of emotion that surges out into the dance, something frightening and potentially dangerous, or disturbingly sensual. In the new poem both these elements are visible. At the start the snake is sleeping 'Through scorching summer ... saving stamina/and sinewed muscle/for the fight', evoking power contained. Then the snake charmer with his flute calls her, little knowing 'the danger he awakens'.[1] In the last stanza the 'harlequin paper skin abandoned' is evidence that the snake has sloughed off her former contained state and is dangerously on the loose. The witches' refrain from Macbeth – 'Eye of newt and toe of frog/wool of bat and tongue of dog' – repeated between stanzas, emphasises the sinister, potentially life-threatening consequences of rousing the snake. The simultaneous power and menace of the creative urge is effectively captured in this poem: in order to write, it suggests, Susanna has to risk accessing the darker side of herself.

Being in the present – turning towards the future

Very quickly then, with 'holding' provided by the tutors and the reading group, Susanna begins her journey out of her stalled vision of the past by creating living, breathing metaphors for her present sense of self. The next exercise pushes this further. For the 'future self' exercise Susanna chooses a safe five years hence, imagining herself now as a working writer. As 'Five Years On' opens, she is sitting with her back 'against a huge floor cushion propped up against a chair', reading and listening to music. She knows that it is 'safe enough to lean back', because there is someone behind her: her lover who is crucial to the atmosphere of trust this piece of writing conjures up. He is the one who helps her to let go of the 'smouldering darkness' and to trust 'the ground beneath [her]'. He helps her to contain her pain, creating a space she can go to, 'tiptoeing gently when I need to visit my dreamland of the dead'. It is also a sensual place, 'where we touch and feel our way through each other's lives'; where desire finds its natural home again.

In this containing space Susanna can be fluidly creative: 'I am always either reading or writing these days, researching and writing, searching and noting, re-writing and shaping, moving and re-arranging'. This activity 'nourishes me in the deepest way'. It gives her a voice: 'I read and I am heard'. But her writing is not always easy; it takes readers 'from one slippery path to a crevice then steeply uphill to the clear light of day'. For some, 'the voice is too loud, too stringent and sometimes the frightened ones call "tone it down"', but she does not. Like Simon's story 'Pencil', 'Five Years On' simultaneously evokes space and movement, in the iterative processes of writing and re-writing, moving and shaping, but there is also a sense of trust that when she 'leans back' she will be held, not just by the other, but by her own internalised sense of safety.

In this piece, then, Susanna dares not only to imagine a future, but one in which she is managing the pain of the past sufficiently to be able to write again, and also, importantly, enjoying a new sexual relationship. This derives, I suggest, partly from her deeper exploration of what the present feels like, and partly from her sense of being 'held' within the reading group. Just doing this piece of writing, Susanna says, is a 'turning point'; 'having it heard in the writing group' is another turning point. Also crucial is the tutor's feedback that helps her not to dismiss the writing as a 'romantic fantasy', but to see it as a legitimate expression of desire. The term 'turning point', although a cliché, captures Susanna's psychic movement away from a fixed focus on the past to a more forward-looking gaze, thus setting her self-narrative in motion again. As she says later, 'I found the act of writing this piece powerful and quite transformational. It moved me from a past and present marked by loss into an area of possibility and future'.

Re-conceptualising the self as multiple and in process

Exposure to the conceptual material of Course 1 also contributes significantly to Susanna's development at this stage. It speaks to her about her own condition: the idea of illness as a narrative in Hilary Mantel's memoir (2004); the potential for psychic splitting under the impact of physical illness (McDougall, 1985); the way medical discourses can construct social identity (Foucault, 1971); and the possibility of having multiple voices and dimensions of self (Neisser and Fivush, 1994). It helps Susanna to articulate and bring conceptual shape to her experience prior to the MA and to understand better the impact of the work of the first term. What begins visibly to emerge from Susanna's experience of the MA is a growing understanding of herself as potentially in process rather than fixed by a label; as having multiple voices and dimensions of self, potentially in conflict with each other; and of writing and rewriting her experience as a means of keeping the process in motion and open to change. This 'new identity' – which she also refers to as a 'new personal typography', revealing her experience of it as spatial – 'includes being part of a writing and learning community that stretches the boundaries between the personal, the creative and the academic'.

Susanna's shift into a more open and fluid sense of self continues in *Writing and Groups*. The issue of disclosure of her medical condition looms large again at the start of this course, with the exercise 'This is Who I Am'. Susanna chooses poetic free verse and a mixture of past and present tense to contain a mini-autobiography spanning birth to the present. A difficult parental relationship comes into view ('They weren't speaking when I was born'), divorce perhaps ('the explosion shattered the fragile family Ming into fragments'), and the need for escape ('a square peg in a round hole in a cold country/I escaped to the sun'). The devastating consequences of that escape ('It was too hot; I got burnt!') become clear in the last few lines of the final stanza: 'Blister packs keep me alive/ I ignore the red and yellow labels/marking me a danger to humanity./Defiant, I use public transport at all times'.

Writing this poem and reading it to the group is, Susanna says, 'enormously cathartic' and is made possible by the holding environment of the group. The 'space in the room' feels safe-enough to begin, at last, the disclosure Susanna is seeking, although when it comes to discussing the poem, she notices that she does not offer explanations of that last stanza. Mutual listening and sharing is enough at this point (although later she regrets not taking the opportunity for a fuller disclosure), but she is glad that the next writing exercise is on: 'This is How I Shelter, When I Shelter'.

Her short fiction on this theme is a series of images of shelter: '... in my bed under cool covers', '... in cafés drinking frothy white cappuccinos', '... the desert of the blank page where the soil is dry and thirsty for words'. Africa is here, drifting into view from the safety of these shelters, and those she has lost – husband and child. Evoking Simon's short story, 'Murder', Susanna uses the image of the ocean here, remembering a time when it was a shelter, when she loosened her grip on the raft she was clinging to and allowed herself to drift to the bottom, where she 'sat curled around myself watching antennae open and close, insects disappear down the gaping mouths of gold-finned fish, tiny pink petals float past and occasionally far above, the heel of a human or a black rubber flipper'. Since that time she has become 'stranded on the land', unable to go underwater again, but a wise voice from the past reminds her that: 'You liked it there ... you've been to the bottom of the ocean before and you know now that you won't drown'.

In a short space of time then, Susanna is able to start working through her sense of loss in the safe-enough holding environment provided by the writing exercises and the group. There are other elements of 'holding' too in this course, including the learning journal, through which she reflects on the experience of the group and the writing. Theoretical readings also bring clarity and structure to experiential learning: Anzieu's (1984) concept of the group as an envelope; Carl Rogers's (1989) idea that it is the ability to change that constitutes learning rather than acquiring knowledge; and particularly Nina Coltart's (1996) notion of silence as an opportunity to reflect deeply and to grow. Whilst the experience of the course, particularly the way it is facilitated, is a hugely important part of Susanna's learning, it is really important for her 'to see some of those ideas formulated in words'.

Re-conceptualising the learning process

The process, begun in Course 1, of relinquishing a dominant identity now begins, in Course 3, to impact on Susanna's sense of what it means to be a learner. Her former conceptualisation of learning as a drive for achievement, a 'terrible compulsion ... to cram everything in', is replaced by a more open and accepting stance. Rather than concentrating 'on delivery and outcome', she now understands the value of concentrating 'on what you're actually learning and being ... in the here and now'. This emphasis on being in the present connects with Susanna's increased ability to inhabit the present in the creative writing exercises. It evokes, in her earlier words, a 'diffuse and less focused' conceptualisation of the self in the learning process than her previous fixed container metaphor of learning as a process of cramming everything in. She also uses the term 'absorbing' to describe her new understanding of learning, with its connotations of porousness and receptivity. This new sense of being open to the process of learning is also helping her to relax her need to be in control as the facilitator of the writing group she is running and to develop a more relaxed, listening-holding stance.

The theme of the final session of *Writing and Groups* is endings, not an easy one for Susanna in the context of her losses. The writing assignment, 'This is What I Remember', gives rise to a free verse poem. Susanna describes this as her 'strongest piece of work so far', allowing her to face 'an aspect of my shadow self – a frightened person, terrified of further abandonment'. Through the gloom of 'the bright seaside sky greyed quickly' at the mention of endings, the catastrophic events of her past life appear as a traffic accident on an African road, 'a thick mud of pigeon guts and liver smeared across the windscreen of our future'. She feels distanced now from the 'long hot summers ... meant for/ children with brown limbs lost in artless play,/ surfers,/ lovers/ and the lioness stalking grasslands, tearing gazelle flesh apart/ with her bare teeth'. There is only the silence of the bush and grandmother's 'sad wisdom'. But it is not all darkness, for there is 'a hairline crack where light seeps through'. The visceral sense of loss this poem conveys is relieved by this final line: it raises the reader's and the writer's imaginative gaze upwards towards the light – and the future.

Finding time again

At the end of the first year, then, Susanna has experienced change in a number of ways. Centrally important is her changing perception of time. From a sense of being 'fixed in the past' and 'dragging myself into the present with great difficulty', she can now inhabit the present and has rediscovered a sense of future. This opening-up to greater psychic movement has enabled her to relinquish her dominant self-concept of a chronically ill person. Her growing understanding of the self as made up of multiple dimensions has enabled her to begin to re-conceptualise her illness identity as 'part of my life and not the only thing'; rather than a portent of ending, it has become 'a companion'. This has relieved the overwhelming pressure to disclose this identity and, whilst she has referred to it in her writing and told 'a few students who have become friends', she hasn't actually 'disclosed' to the student group as a whole.

Whilst the opening-up has been challenging, anxiety is now 'hugely reduced'; she has a 'stronger sense of myself as an individual'; she is able to write more consistently, to be bolder and take risks with it, to allow 'ideas [to] come on trains and buses' and to be in process before they become fixed in words. She is also 'beginning to get more sense of trusting my *self* as a learner', learning 'to work between aspects of myself', which gives her 'a stronger sense of "whole"'. These are major changes, yet Susanna describes the process of change as subtle and personal, 'like homoeopathy where nothing necessarily *happens* but everything *changes*'. All the things she has been working with, she says – her writing voice, her ideas and material, readings of all kinds – have always been there, but 'the exercises and discussion and listening and reading of our own and each other's work [have] synchronised into a self-respect and validation that has allowed me to write about it in some way'. This conjures up for me a stalled process being set in motion again, or perhaps better the re-setting of a mechanism that has never quite worked properly, so that the process it motors begins now to function more smoothly. That process, as in Simon's story, involves cognitive fluidity, a more ready access to feeling and emotion, and an ability to 'hold' the challenging space for the imagination. Thus the sense of fixity and fragmentation into discrete identities, with their inhibiting consequences for feeling and thinking, has given way to a more fluid but manageable sense of multiplicity. As a result, learning and writing processes have speeded up: 'I learn something [every session] and in shorter and shorter time spans …On [one journey home] I wrote 14 short passages of prose – one for every station at which the train stopped'. Even in therapy, 'I've kind of moved along at a much quicker pace'.

Consolidating a more reflexive self-experience

The start of Year 2 is complicated for Susanna by a period of hospitalisation. But her newfound facility for poetry provides a tool for reflecting on that experience through metaphor and imagery. During the enforced passivity of her hospital stay, rather than pressing herself to read all the theory books on her list, she begins to write a sequence of poems. These form a connected narrative from the end of the summer term, with its 'golden glow' of the intense relationships developed in Course 3 and expectations of journeys to be made over the vacation, to finding herself at the mercy of the 'howling dog' of physical pain. Waiting for hospital admission evokes difficult memories of an absent father at a time of childhood hospitalisation, but there is also a lighter, more ironic tone, that gently subverts the serious business of the psycho-geriatric ward in which she finds herself and her preparations for her operation. What she learns from this period of reflection and writing is, again, 'to be much more in the here and now'.

In spite of the new challenges, Course 4 (*Contexts for Practice*) is a period of consolidation, enabling Susanna to bring together some of her learning from previous courses: how to facilitate effectively for others the kind of 'bonding and … opening of the valves of creativity and self-examination' she experienced in Course 1; how some of the theory from Course 2 becomes more intelligible in a practice context. This term's student-led writing workshop provides an opportunity to develop her sequence of hospital poems, and she learns the value of re-working her initial 'energetic expression' of ideas. She ends the term with a deeper sense of trust in herself as a writer; it is invaluable, she says, to listen to others and take their comments on one's work, but 'in the end one relies on one's own feelings and judgements'. This involves being able to 'learn through mistakes'. She realises that this applies also to her work as a facilitator of therapeutic writing groups, and equally well to the way she evaluates herself: 'owning oneself rather than taking on an identity through the blame or praise of others'. All of this echoes the theme of opening-up to a more fluid and multiple sense of self that is also grounded in a growing sense of personal agency.

Creating a space for relationship

For her *Independent Study* project Susanna embarks on a 'travel memoir', exploring her time in Africa and her relationship with her former partner, continuing the process of purging and clearing a space for new thoughts. She has a sense of 'leaving home', of relinquishing the holding environment of the MA and going out into the world alone to show what she has learnt. In a conscious attempt to free herself of the need for 'chronology and accuracy' of an autobiographical account of her past and to continue the process of opening-up, Susanna chooses creative life writing and a non-linear, episodic structure for the memoir. Using flashbacks, she can move back and forth in time and place, dramatising key events: her arrival in Africa by native bus to be reunited with her lover after their initial coming together; their first meeting in a neighbouring African country; her subsequent sojourn in England before returning to Africa; then the traditional wedding in her partner's home village.

She wants to locate her story in the political and historical context of the time and in a first draft she intersperses newspaper extracts, maps, and photos of African leaders in between episodes. But the members of her reading group find that these distract from the memoir, so she begins afresh, this time keeping these 'actual' readers' needs – for living characters, and dialogue and commentary – more clearly in mind. This is 'a pivotal moment' in her understanding of how to start shaping the memoir and another example of how crucial the group is as audience to the developing work and the developing self. The revised version is a multi-voiced narrative, within a first person, past tense frame, with the historical and political context brought alive through imagined dialogues between the narrator and local people, such as students she is teaching, who relate their experiences of the struggle for liberation in their country. These dialogues – imagined re-renderings of conversations Susanna had at the time – enable her to place her story, and her suffering, into a larger context. Thus in creating this relational piece of writing, she confronts her difficult past in the company of others with difficult pasts. Relationality is strongly present in this piece in other ways too. In the preparations for the narrator's wedding festivities and the ceremony itself there is much collaborative music-making and dancing and, by contrast with 'Beginnings' where Susanna's dancing is an expression of rage and pain in isolation, here it is sensual and joyful and in the presence of family and friends. In this final piece of writing Susanna has created a moving, bodily-felt space for herself in the company of others.

Having successfully sustained a long piece of creative writing in the relative isolation of *Independent Study*, Susanna feels increased confidence in herself as a writer and a sense of 'self-reliance'; readers' comments and tutorial feedback have helped her to sharpen her 'critical eye' on her writing. She is also, she says, 'more self-accepting'. This latter is the result of the 'very powerful effect' of writing 'creatively' about a period of her life 'that was full of contradictions'. Being given permission to fictionalise it has allowed her 'to acknowledge it and make something of it without it disturbing me or feeling like a confession'. It has brought her a sense of 'freedom with myself'. What she means by this, she says, is that she is

> much less frightened of exposure and writing about myself ... I was almost frightened to write in case of what came out. Now I feel that what comes out is fine, it can stay on the page as private writing or be shared or be changed into a fictional or other format.

The phrase 'frightened of exposure' is seemingly at odds with Susanna's previous pressing need to 'disclose' her illness identity, and the two verbs carry very different connotations: 'expose' implies opening-up to something raw and vulnerable, whilst 'disclose', as I said above, implies revealing something complete or closed. It also links with Susanna's intense experience of needing to be heard: if what needs to be heard is closed off, it cannot be expressed. I would suggest that the idea of disclosing her illness was a safer option than exposing her grief and anger. Whilst imposed from outside and freezing time, the illness identity created a sense of coherence at a time of huge emotional upheaval. Susanna hints at this when she says at the outset that she was unable 'to be with myself' and that this had 'frozen my ability to express myself in creative writing' and inhibited the work she could do in therapy.

After the MA Susanna talks about getting back into teaching and says: 'I am easing into myself a lot more'. And then trying to define this more closely, she says she is 'pushing back ... into a kind of area of not so much familiarity or comfort but [pause] being more myself'. Elsewhere in the interview she describes this sense of being more herself to being 'much more timely with myself and other people'. Being 'more timely' evokes fluidity and movement and contrasts with Susanna's previous stuckness in the past, no longer having a tolerable present or future. This increased sense of psychic movement allows the different aspects of herself – her writer-self, her ill self, her teaching self – to feel more integrated. She has moved from a fixed self that needs to be revealed towards a looser, more fluid and bodily-felt sense of self in time. The work she has done through the MA, alongside her therapy, has set the process of self-making in motion again.

Note

1 Later, Susanna identifies the snake charmer as her therapist.

Part II

Understanding mechanisms of change in transformative learning

There are two main strands of thinking in the attempt to understand the nature of deep individual change taking place in transformative learning: the original one deriving from Jack Mezirow and the early response to this by Robert Boyd and colleagues. For Mezirow, transformative learning:

> transforms problematic frames of reference – sets of fixed assumptions and expectations (habits of mind, meaning perspectives, mind-sets) – to make them more inclusive, discriminating, open, reflective, and emotionally able to change. Such frames of reference are better than others because they are more likely to generate beliefs and opinions that will prove more true or justified to guide action.
>
> (Mezirow, 2003: 58)

Achieving transformation involves 'critical reflection', both on the views of others that make up one's own 'frame of reference' ('objective reframing'), and on one's own views ('subjective reframing') (Mezirow, 1998). With the emphasis on assumptions that form the way we see ourselves and the world, this theory primarily focuses on cognitive constructions rather than psychodynamic processes, and on consciously intentional and rational methods of liberating oneself from them. Mezirow does, however, acknowledge the role of the emotions in this process, suggesting that 'subjective reframing' can be 'an intensely threatening emotional experience' (Mezirow, 2000: 6–7).

For Jungians Boyd and Myers, 'transformative education' involves liberating oneself from 'old patterns of thinking, feeling, and acting' resulting from upbringing, which '[prevent] growth' (Boyd and Myers, 1988: 279). Rather than critical reflection, they see emotional release or 'discernment' as the key mechanism of transformation. This consists of three stages: 'receptivity' or 'assum[ing] the posture of listener, open to receive the symbols, images, and alternative expressions of meaning that surface from the [unconscious]'; 'recognition' or confronting authentic thoughts and feelings that become available through increased receptivity; and 'grieving' in response to the 'involuntary disruption of order [and collapse of] previous assurances and predictable ways of interpreting reality and of making meaning', that can be 'poignant and painful'. The consequence of discernment is 'an expansion of consciousness' that:

> moves the person to psychic integration and active realization of their true being. In such transformations the individual reveals critical insights, develops fundamental understandings and acts with integrity.
>
> (ibid.: 262)

As in Mezirow's theory there is a shift to a more agentic way of being, here indicated by the development of a more critical stance and the ability to act with integrity, but the shift is more embodied and less consciously intentional or rational. John Dirkx provides a more recent Jungian rendering of this expansion of consciousness:

> [The] paradigm shift [in transformative learning] involves decentering the ego and ego consciousness in the learning process and allowing our inner selves greater expression and voice, allowing for a deeper and more meaningful presence of the imagination and the spontaneous and semi-autonomous forces of the unconscious to which it is giving voice. This paradigm shift requires a reconnection, an ongoing dialogue of the ego with these deeper, unconscious, and extrarational aspects of the human psyche, both individually and collectively.
>
> (Dirkx, 2012: 127)

Both the Mezirowian and Jungian understandings of the shift in transformative learning are helpful in my attempts to understand CWPD students' experience of change, but they also have their limitations. Mezirow's idea of liberating oneself from 'frames of reference' that have become fixed resonates with the idea I discuss in Chapter 7 that social self-concepts containing a narrative of how one should be in the world can become rigid identities and that transformative learning involves their dismantling. However, his exclusive focus on the constructed nature of meaning-making gives a one-sided picture of mechanisms of transformation, as does his privileging of highly intentional, conscious processes over the less conscious and embodied. This latter has, in fact, become a major theme in recent thinking in the field (Taylor, 2001). Boyd's idea that change involves an 'expansion of consciousness' resonates with what I have called the expansion of the psyche, but his reliance on the exploration of Jungian archetypes in the collective unconscious for understanding this is limiting. Dirkx's understanding of the 'paradigm shift' as involving the 'decentering of the ego and ego consciousness' which facilitates a 'reconnection' with deeper and less conscious dimensions of the psyche, is similarly helpful. However, there is scope for unpacking terms such as 'ego' or 'ego-consciousness' and for understanding more deeply how the ego can be 'decentered' or engage in a 'dialogue' with other aspects of the psyche. Some of Dirkx's terms could also usefully be reconsidered in light of the cognitive neuroscience of self and consciousness: for example, his distinction between conscious processes that are rational and unconscious processes that are extrarational. In the thinking of Damasio and others, rationality is both conscious and unconscious (cf. Taylor, 2001).

Thus in the two chapters of Part II I attempt to open up some of the meanings inherent in these two main theories of individual change in transformative learning and, working within a bio-psycho-social conceptual framework, to understand in greater depth the psychic shift that transformative learning brings about, as well as what necessitates it in the first place.

Chapter 6

Reflexivity and the psyche as a dynamic system

Part I provides a detailed picture of students' shift from cognitive control, where certain emotional feelings and parts of the personality are repressed or in conflict, towards a more open, flexible, embodied, and agentic self-experience, whether for writing, learning, or simply for being. As I have shown, this shift is evident not only in students' conscious descriptions, but also comes through less conscious metaphors and imagery, especially in their creative life writing. The opening-up of space for the imagination and the growing ability to manage it is visible, for example, in Simon's change of metaphor for his sense of self as a writer from closed, unspeakable psychic territory to more confident management of the 'wild prairie' of the imagination. Increased psychic space is visible too in Susanna's change of verb from the need to 'disclose' her identity as an ill person, to her subsequent willingness to 'expose' more of the raw emotional feelings this identity was keeping under control. Similarly increased psychic flexibility is visible in images of movement in the later creative writing, as in Susanna's shift from a sense of 'stumbling and staggering' along overgrown paths at the start of the MA to the fluid and sensual dancing at the wedding feast at the end. The creative writing Maria produces in her second year is also full of dancing, and Simon's later work is full of movement, with Ian Ferris rolling weightlessly in the 'cool womb' of the sea in 'Murder' and the constantly regenerating life cycle of 'Pencil'. Thus at the phenomenological level the shift to a more open, flexible, embodied, and agentic psychic state seems to be experienced as an increased sense of inner space and movement.

In previous attempts to understand this shift I have referred to it, drawing on Mikhail Bakhtin's work, as the development of a more 'dialogic relationship', whether with others or with oneself (e.g. Hunt, 2000), and it is interesting that Dirkx and others in transformative learning (e.g. Taylor, 2000) use this concept too (although not the Bakhtinian version). Dialogue in Bakhtin's sense means being psychically open and flexible, able to suspend one's own preconceptions and engage with the other on equal terms (Bakhtin, 1981). More recently I have also been referring to this shift as the development of a more 'reflexive' psychic state (Hunt, 2004a), which I have come to understand as consonant with 'dialogic'. Mezirow also uses 'critical reflexivity' or 'critical reflectivity' – the two being, for him, interchangeable – to describe the 'crucial' feature of perspective transformation, suggesting that it 'needs phenomenological study' (Mezirow, 1981: 11). Seeing that reflexivity, being a form of metacognition, is a fundamental mechanism of consciousness (Koriat, 2007), it is also relevant to Boyd and Myers's idea that transformative learning involves an 'expansion of consciousness'. So reflexivity could be said to be a key concept in transformative learning theory. However, there is a considerable amount of confusion about what it actually means. Thus, in an attempt to throw light on the fundamental mechanisms of transformative change, I focus in this chapter on trying to make better sense of reflexivity by placing it within a bio-psycho-social conceptual framework.

The concept of reflexivity

For social theorist Anthony Giddens reflexivity is 'a defining characteristic of all human action', 'a methodology of practical consciousness' by which 'human beings routinely "keep in touch" with the grounds of what they do as an integral element of doing it' (Giddens, 1990: 36, 99). In traditional cultures where social change was slow people reflexively monitored their actions so as to reproduce the structures of society. In the modern world by contrast, where social change is rapid, reflexivity involves constantly examining and reforming social practices 'in the light of incoming information about them'. This means constantly engaging in reflection, including '[reflecting] upon the nature of reflection itself' (ibid.: 36–38, 99). Consciously reflecting on reflection is how reflexivity is generally understood in adult education (e.g. Illeris, 2004a), including by Mezirow.

In my own attempts to understand reflexivity, I have tended towards Donna Qualley's view that reflexivity is not just reflection on reflection, but a somewhat different process:

> Where reflection could be said to involve taking something into oneself – a topic, an event, a relationship – for the purpose of contemplation or examination, reflexivity involves putting something out in order that something new might come into being. It involves creating an internal space, distancing oneself from oneself, as it were, so that one is both inside and outside of oneself simultaneously and able to switch back and forth fluidly and playfully from one position to the other, giving oneself up to the experience of 'self as other' whilst also retaining a grounding in one's familiar sen e of self.
> (Hunt, 2004a: 156; Qu "ey, 1997: 11)

The idea of reflexivity as involving 'putting something out in order that something new might come into being' seems crucially important here in light of the findings from the current project. It precisely evokes students' experience of allowing new knowledge to come into being through loosening cognitive control – 'giving oneself up' to experience – rather than actively pursuing knowledge through conscious reflection. This makes reflexivity more passive than active and perhaps also less conscious. Jerrold Siegel supports this active/passive distinction, suggesting that whilst reflection – or what he calls 'reflectivity' – is intentional and wilful, reflexivity is automatic, involuntary, something like a reflex (Siegel, 2005: 12–13). Yet reflexivity cannot be completely passive, as learning, no matter how relaxed, always involves an element of will. It also *gives rise* to action, in the form of carrying forward the new knowledge into writing or learning processes or engagement with others, or indeed into conscious reflection. Thus, as a starting definition, I would suggest that reflexivity is a cognitive–emotional[1] mechanism that enables knowledge of the world and of oneself to be acquired through a relaxed kind of intentionality operating intuitively at a low-level of consciousness but giving rise to conscious reflection and action. Reflectivity, by comparison, is more conscious, intentional reflection, including reflection on psychic processes. On this definition Mezirow's active and highly conscious process of 'critical reflection' is reflectivity, whilst Boyd and Myers's more passive 'discernment' is closer to reflexivity.

But what about the role of the self in reflexivity: the switching back and forth between what I called our familiar sense of self and the sense of self as 'other'? Dirkx's dialogue between the ego and the deeper, unconscious aspects of the psyche has certain similarities with this, but does not take us further. Social realist Margaret Archer's schema for understanding the self in reflexivity, by contrast, provides a useful starting point. She sees reflexivity as the individual's ability to become a 'social agent' capable of transforming society, that is, the ability to think outside of the conceptual frameworks we imbibe from family, education, and society, which echoes the idea of being able to be inside and outside of oneself in my starting definition. For Archer, being a 'social agent' necessitates distinguishing between the '*concept* of self (which is ... social) and the universal *sense* of self (which is not)'. The 'concept of self' is associated with 'social identity', which emerges out of our immersion in existing conceptual frameworks; the 'universal sense of self' is associated with 'personal identity' – a sense of being the same person over time. 'Personal identity' is crucial in becoming a 'reflexive social agent', because it enables us to avoid being 'swamped' by 'social identity' (Archer, 2003: 19–20).

Archer's idea that reflexivity takes place between the self-concept and the continuous sense of self arising out of the body is helpful, but her suggestion for how the latter comes into being ignores empirical evidence. Working from a neo-Lockean position, according to which we come into the world as a 'blank slate', Archer sees the 'universal sense of self' emerging naturally out of the 'practical activity' of the body's engagement with its physical environment, starting with the infant's rubbing itself against the bars of its cot (Archer, 2000: 122–26). In light of extensive research in developmental psychology indicating that newborns are able to distinguish between their own bodies and other entities in their environment (Rochat, 2011), it seems more likely that they have an innate but pre-reflective bodily sense of self and agency, that is, a sense of being a connected physical whole that can engage with the world rather than a series of disconnected parts, and that it is this sense of wholeness that enables them to *own as theirs* their early encounters with the environment, including with their carers.[2] Indeed in recent years the idea that there is an innate base level of bodily subjectivity and agency – a minimal or core self – pre-existing the acquisition of language has become a dominant theme in a wide range of scientific and science-related disciplines. Thus I would suggest that reflexivity is more likely to take place between this innate bodily subjectivity and a higher level of subjectivity in the form of the self-concept. I will now explore this idea in more detail.

The core self and bodily agency

Extrapolating from his research into the experience of people suffering brain damage, cognitive neuroscientist Antonio Damasio posits the existence in human functioning of two levels of conscious self – the 'core self' or 'core consciousness' (consciousness for Damasio is always accompanied by a sense of self) and the 'autobiographical self' – neither of which rely on language for their existence, although in humans the latter becomes enhanced by language (he calls this the 'extended self' or 'extended consciousness'). The core self emerges out of what Damasio calls, following Panksepp (1998), the non-conscious[3] 'protoself', which he locates in the most ancient parts of the brain.[4] The protoself results from the brain's perpetual activity of 'mapping', that is sensing and feeding back to itself information about the body's internal states, such as metabolic processes (e.g. temperature control) and innate drives and motivations (e.g. hunger, thirst, curiosity, sexuality), for the purpose of maintaining physiological balance (homeostasis) and ensuring the organism's survival (Damasio, 2003: 34–5). The global 'map' of the state of the body that results from this feedback loop emerges in the form of 'primordial feelings', which occur spontaneously and continuously whenever we are awake. They have a definite quality, 'somewhere along the pleasure-to-pain range' and provide a background sense of bodily ongoingness. They are the basis of the emotions, which constitute a central part of the homeostatic process, enabling the organism to evaluate the safety or otherwise of external environments (Damasio, 2010: 21, 109–10, 185, 193, 201).[5] The protoself and its primordial feelings constitute for Damasio the basic 'material me' or the 'self-as-object' (ibid.: 9, 202). Panksepp (1998) calls it the 'affective core'[6] of the self, which we share with many animals.

The conscious core self emerges in pulse-like fashion whenever the protoself has to adjust the body as a result of the organism's encounters with 'objects', by which Damasio means here events in the external world such as sights, sounds, smells, tastes, and bodily movements, and when those encounters are momentarily linked in a series of 'images' or mental patterns resulting from these sensory experiences (Damasio, 2000: 318); that is, the image of the organism, the image of the object now enhanced by attention, and the image of the emotional response to the object (Damasio, 2010: 203). At the experiential level this series of images (or moments of felt awareness, as Mark Johnson more intelligibly calls them)[7] provides a momentary 'feeling of knowing', consisting of a bodily felt *perspective*, or *orientation*, from which objects are being encountered, a sense of *ownership* of the phenomenal experience of the objects, and a sense of *agency* with regard to any actions carried out in relation to the objects. Damasio calls this the 'simple self at the bottom of the mind'. It is our basic experience of the self-as-subject, the bodily-felt first person of consciousness in the present moment which is not yet reflected upon (Damasio, 2010: 9, 180–86, 202–4; 2003: 208).

Damasio attempts to capture the experience of this pre-reflective bodily self-awareness (Gallagher and Zahavi, 2008) from the perspective of higher consciousness as a form of aesthetic cognition: it is being 'the music while the music lasts' (Damasio, 2000: 191) or 'a lot like music but not yet poetry' (Damasio, 2010: 186). These musical metaphors of movement are echoed in phenomenologist Maxine Sheets-Johnstone's attempts to capture it. She draws on Luria's terms 'kinetic' or 'kinaesthetic melodies' (Luria, 1973) to describe the feeling of 'a certain dynamic flow' in the body that is different from sensory perception (Sheets-Johnstone, 2009: 332). Developmental psychologist Daniel Stern's term 'vitality affects' is also an attempt to capture the 'dynamic, kinetic' quality of this bodily-felt experience; they are sensations of 'surging, fading away, fleeting, explosive, crescendo, decrescendo, bursting, drawn out …'. These vitality affects, he argues, are the earliest form of self-experience in infants and remain with us throughout our lives as the source of thought (Stern, 1998: 54, 67). However, this subtle bodily-felt self-experience is difficult to access once extended consciousness has developed. As Damasio says: 'the images that constitute knowing and sense of self' at the level of the core self 'generally remain to the side … are in subtle rather than assertive mode. It is the destiny of subtle mental contents to be missed' (Damasio, 2000: 128). In fact the core self could easily be described as 'the self as other', in the terms of my starting definition of reflexivity. To become aware of it we have to relax our familiar, everyday sense of self-identity or actively shift our attention inwards for the purpose of introspection (Petitmengin, 2007). This happens most readily, of course, in psychotherapy, so it is not surprising to find psychoanalysts trying to conceptualise it.

Indeed this is what I believe Karen Horney was trying to do with the concept of the 'real self' (Horney, 1939b: 130), which she coined to capture her own and her patients' experience of connecting or reconnecting in the therapeutic process with 'the most alive center of psychic life' (Horney, 1942: 291), and on the basis of which it then became possible to develop a sense of agency and individual values (Horney, 1999: 132–42). For Horney the real self is an innate, positive 'force toward individual growth and fulfilment'. It consists of 'temperament, faculties [and] propensities', which constitute a set of 'intrinsic potentialities' that are part of the individual's genetic make-up and are likely to develop in favourable life circumstances (Horney, 1951: 13, 158). That she refers to the real self as a 'force' makes it sound like a process, although reifying it as a noun makes it sound like an entity, but her descriptions in her last book, drawing on William James (1901: 296–305), move it more towards a temporal bodily process:

> [The real self] provides the 'palpitating inward life'; it engenders the spontaneity of feelings, whether these be joy, yearning, love, anger, fear, despair. It also is the source of spontaneous interest and energies, 'the source of effort and attention from which emanate the fiats of will'; the capacity to wish and to will; it is the part of ourselves that wants to expand and grow and to fulfil itself. It produces the 'reactions of spontaneity' to our feelings or thoughts, 'welcoming or opposing, appropriating or disowning, striving with or against, saying yes or no'. All this indicates that our real self, when strong and active, enables us to make decisions and assume responsibility for them. It therefore leads to genuine integration and a sound sense of wholeness, oneness. Not merely are body and mind, deed and thought or feeling, consonant and harmonious, but they function without serious inner conflict.
> (Horney, 1951: 157)

The key elements here are the spontaneous, dynamic experience of bodily feeling, its role as a basis of agency and cognition, and the sense of wholeness it brings, all of which are features of Damasio's core consciousness. Under the influence of her friendship with Zen scholar D.T. Suzuki towards the end of her life, Horney comes even closer to thinking of the real self as a temporal process, conceiving of it as 'something akin to Suzuki's "state of utmost fluidity or mobility"' (Westkott, 1998: 297–99; Suzuki, 1959: 14). This is visible in her *Final Lectures* where, in describing 'real self' experience, she puts a much stronger emphasis on being able to tolerate the *movement* of emotional feelings, the importance of 'accepting oneself feelingly' and the 'feeling of liberation' this brings (Westkott, 1998; Horney, 1987: 98–9). In fact, Horney's 'real self' could be thought of as a composite of Damasio's bodily-felt core self and elements of what he calls the 'genomic unconscious' such as drives and motivations, and 'spontaneous preferences one manifests in early life' (Damasio, 2010: 278–9), of which we can become aware through higher or extended consciousness. This comes close to the idea of reflexivity I am developing here (cf. Danielian, 2010).

Higher consciousness and the agency of the autobiographical self

In Damasio's schema the higher 'autobiographical self' emerges out of the bodily-felt sense of agency in the living present provided by the core self. Once language is acquired this becomes the 'extended self' or 'extended consciousness', an awareness of existing not just in the present, but across past, present, and future. This has been called the 'narrative self', where narrative or storytelling is seen as a natural mode of the broad temporal sweep of extended consciousness

(Oatley, 2007). Damasio refers to the autobiographical self as both the 'social me' and the 'spiritual me' in William James's terms, where 'spiritual' means the inner psychic faculties or dispositions (Damasio, 2010: 23, 168–9); it is what we think of as our identity, our personhood (Damasio, 2000). This higher level of self emerges into consciousness when memories of lived experience or anticipated future experience 'interact with the protoself and produce an abundance of core self pulses' (Damasio, 2010: 181, 212–3). This category of felt 'objects-to-be-known' – this time internal rather than external – are brought together and transiently held in what Damasio calls 'image space' in the most recent part of the brain, the cerebral cortex. This facilitates forethought and planning, as well as complex mental processes such as creativity, which 'require the display and manipulation of vast amounts of knowledge' (Damasio, 2003: 177).

In psychodynamic thinking the autobiographical self has been equated with Freud's ego (Solms and Turnbull, 2000). However, the ego is the inhibiting function of the psyche, keeping at bay the unruly instincts of the id on the one hand and on the other defending itself against the demands of the civilizing forces manifested in the superego and is therefore much narrower than Damasio's formulation.[8] Karen Horney's holistic concept of the 'actual self' has certain similarities with the autobiographical self, as she, like Damasio, was working with William James's ideas. She describes the 'actual self' as everything a person *actually* is in the present, mind and body, whether well-functioning or not (Horney, 1951: 110). This is clearly derived from James's description of the 'empirical self' as 'all that [a person] is tempted to call by the name of *me*', including not only 'his body and psychic powers' but all the things invested with the sense of 'me', including the sense of who one is in the world. Thus, as in Damasio's formulation, Horney's actual self embraces the self in the world James calls the 'social self', including different self-concepts[9] and self-narratives[10] derived from immersion in society and culture, and the inner psychic faculties or dispositions he calls the 'spiritual self' (James, 1901: 291).

Neither Horney nor Damasio devote much attention to the development of James's 'I' or agency at the higher level of self-functioning. However, Damasio does mention that the 'I' (which he associates with the extended self) is created by language, whilst the autobiographical self is not (Damasio, 1994: 243), which indicates that he distinguishes between the two. Freud's ego is closer to James's 'I' than to the autobiographical self as a whole, but Horney rejects Freud's concept as essentially too weak and defensive to be the central agency of the psyche (Horney, 1939a: 184): it is 'an employee who has functions but no initiative and no executive powers' (Horney, 1951: 173). Indeed she sees Freud's ego as a defence which, when dismantled in therapy, will lead to the retrieval of spontaneity and the 'faculties of willpower, judgment and decision making' (Horney, 1939a: 190; 2000: 214–5). Damasio also identifies the will as a central feature of the agency of the extended self (Damasio, 2010: 280), drawing on Wegner's view that the conscious will is 'an emotion that authenticates the action's owner as the self' (Wegner, 2002: 327).

Attachment theorist Peter Fonagy, who sets out to explore the distinction between James's 'me' and 'I', sees the agency or 'I' of the autobiographical self not as a given but as a 'developing or constructed capacity' that is 'hard won' across a number of stages (Fonagy *et al.*, 2002: 3–4). He acknowledges that infants manifest an innate sense of bodily agency. This enables them 'to represent their bodily self as a differentiated object in space that can initiate action and exert causal influence on its environment'. A non-verbal self-concept is thought to develop during the second year of life, once the neural equipment for autobiographical memory is in place. But this is a 'present self' – the 'single representation of the self's actions and physical features' – rather than a self across time.

The higher-level self-agency or 'I' does not emerge until 4–5 years of age when language is in place and when infants can be seen to understand that their desires and beliefs are the cause of events in the world. This implies an ability to conceptualise themselves as an object and to connect this self-concept with external reality (ibid.: 3–4, 206–8). A unified self-concept that includes a sense of continuity across time requires the ability to hold in mind multiple representations or models of the world simultaneously (ibid.: 247), a description which echoes Damasio's concept of 'image space' at the level of extended consciousness. So the autobiographical 'I' or higher self-agency can be understood as the infant's ability to conceptualise the autobiographical self as a felt, holistic structure and to link this self-concept with its desires and beliefs, which gives rise to a more conscious sense of intention to act in the world. It has been suggested that 'higher-order, conceptually informed attributions of ownership or agency may depend on [the] first-order experience of ownership or agency' derived from the core self (Gallagher and Zahavi, 2008: 161). Thus, what is being objectified in the higher-order self-concept is (at least in part but importantly) the orientation, sense of ownership and agency provided by the bodily core self, as discussed above.

Crucial for the development of higher self-agency or the 'I' is what Fonagy calls the 'reflective function' or 'mentalization' – the ability to make sense of one's own mind as well as recognise mind states in others – which emerges out of the engagement with carers in the early stages of the child's life (Fonagy *et al.*, 2002: 23–64). For this to occur, carers need to be able to reflect back to their infants their mental processes, that is, their perceptions and intentions. Also important is the reflecting back of infants' spontaneous affects, but through simulation rather than direct mirroring, to enable the child to recognise that these are *its own* feelings rather than the carers'. This ability to experience affects whilst simultaneously thinking them, rather than reflecting on them 'from a position of distance', Fonagy calls 'mentalized affectivity' (ibid.: 439). I translate this as 'thinking feelings'. It is a core feature of reflexivity and a good description of a central dimension of the work of the CWPD programme (see Part III).

Feeding back to the child its own experience of mental states and affects facilitates, on this view, not only its cognitive development but also, crucially, the discovery of, and developing ability to regulate, its feelings. Thus developing a robust sense of agency at the level of the autobiographical self involves beginning to understand one's own mental states and making sense of what feelings mean, which leads to the ability to manage or regulate the self as a whole (ibid.: 436). It facilitates the development of what is known as the 'executive function' of the mind, which includes metacognition (i.e. the ability to reflect consciously on one's own mental processes), selective attention (i.e. the willed shifting of attention), working memory (i.e. the area of memory readily available to consciousness), inhibitory control (e.g. of automatic mechanisms such as emotions), and rule use, and is responsible for 'flexibly and dynamically' organising phases of problem solving in the pursuit of specific goals (Zelazo and Cunningham, 2007: 136–8). This is precisely the part of the mind we associate with the will, so corresponds to what Horney and Damasio see as the central agency of the actual or autobiographical self.

The role of agency in reflexivity

How, then, do these two levels of conscious self with their different senses of agency help to understand the concept of reflexivity and, by extension, what is happening in transformative learning? Damasio does not use the term reflexivity, but his description of the way consciousness 'fluctuates' between the temporal frames of core and extended consciousness sounds very much like the mechanism I am seeking to understand. Core consciousness provides the mind with 'minimal scope', the sensing of the self in the present moment, whilst extended consciousness provides 'big scope', the sensing of the self over time past, present, and future. The shift upwards and downwards between big and minimal scope happens fluidly all the time as if 'on a gliding cursor' (Damasio, 2010: 168–69), so that one minute I can be immersed in the sensation of the sun on my face whilst sitting quietly in the garden, and the next negotiating with my neighbour about his plans to rebuild the dividing wall that involves knowledge of previous discussions and the projected outcome. As Damasio says, in the former state the big scope of extended consciousness is not needed: 'it would have been a waste of brain-processing capacity, not to mention fuel'. The 'downshift to core self' provides the brain with rest, but it also opens the mind to a less focused and more daydreaming state (ibid.: 169–70). This latter point indicates that there is a *spatial* as well as a temporal dimension to this switch, for if the downshift to core self facilitates a less focused, more daydreaming state, then it can be thought of as a shift from *narrow* focused attention on specific objects or events taking place within the broad time-frame of extended consciousness to a *broader* bodily-felt immersion in spontaneous phenomenal experience provided by core consciousness.

The existence of two such *spatial* modes of consciousness is exactly what psychoanalyst Marion Milner discovers in her reflections on her attempts to draw. She calls them 'thinking mode', the sharp-pointed focusing with the mind, and 'feeling mode', the broad, hovering attention with the body, which she calls the 'imaginative body', because it feels like an extension of her bodily self into space (Milner, 1971: 36). In order to animate her drawings she found that she had to let go of thinking mode, which usually resulted in lifeless, unsatisfying representations, and shift into feeling mode. She describes this as an 'internal gesture', which involved relinquishing control of her everyday sense of self and taking an inner 'step back', so that psychic space could open up. She experienced it as a physical sensation of becoming 'fatter', even though it was a gesture of the mind (ibid.: 70–4). In Damasio's terms Milner's internal gesture – a good example of Damasio's images or Johnson's moments of bodily felt awareness (cf. Nicholls, 2006) – involves the softening of the autobiographical 'I' to make way for the agency of the bodily-felt core self, but the former remains in the background holding the space open for sensuous thought processes at the level of core consciousness to emerge. As Damasio puts it, a sense of self as the protagonist of the psyche never goes away completely. If it did, 'the mind would lose its orientation, the ability to gather its parts' (Damasio, 2010: 170). It always functions as a frame for thinking.

It is significant that both Damasio and Milner highlight the flexible shifting of *attention* as the core mechanism of the experiences they are describing, with attention at the level of bodily feeling characterised as a relaxation from, or loosening of control of, the demands of sharply focused attention. Damasio regards attention as a key component of the 'feeling of knowing' provided by the bodily core self (Damasio, 2000: 182–3), presumably part of the orientation, ownership, and agency the core self provides, although at this level it is not *reflective* attention. Attention is also a central feature of 'executive function', as noted above, where it regulates thoughts and feelings, and processes such as planning and decision making (Raz and Buhle, 2006: 374). Damasio's description implies that the oscillation between higher and lower level attention (or between attention and immersion) takes place effortlessly and without conscious awareness. By contrast Milner has to 'open up' to the mechanism and bring it into conscious reflection so that she can 'practice' it. This involves loosening her usual cognitive control, so that the two modes of attention can begin to work together and become spontaneously reflexive. This connection between openness and self-reflection as a prelude to reflexivity is also at the core of Daniel Siegel's discussion of mechanisms underlying mindfulness, a method of attention training which, he argues, renders the executive function simultaneously robust and flexible for the purpose of self-regulation. In his view reflexivity is a deeper and 'more automatic meta-awareness within the larger framework of reflection'. It 'implies a more immediate capacity of the mind to know itself, without effort, without conscious observation, without words'; it facilitates openness to whatever arises into awareness in the moment whether 'sensations, images, feelings, thoughts' (Siegel, 2007: 126–33; cf. Gunnlaugson, 2007). This description supports the understanding of reflexivity I am developing here.

Thus I would now describe the role of the self in reflexivity as follows: the autobiographical 'I', that is, the higher self-agency of extended consciousness, when in spontaneous contact with the bodily agency of the core self, provides a robust but flexible temporal and spatial frame for the mind's attention, enabling it to operate spontaneously and fluidly between higher cognition located in the prefrontal cortex of the brain and bodily cognition located in the reality-evaluating function of the more ancient emotion-based functions of the brain. Optimally this process takes place effortlessly, without full conscious awareness, although it can be brought to conscious awareness and reflected upon in order to improve its functioning (see Chapter 8 re 'practising reflexivity'). Seeing that the function of the self is to enhance the mind's operation (Damasio, 2010: 267), it is reasonable to conclude that when the self functions optimally, the mind will function well too. Thus the consequence of reflexivity is that the mind and the affects can be flexibly regulated rather than controlled (Fonagy *et al.*, 2002: 95–6), so that the psyche as a whole becomes simultaneously grounded and agentic and open to change. To put it another way, it functions as a *dynamic system*.

The psyche as a dynamic system

The idea that the psyche is a dynamic system has been suggested by a number of writers (e.g. Tershakovec, 2007; Siegel, 1999) and helps to consolidate the picture of reflexivity I have been working towards. Systems theory was developed originally by Ludwig von Bertalanffy (1968) and has been widely applied to understanding how complex organisms – from eco-systems, to large-scale social organisations such as schools or businesses, to small-scale social units such as families, to the biological structure of the brain – function holistically. Dynamic systems are seen as having inherent self-organising processes that are naturally motivated to move from (relative) disorder,[11] towards maximal complexity,[12] with holistic structures emerging out of the interaction between different parts (Lewis, 2005: 173–4; Siegel, 2003: 4). They tend to evolve hierarchically toward ever higher levels of organisation, with new and more advanced organising principles emerging spontaneously at each level. This is achieved not through linear causality but through constant cycles of feedback, or circular causality. As dynamic systems develop, the operation of lower levels tends to become mechanised, whilst higher levels become more specialised and segregated (Tershakovec, 2007: 27–31). So there is a drive to differentiate the parts of the organism, but the overall trajectory is towards integrating them into a maximally complex whole that is both stable and flexible (Siegel, 2003: 23–4).

In the model of the psyche as a dynamic system the mind is seen as an energy and information processing system, with the two hemispheres of the brain fulfilling different functions and having different modes of operation that complement each other. The left hemisphere is a serial processor that contains the main language faculty. Its mode of operation is characterised by logic and clarity, and linear sequencing in time. It interprets and makes explicit what is experienced by the right hemisphere. The right hemisphere is a parallel processor with a holistic mode of operation that means that it is has a broader scope for establishing levels of meaning and context (Tershakovec, 2007: 56–63; Bowden *et al.*, 2005) and can tolerate ambiguity and uncertainty (McGilchrist, 2009: 82, 187). The holistic mode of operation of the right hemisphere comes from its being connected to the body through the protoself's global mapping (Devinsky, 2000), and it is therefore more spatially oriented than the left. It is also dominant for the understanding, expression and regulation of the emotions, particularly the primary emotions,[13] although the left hemisphere is involved in the expression of anger and the social emotions. The right hemisphere is therefore more relational, empathic, and responsive to nonverbal aspects of language, such as tone of voice and gesture, all of which are emotion-based (McGilchrist, 2009: 58–64; Tershakovec, 2007: 78–9; Siegel, 2003: 14–15).

Importantly for understanding reflexivity, the right hemisphere is associated with unconscious modes of processing and the left with conscious modes (McGilchrist, 2009: 187), although there is evidence indicating that both hemispheres are 'capable of supporting personal consciousness' (Trevarthen, 2009: 162). In the context of Damasio's two-tier model of consciousness one could perhaps think of the hemispheres as rendering different *degrees* of consciousness, rather than the either/or of conscious/unconscious, with focused attention bringing sharper conscious awareness to phenomena previously in low level consciousness. Indeed attention and intention are key factors in the different modes of operation of the hemispheres, with the right yielding attention that is broad, flexible, and 'patiently open to whatever is' and the left yielding attention that is narrow, focused, and purposefully active (McGilchrist, 2009: 25–9, 171–5). As these modes are very similar to those identified by Damasio and Milner in connection with reflexive mental functioning, it sounds as if reflexivity is fundamentally an inter-hemispheric mechanism involving different degrees of consciousness and will. This also follows from the dependence on the right hemisphere of the sense of self as bodily and holistic (Damasio's core self) and the basic self-concept and theory of mind (key features of the pre-linguistic autobiographical self), and the dependence on the left hemisphere of 'the objectified self', which I take to include social self-concepts, and 'the self as an expression of will' (ibid.: 57, 87–8).

However, whilst reflexivity can be understood as an inter-hemispheric mechanism, for optimal functioning of the psyche the right hemisphere needs to be the 'leading edge' (Tershakovec, 2007: 40–2).[14] This is von Bertalanffy's term for the mechanism of the dynamic system that governs the behaviour of the organism at the highest level of the hierarchy and promotes integration. This finds support in McGilchrist's argument for the 'primacy of the right hemisphere' in human functioning (McGilchrist, 2009: 176–208), according to which the right hemisphere is the primary interface with the world, whilst the language-based left hemisphere receives and interprets what is transmitted to it by the right and then transmits it back again, that is a 'bottom-up' (bodily-felt) rather than 'top-down' (linguistic) structure. Indeed the top-down nature of the left hemisphere seems particularly unsuited to being the leading edge, seeing that its characteristics include 'stickiness', which I take to be a tendency to psychic perseveration, the need to be right, a 'black and white style', a lack of realism, and a tendency to confabulation (ibid.: 82–91), all of which feature significantly in Group 2 students' difficulties with being creative. By comparison, the right hemisphere's mode of operation is characterised as 'betweenness', which evokes relationality, getting close up to 'whatever it is that exists apart from ourselves' (ibid.: 93). Thus, when the psyche is led by the right hemisphere the 'objectified self' or autobiographical 'I' in the left hemisphere can remain in reflexive contact with the core bodily self, rendering open and flexible the relationship with social self-concepts and the self as an expression of the conscious will. This collaboration is crucially important for the formulation of a realistic mental model of the self-in-the-world (internal mental self-representation) that, whilst implicit, will be open to reflection and modification in the light of experience (Tershakovec, 2007: 122–4, 155; Johnson-Laird, 1983). Such a mental model would make it possible to be a 'social agent' in Archer's sense, able to engage reflexively with familial, social, and cultural narratives and discourses.

Reflexivity, then, turns out to be a right hemisphere-led function that facilitates collaboration with the left hemisphere and renders the psyche both stable and flexible. It could be described as a fundamental mechanism of learning involving two different modes: one broad, intuitive and bodily-based, which I will call embodied–experiential learning, and the other sharply-focused and language-based, which I will call critical reflection. These are, in fact, the two modes of learning articulated by the Jungian and Mezirowian strands of transformative learning theory, which can thus be seen as two parts of what I am calling the 'cycle of transformation', with the embodied–experiential mode preceding the critically reflective (see Chapter 10). According to Daniel Siegel, it involves a process of beneficial neural integration (Siegel, 2007: 119–20; cf. Cozolino, 2002).

Reflexivity, however, is difficult to achieve and, even if achieved, is a precarious process. The psyche's constant openness to change means that it is always in process between order and (relative) chaos (Siegel, 2003: 3–4, 23). Indeed, very small changes in the leading edge can trigger massive changes throughout the whole dynamic system (Tershakovec, 2007: 28–30). For example, if spontaneous access to everyday reality via the feeling- and emotion-processing right hemisphere becomes too painful or difficult, the left hemisphere is likely to become dominant, shifting the leading edge from bottom-up to top-down and limiting the amount of information that can be processed (Ward, 2001: 320). Without a spontaneous grounding in bodily agency, the left hemisphere tendency to 'stickiness' and control will result in psychic inertia or stasis, with adverse consequences for thinking and creativity. Seeing that for many Group 2 students there is a marked shift from top-down cognitive control towards bottom-up reflexivity as a result of their studies, as demonstrated by their marked increase in cognitive flexibility, it seems reasonable to suggest that a change in the leading edge of the psyche has occurred, freeing up the bodily flow of experience.

Thus I would suggest that the mechanism underlying students' experience of change can be understood as a fundamental shift in the functioning of the self. It involves the relaxing of the autobiographical 'I' in the left hemisphere, which allows more spontaneous access to core consciousness in the right hemisphere. This in turn gives rise to a more authentic and holistic sense of self, which facilitates the development of a more grounded sense of bodily agency and the ability to regulate rather than control the affects. The result of this development is an enhanced ability to think creatively and independently. But why did the shift to top-down control occur in the first place? The next chapter offers some possible answers to this question.

Notes

1 I use the view of cognition as 'any mental operations and structures that are involved in language, meaning, perception, conceptual systems and reason', which are at least 95 per cent unconscious and fundamentally bound up with emotion (Lakoff and Johnson, 1999: 11–13).
2 Archer discounts the role of carers in the development of bodily agency.
3 Damasio distinguishes between 'non-conscious' mechanisms, which will never become conscious, and 'unconscious' mechanisms that may.
4 Damasio has moved towards Panksepp's position on this (Gallagher, 2008: 106–7; Damasio, 2010: 322–3, n.17).
5 Damasio distinguishes between emotions, which are non-conscious, and emotional feelings, which are conscious.
6 The term 'affect' encompasses emotions, feelings and moods (Fox, 2008).
7 Johnson suggests that the term 'images' is problematic, as they are generally thought of as visual. He suggests understanding them as 'just our awareness of certain aspects of our current body state' (Johnson, 2007: 64). This makes more immediate sense.
8 Laplanche and Pontalis (2004: 134) suggest that: 'Freud does not identify the ego with the individual as a whole, nor even with the whole of the mental apparatus: it is a part. […However…] he does locate the ego in a privileged position in regard to the individual' considered both biologically and psychically.
9 I understand self-concepts as dominant categories of self-understanding available in a society or culture (Neisser, 1988).
10 Self-narratives are the ways of self-telling available in a society or culture (Bruner, 1990).
11 'Relative' because there will always be internal and external constraints to the disorder (Siegel, 2003) (see below pp. 147–8).
12 Dynamic systems theory has become incorporated into what is known as complexity science.
13 Damasio defines the primary emotions as fear, anger, disgust, surprise, sadness and happiness and regards them as innate, although their expression will be influenced by cultural factors (Damasio, 2003: 44).
14 Tershakovec suggests that Horney's 'real self' located in the right hemisphere is the leading edge of the optimally functioning psyche (Tershakovec, 2007: 42–4). This makes sense if, as I suggested, the real self is a combination of core consciousness and aspects of the genomic unconscious of which we can become aware via extended consciousness. Horney's idea of reconnecting with the real self could be thought of as the process of becoming more reflexively aware of right hemisphere functioning, which brings us a more spontaneous and authentic feeling of our engagement with the world than the left hemisphere.

Chapter 7

Vicissitudes of the dynamic psyche and their consequences for learning and creativity

In the early stages of transformative learning theory change was understood as an individual process of freeing the self from inhibiting psychic mechanisms resulting from upbringing or other negative effects of socialisation, similar to psychodynamic psychotherapies. Mezirow's ideas were strongly influenced by his relationship with psychoanalyst Roger Gould, who was applying a 'popularised version of psychoanalytic theory to adult development' (Finger and Asun, 2001: 55). This is visible in his descriptions of 'perspective transformation' as fraught with psychological difficulties, including 'unresolved problems from childhood' (Mezirow, 1981: 6, 9) or 'rigid and highly defended thought patterns' in some people (Mezirow, 1991: loc. 1771). Boyd, from his analytic psychological perspective, also saw transformation as liberation from 'old patterns of thinking, feeling, and acting which previously prevented growth' (Boyd and Myers, 1988: 279).

However, in Mezirow's subsequent work the depth psychological element has more or less disappeared, whilst the constructivist dimension of his thinking, influenced particularly by Kuhn's (1962) idea of 'paradigm shift', has become more dominant (Kitchenham, 2008: 113). This has shifted the focus from problematic psychic mechanisms afflicting some people to problematic sociocultural discourses in the world (Mezirow, 2003: 58). Whilst the depth psychology strand originating from Boyd continues to focus on psychodynamic processes, there has also been a similar shift away from problems for some learners of 'patterns of thinking, feeling, and acting' that prevent growth to the universal process of individuation, or self-formation: 'a process in which we gradually differentiate the self from the conditioning of early family and other external contexts, as well as from one's current environment' (Dirkx, 2008: 73).

This shift away from problems with thinking and feeling that afflict some people avoids, of course, what is often seen as the tendency of depth psychological thinking to pathologise individuals by positing a healthy norm (e.g. Dirkx, 2006; Cranton, 2000). But I would suggest that it discourages research that attempts to distinguish between more or less workable psychic states in individual learners,[1] which may account for the absence of work in the field on why some people are less open to transformative learning than others (Taylor, 2007: 187).

This is a pity because, as Illeris says, 'When it comes to non-learning, it is not about processes that are fulfilled but about processes that are blocked or derailed partially or totally' (Illeris, 2004b: 86), and it is these processes at work in individuals that are my main concern. This is not to stigmatise or pathologise individual learners but to try to understand, and find ways to ameliorate, the effects of psychic mechanisms that interfere with thinking and creativity. Thus, in an attempt to understand better the process of individual change in transformative learning, I use psychodynamic theory to explore mechanisms underlying cognitive control and its origins.

Trauma and the closing down of the psyche

I have argued that reflexivity between the language-based autobiographical 'I' and the bodily core self is a key mechanism in the optimal functioning of the dynamic system of the psyche involving a process of neural differentiation and integration that results in psychic flexibility and stability. Yet it seems intrinsically difficult for the psyche to become and remain reflexive; even if we are fortunate enough to develop a sense of self-agency in childhood, the autobiographical 'I' can lose its flexibility at later stages of life, with adverse consequences for learning and creativity. One of the reasons for this may be that maintaining spontaneous contact with core consciousness is intrinsically difficult. I have already noted Damasio's view that our awareness of it gets easily obscured by the workings of consciousness extended by language, so that even under optimal conditions, we do not pay much attention to core consciousness unless we are specifically trying to articulate what our experience feels like. This echoes philosopher Eugene Gendlin's view that the 'forms, concepts, definitions, categories, distinctions, rules' that make up our everyday language are fixed patterns that obscure the 'felt sense' of our own meaning (Gendlin, 1991: 21). It is further supported by McGilchrist's view that the brain's hemispheres work by mutually inhibiting each other and that, whilst the right hemisphere has overall primacy, in the mutual inhibition stakes it is the left that has the advantage. This is because it is more conscious and self-aware than the right, the knowledge it provides is more linear and logical and therefore more readily graspable, and of course it has language at its disposal. Thus in a language-based culture left hemisphere knowledge easily takes priority over the more intuitive, complex knowledge of the right (McGilchrist, 2009: 227–9).[2]

There is also a logical reason why we might need to retreat from right hemisphere functioning and seek left hemisphere fixity in concepts, categories, rules, and distinctions. 'The first-person body', as Sheets-Johnstone calls the bodily core self, 'is in and of the world, a felt lived world'; it is our primary point of sensory and emotional contact with inner and outer worlds. Optimally we can have more or less stimulation; we can open ourselves to engagement with others, or to learning or physical or artistic activities; or we can withdraw and reduce stimulation, create a balance. But when the felt lived world 'becomes too much for us' – when it causes us pain or makes us anxious – we have to defend ourselves against it (Sheets-Johnstone, 2009: 24). An effective way of doing this is to develop a relationship with the world that is more fixed and safer-seeming – more left hemisphere – rather than one that involves constant openness to change. This seems to be a common experience for many Group 2 students.

One of the main causes of the closing down of core consciousness is trauma. Emotional feelings that are too overwhelming or too painful have to be blocked off. When this happens, the left hemisphere, deprived of the holistic, largely unconscious meaning-making function of the right hemisphere, loses its grounding in everyday reality (Siegel, 1999: 35–6; Tershakovec, 2007: 56–63). Thus the trauma sufferer can lose the sense that time is moving between past, present, and future, and there is also a tendency for awareness to become split and the personality to become dissociated (Rothschild, 2000: 13). This can lead to mental chaos and confusion or to the freezing of the psyche (Siegel, 2003: 5). Susanna's experience of multiple losses combined with her illness diagnosis is an example of the freezing and splitting effects of trauma. She cannot confront the pain of her losses nor can she think about her future, rather she is fixated on her regrets about the past, so that time has ceased to flow. Her primary mental model of herself in the world is of a person with an illness and no future, which is partly a consequence of her feeling labelled by the medical system but, as I have suggested, might also be a necessary defence against psychic pain. Her illness identity, whilst challenging, provides a sense of wholeness and keeps the dissociated psyche under control, but the psychic freezing impairs her ability to function and for a while creativity is lost.

Ruth's defence against the unresolved trauma of unexpectedly losing her father when she is at university takes the form of an obsessive concern with protecting and containing her former boyfriend who suffers from alcoholism. This displacement of painful feelings onto another person distances her from experiencing them head-on. Her profession of actor also enables her to distance herself from her feelings: 'I barely perform as myself', she says. Both these devices provide a means of control, but the closing down of the psyche that results impairs her ability to think flexibly, whether in relationships or in her writing. She gets stuck in a rut and continues endlessly, 'like a rat in a maze', even though at some level she knows that another perspective is needed.

For Miranda the trauma of losing her mother to mental illness in childhood results in her existing for a long time in a 'stunned fog', a metaphor that aptly captures her freezing and withdrawal from the distress. This distancing from her feelings and the world provides a means of self-protection, but adversely affects her functioning. For example, it makes it difficult for her to have a sense of agency in relations with others, although she says this has improved somewhat in recent years:

> when I said yes [to a friend's request to look after her cat for two weeks] I didn't qualify the yes. I didn't say oh but who's going to help me, or who's

going to whatever. You say you can or you will do things that are just too much. And that which again goes back to family, it says yes I *can* be there at six and I *will* go to your house and I'll have another second dinner and oh until you're exhausted.

Not having spontaneous access to her feelings also makes it difficult to write her personal story: she has no sense of what is true for her (see Chapter 2). Both of these developments are intelligible in the context of trauma: when spontaneous access to core consciousness is lost, the ability to know intuitively what is right or wrong for oneself is impaired. As Siegel suggests: 'One way of understanding unresolved trauma and unresolved grief is from the view of impairments to the process of neural integration' (Siegel, 2003: 23, 31). Without the differentiating and integrating process of hemispheric reciprocity, different parts of the psyche become detached from each other and an ad hoc holistic structure has to be constructed and maintained by the left hemisphere.

The need to defend the psyche against anxiety

What we see happening in these three instances of trauma is a shift towards a defensive way of being that keeps painful feelings at bay but results in fragmentation of the psyche. A similar process can be observed in the need to defend against anxiety caused by on-going stress in childhood. For Claire and Jill there is a marked shift away from their spontaneous feelings in childhood because of having to deal with the long-term effects on the family of a difficult sibling. For both of them the shift is to compensate by being the good child. Being good means not being angry, so a way of relating to others without it has to be instituted. When Jill's anger against her father begins to emerge during the writing of her dissertation she notes that: 'Up till now my self-narrative has been one of the "good child", frightened of failing to live up to my father's expectations, wanting to gain his approval, not wanting to provoke his anger', and this set the pattern for relationships with men throughout her life. But she remembers not being like that:

> when I was young, I mean I suppose under ten, I used to think I could do anything, I mean really anything at all, anything I wanted to, it was all possible and I felt very sort of boy-girlish then, I didn't feel I had to please too many people and had an immense feeling of capacity, and I'm feeling some of that starting to come back … .

The mention of her child self as originally boy-girlish implies that for her being 'good' is a characteristic of being female and highlights the strong presence of a cultural self-concept in her shift (Symonds, 1978: 195). That this shift to compliance then becomes a standard feature of her mature psyche indicates the power of this cultural self-concept to provide an acceptable mental model for women coming to maturity in the 60s and 70s, but the shutting off of anger impairs her sense of agency in close relations and makes creative self-expression difficult. This is also the case for Claire.

For a significant number of Group 2 students the closing down of the psyche is a reaction to carers' inability to recognise and nurture their spontaneous temperament. Temperament is generally regarded as innate and can be thought of as 'dispositions to react in certain ways to a variety of situations', with the different ways infants express and regulate the emotions being a central feature (Fox, 2008: 53–5). The emotions will of course be modulated by life experience, particularly by upbringing (ibid.: 61), and sometimes the family environment forces children to repress aspects of their spontaneous temperament. We have seen this at work most painfully in the case of Maria, where a combination of the oppressive Catholic environment of her upbringing and her mother's inability to help her manage her emotions undermines her confidence to express herself and impairs her ability to learn. Her comment that she cannot 'contain' her learning echoes the view that learning necessarily involves opening ourselves to change (Rogers, 1951); thus if we cannot be psychically open because we cannot manage our emotions, we will have difficulties with learning.

There are other instances where spontaneous moves to self-expression are discouraged by carers, with adverse consequences for development. Rhiannon's mother's intrusiveness by reading her daughter's diary where she records her early attempts at poetry brings this 'first love' to a premature end, blocking her creativity for many years. Like Jill and Claire, rather than pursuing her spontaneous desires she becomes adept at fitting in with what others want her to be: 'I had become very adept at not being me, being the person that I *thought* I wanted to be, or that other people wanted me to be and I was quite good at that'. Repressing her spontaneous temperament results in the closing down of inner space for learning and creativity, which may account for the difficulties she experiences as an adult when trying to structure her burgeoning ideas into a coherent whole, particularly in her academic writing: the intuitive 'felt sense' (Gendlin, 1991) for what makes a rounded piece of writing is absent. Harriet's retreat into compliance under the impact of her mother's oppressive rules and negativity towards her spontaneous desire to write creatively provides another example.

That schooling sometimes has a similar detrimental effect on spontaneous manifestations of temperament is visible in the experience of several students. As we have seen, Claudia remembers having idiosyncratic ways of thinking as a child, making unusual connections between things and endlessly weaving stories, which were disapproved of by the nuns at school and came to be labelled as bad. Stacey also remembers having her own particular ways of learning – needing to do things in her own time and on her own – that were not validated by teachers, and Tess is oppressed by teachers at her boarding school for not conforming to the tidy, organised child they expected her to be. Seeing that temperament includes the amount of energy children bring to an activity, their reactions to unfamiliarity, responsiveness to stimulation, distractibility, and attention span (Thomas and Chess, 1977, quoted in Fox, 2008: 55), it seems perfectly possible that they will develop idiosyncratic ways of learning early on that may feel organic to them but may not be understood by teachers or parents, or may be at odds with standard teaching methods. As we have seen, Simon retreats from his school's 'cramming' approach into playing with painting, with the result that his playful, creative side does not integrate and subsequently gets overlaid by the demands of the army, career, and family. Stella does not have time to find out what she is naturally good at, because of her mother's mantra that she is generally not good enough by comparison with her older sister, 'the academic one'. The anger associated with these oppressive childhood environments would in all likelihood have had to be repressed or defended against, leading to anxiety and impairing the development of confidence in actual talents and abilities (Horney, 1937).

Compliance as a 'solution' to fear and anxiety

It is striking that for a good proportion of the female students in Group 2, the default mode in response to anxiety in childhood is to become compliant to other people's wishes and expectations. This is not surprising in view of children's primary need for safety, which means retaining their parents' love and approval. Apart from those students already mentioned, a tendency towards compliance is visible in Harriet's, Stella's, and Stacey's struggles to legitimise their strong desire to develop their creativity in the face of their dominant self-concepts as carers, where others' creativity or welfare are seen as more important. Compliance as a dominant strategy is also visible in Lucy's tendency to lose her identity in close relationships:

> something I've always struggled with is, particularly in partnerships and in friendships, is losing bits of myself to the other person and becoming drawn in by what they would like me to be as opposed to what I am, which given that I am quite kind of opinionated always seems quite surprising to other people, but I think women sometimes do have other female friends who seem to do it, but I'm terrible at it, so I'll just lose who I am bit by bit by bit … .

Again, the mention that this tendency is prevalent amongst women implies that it is usual for them to become compliant in close relationships. As I said in connection with Jill, there is clearly a cultural element here, but whilst compliance is fully intelligible in the generation born in the 1940s and 1950s where it was the dominant model for women, it is not so intelligible in the younger generation for whom there is a wider range of models. This may indicate that compliance is a safer and more powerful option than other cultural models available to women when the primary need is to defend against anxiety.

The presence of a dominant self-concept such as compliance with its demands that we fit in with or prioritise others' needs and desires rather than our own can be understood in the context of Karen Horney's concept of 'life solutions', which she sees as a long-term response to anxiety in childhood (Horney, 1951). The child's short-term response is to defend itself by moving against people and becoming aggressive, or away from people and becoming withdrawn, or towards people and becoming compliant (Horney, 1946), moves that mirror the emergency reactions of fight, flight, and submission observed in nature (Paris, 1994).[3] Horney suggests that under optimal conditions we can move back and forth between our need for self-assertion, distance, and closeness in our relations with others, but where anxiety has to be defended against, these ways of relating lose their flexibility. Unless ameliorating circumstances intervene, these initial moves develop, in adolescence and adulthood, into 'life solutions': moving against people becomes expansiveness (or 'the appeal of mastery'), moving away from people becomes detachment (or 'the appeal of freedom'), and moving towards people becomes compliance (or 'the appeal of love') (Horney, 1951). For Horney the usual pattern is for one of the three 'solutions' to become dominant, whilst the other two are repressed but continue to operate under the surface, giving rise to inner conflicts. However, from my own experience and that of my students the pattern seems to be that one solution becomes dominant and the emotions and parts of the personality that do not fit get split off and operate as 'sub-personalities' (Rowan, 1990).[4] Those that do not conflict unduly with the main solution will operate in tandem with it, whilst those that do conflict will be repressed, although, in line with Horney's view, they will continue operating in the background, causing inner conflicts.[5]

Horney suggested that life solutions are best understood as 'directions of development' rather than as personality types (Horney, 1951: 191). It seems likely that the solutions people adopt and the way they combine them depends not only on individual temperament, but also on existing models in their childhood environment, particularly those of parents, and in the culture at large. Thus compliance finds fertile ground in the traditional cultural stereotype that a woman's role is to be a carer or facilitator of others, and institutionalises it as a self-concept that can provide a sense of unity and wholeness. This is not to suggest that compliance cannot be adopted as a strategy by men; indeed Simon says more than once that his main strategy is to be nice to people when underneath he's really a grumpy old man, and it is perhaps significant that one of the two characters he creates in the 'Self as Source' exercise has 'a deep need to be liked'. Nevertheless compliance does seem to be more prevalent amongst women.

The splitting-off of expansiveness and the need for control

Becoming compliant is a logical strategy where anger cannot be expressed for fear of losing the love or approval of powerful adults. Adapting our behaviour and wishes to fit in with what we imagine others expect or need means that anger automatically gets repressed because it is expansive and therefore inappropriate. This, however, compromises our ability legitimately to assert ourselves against others, and there will also be a taboo on personal ambition and competing with others (Horney, 1951: 318–20). This means that important aspects of spontaneous temperament, particularly the natural vitality or playfulness required for developing creativity, are likely to be repressed too or at least split off into an expansive sub-personality. The result is a general weakening of the psyche, so that it becomes more difficult to develop confidence and a sense of agency.

I derive this picture from a dialogue between Horney's theory and what I see happening in students' experience. For example, it is striking how many Group 2 students unearth both anger and a part of themselves that feels authentic and creative. It is as if the repression of anger entails the repression of a whole dimension of spontaneous temperament, rather than just the emotion itself. This may be because emotions and the way they are regulated are an integral part of temperament, as I said above. Needless to say, this powerful composite of emotion and temperament, repressed beneath a compliant life solution, does not cease to operate; rather, without opportunities for expression, it grows larger and potentially more disruptive. It also fails to mature along with the rest of the personality. Thus it becomes a dangerous expansive presence in the psyche, which then requires additional means of control.

Some of the students unearth not just a tendency towards compliance in relations with others and an unruly, expansive part of the personality, but a rule-bound, perfectionistic sub-personality whose role is to keep the expansive part under control. This is particularly visible for Claire, who associates her rule-bound tendency with the 'strict parent' part of herself that needs to get everything right. Both Megan and Tess become similarly aware of a conflict between a rule-bound part of the psyche and a rule-flouting part. Tess thinks that she opts for the rule-bound part in order to escape from the rule-flouting part that is too difficult for her to manage. This is a legitimate response in view of how the unruly or childish parts of the personality manifest themselves when they are liberated. As we have seen, when Simon's writer-self is given its freedom to create characters, it turns to rape and murder, which Simon finds shocking. Claudia's creative side emerges manically, leading her to feel that she can achieve anything regardless of the circumstances, but is quickly followed by a plunge into depression and self-torment when it is clear that she cannot. Maria's sensuous gypsy side also leads her into dangerous personal territory at one point.

The emergence in the psyche of a rule-bound sub-personality is a defensive top-down way of keeping the unruly side under control.[6] It may be an internalisation of a parent figure whose voice was dominant in childhood (Lewis, 2002), which certainly seems to be the case for Harriet, who associates her tendency to repress her spontaneous desire for self-expression with her mother's mantra that men are the creative ones. The controlling sub-personality can be effective, allowing everyday life to proceed reasonably well as long as the unruly sub-personality is kept out of sight. But if the desire to be creative remains strong, as it clearly does for many of the students, who have specifically come to the MA to learn how to free up their creativity, the resulting tug of war between the controller and the controlled can seriously interfere with the creative process.

As I have argued elsewhere (Hunt and Sampson, 2006: 65), creativity is an essentially reflexive activity that involves spontaneous psychic movement back and forth between bodily-felt immersion in our material and distancing ourselves from it sufficiently to craft it into shape. I call this accessing and objectifying the material (Hunt, 2001). Where the rule-bound part of the psyche has to keep the unruly creative part under control, there are likely to be problems with both of these cognitive tasks, as there will be insufficient psychic space and movement. For example, Megan says that her creative side is too risky and unconventional, and she fears giving it its freedom in case it exposes things about her that she does not want others to see. So she sticks with the safer, more conventional side of herself, which is why she gets bored with her writing and does not persist. The problem here is connecting sufficiently with bodily-felt material for writing that will be more personally meaningful and prevent her becoming bored. A similar problem afflicts Simon's creative writing.[7] Lucy indicates that both accessing and objectifying her material is a problem in her academic writing: 'I can lack attention to detail and the ability to step back and see the wood for the trees'. Like Simon and Megan, she skids along the surface 'making do the whole time', although she is aware that she needs to delve more deeply. She can neither get sufficiently in touch with her material nor distance herself sufficiently from it, to develop what, she feels, would make a good essay. She ascribes this difficulty to a lack of confidence.

The consequences for agency of the shift away from the core self

Lucy's mention of a lack of self-confidence is echoed by many of the other students, whether in connection with their creative or academic writing, or generally. As I have shown in Chapter 2, this is often accompanied by very high expectations of what they believe they 'should' be able to achieve. This is likely to be in part the consequence of unhelpful schooling methods or parental attitudes, with deeper intrapsychic mechanisms at work associated with the shift away from spontaneous connection with the bodily core self and the conflict between different parts of the personality where this has developed.

For Horney the loss of spontaneous contact with the core self and the formation of a 'life solution', which she refers to as 'alienation from the real self'

(Horney, 1951: 157), is a move away 'from [one's] own feelings, wishes, beliefs and energies. It is the loss of the feeling of being an active determining force in [one's] own life. It is the loss of feeling [oneself] as an organic whole'. This last sentence is particularly relevant in a dynamic systems' context: we are no longer in touch with the bodily-felt sense of *wholeness* originating in the right hemisphere core self. This means that the psyche lacks an adequate centre for the development of a realistic mental model of the self-in-the-world, with genuine self-worth and robust self-agency; the naturally occurring 'leading edge' of the psyche is lost.[8] To compensate, an 'idealised image' (Horney, 1951) emerges as the leading edge (Tershakovec, 2007: 178–9). In compliance, for example, being good or nice in the eyes of others becomes idealised; in perfectionism what is idealised is being right; in expansiveness it is triumphing over others. These idealised characteristics will be underpinned by a set of rules for behaviour, which Horney calls 'shoulds', and these must be adhered to rigidly in order for any sense of self-worth to be generated (Horney, 1951). However, this is not grounded self-worth, as it is rooted in the extent to which we can fulfil the rules rather than in realistic self-evaluations. It is also short-lived, so that it must be continuously generated. This sets up a vicious circle (positive feedback)[9] of seeking short-term 'highs' or validation from others and means that the activities from which we derive these take priority. If this is pleasing others, then we will find endless ways and opportunities for doing this at the expense of our real needs. This might account, for example, for the struggles that some of the students experience in making legitimate space for their own creativity within their dominant caring roles.

Once the system of idealisation has been set in motion it becomes very difficult to relinquish, because what we *actually* are – our 'actual self' in Horney's terms – falls far short of what we have now come to expect of ourselves. It becomes the 'despised image', constantly subject to inner attack (Horney, 1946: 112). The whole complex of idealised and despised images, and the mechanisms that come into play to support the demands of the idealised image, Horney calls the 'pride system' (Horney, 1951: 111). I understand this as a complex of cognitive mechanisms, particularly vicious circles, that strategically employ emotions such as fear or anxiety to alert the system to infringements of the 'shoulds' so that defensive action can be taken. This is a form of top-down self-regulation.

To put this in the context of my previous discussions, when the psyche moves away from, or fails to develop, its grounding in the right hemisphere core self, it loses the spontaneous emotional feedback system that enables us to evaluate realistically our relations with the world or our own abilities and level of development. This may account for why so many of the students have unrealistically high expectations for what they 'should' be able to achieve in their creative or academic writing, and why they easily become depressed or tormented when brilliance or excellence is not instantly forthcoming, even when they are in fact doing rather well. Recall Lucy's comment that: 'even if I'd got 100% on each essay [I] would not be satisfied', which indicates idealised expectations that can never be fulfilled.

This inability to gauge our actual level of development is perhaps not surprising if the psyche is dominated by idealisation backed up by self-punishment. No doubt for some people the urgent need to excel is understandable against the background of over-critical parents or punitive schooling methods, but there is, for some at least, a marked lack of realism in what can be achieved in a short space of time. The urgency to excel, which is an expansive drive, also makes sense in the context of a conflict between compliance and expansiveness, which Horney sees as a major inner conflict (Horney, 1951: 112).[10] Neither side of this divide allows space for the *gradual* development of actual talents; rather what is important is the short-term high of being the best, whether in goodness or brilliance.

The fear of self-exposure through creative writing, another dominant theme I highlighted in Chapter 3, is also partly intelligible in this context: doing the writing and sharing it with others threatens to reveal our actual level of development as an academic or creative writer and therefore risks exposing us to inner attack when this fails to live up to our idealised expectations. In the light of the above it is clear that making space for developing our actual talents and abilities, as much as we might want to do this, presents formidable difficulties. Surprisingly, it is possible for many of us to function reasonably well under these conditions as long as we limit our lives to what is possible given the restrictions. However, the pushes and pulls of the pride system are likely to be exhausting, and there will be a sense of frustration. Sometimes there will be a pervasive feeling of inauthenticity, as indicated by some students' feeling of 'being an imposter' or 'a big sham' in relation to their writing or learning. The other dimension of the fear of exposure through creative writing, which I highlighted in Chapter 2 – the fear of disrupting the existing configuration of the psyche – also makes sense in this context. Whilst the psychic status quo might be confining and frustrating, it is at least familiar and provides a degree of safety. Opening ourselves up to the chaos of creativity and learning can be terrifying if there is a potentially dangerous and disruptive presence in the psyche that we have not learned to manage effectively. Thus control is essential.

Fragmentation versus multiplicity of the psyche

It has been suggested that it is a standard development to have different selves with different voices in the psyche (Hermans, 2002), and it seems likely that different dimensions of our personality might well manifest themselves as different 'characters',[11] especially if they are associated with different roles we play in life. Where the psyche is dynamic and open, it may be possible to move between them as occasion demands or allows. But the sub-personalities that manifest in students' experience are often at odds with each other, inhibiting creativity. Damasio's view is that whilst it is likely that there can be only one core self, it is possible for there to be more than one at the level of the autobiographical self, but he links this with multiple personality disorder (MPD) rather than optimal development (Damasio, 2000: 142–3). Indeed the painful reality of being truly fragmented is evident in the distress experienced by people suffering from such disorders.[12]

Clearly, the sort of fragmentation visible amongst the students does not constitute MPD, since all of them are functioning reasonably well, albeit with a degree of struggle and distress in some instances. Rowan, building on Beahrs (1982), suggests that dissociation or splitting of the psyche exists along a continuum with dream and drug-induced states of boundary-loss at one end and the extreme fragmentation of MPD at the other, and in between a range of everyday psychic multiplicity from fluctuations in mood to sub-personalities to 'possession' (Rowan, 1999: 11). Ross argues against the idea of a continuum because MPD, or dissociative identity disorder (DID), as it is now called, has discrete characteristics not present in what he refers to as 'normal polypsychism', the normal multiplicity of the human mind. The difference between DID and normal psychic multiplicity 'is in the degree of personification of the ego states, the delusion of literal separateness of the personality states, the conflict, and the degree of information blockage in the system' (Ross, 1999: 193). Whether or not there is a continuum, it would not be surprising – in view of the complexities for human beings of having large and powerful brains with different levels of self and consciousness, and the two hemispheres of the brain providing very different views of the world, not to speak of the vicissitudes of upbringing and of living in complex societies – if psychic multiplicity was the norm, with different degrees of fragmentation representing less workable configurations. Thus, when the psyche is grounded in the body, we can be fluidly multiple, using the different dimensions reflexively in our engagement with the world and the development of our talents and abilities without being overly aware of them as separate. When the psyche is not so grounded, these dimensions become fragmented and potentially in conflict. Only in extreme circumstances might this give rise to what we designate as multiple personality or dissociative identity disorder.

McGilchrist refers to empirical evidence indicating that dissociation involves 'a disconnection from the right hemisphere and an interhemispheric imbalance in favour of the left' (McGilchrist, 2009: 236). Seeing that one of the features of the narrow attention of the left hemisphere is that it isolates and fixes phenomena – reifies them as objects, one might say – (ibid.: 3), the mental model of the self-in-the-world resulting from left hemisphere dominance might well be a whole consisting of separate, unintegrated parts, rather than the bodily based sense of wholeness generated by the right hemisphere. However, Platt argues that it is not the fragmenting attention of the left hemisphere that leads to dissociation, rather the left hemisphere, deprived of the reality-evaluating input of the right hemisphere, 'confabulates the dissociative story' (Platt, 2010: 11–12). This makes sense when applied to Horneyan life solutions, in which the imagination is placed in the service of idealisation, where it creates impossibly glorious images of what we 'should' be in the world and punishes us when we fail to achieve them

(Horney, 1951: 31–9). However, I would not rule out McGilchrist's view; the confabulating story may well be the left hemisphere's attempt to create a sense of wholeness out of the fragmentation.

Dominant self-concepts as a quest for wholeness

The picture that emerges from the experience of many of the students, then, is of insufficient grounding in, or disconnection from, felt bodily agency, which has resulted in a number of different parts of the personality pulling in different directions, making creativity or learning difficult. It is not surprising that many of us so afflicted, whether in response to short-term trauma or long-term anxiety, restrict ourselves to what is possible within the constraints of, say, one particular dimension of the split, or find some other overarching means of keeping the psyche under control and feeling whole. When I look at the ways students do this, I can see that there is a strong conscious tendency to identify with social self-concepts that are rooted in their actual lives, such as professional or formal identities. This is certainly the case for Claire, Rhiannon, and Lucy, who are all strongly defined by their professional roles, which make it possible to function well in those areas of life, although creativity is compromised. This is also the case for Jill before the MA, as she only discovers her problems with creativity once she retires. Harriet is strongly defined by her academic identity and has accumulated an impressive array of qualifications, but again at the expense of space for her creativity. It may be that academic study and writing have been possible for her because they do not involve deep engagement with self and emotions, in a similar way to Ruth's acting. Harriet also has a strong identity as a carer of others, as do Stacey and Stella, whether professionally or as mothers. Whilst Maria does not talk much about what contained her sense of being split before she began the MA, there is an indication that it was her strong identity as a healthcare professional, as she says at one point that this has been badly disrupted by the MA and has had to be re-made. For Simon it is his roles as husband, father, and grandfather that hold his fragmented psyche together, although he has constantly to adjust himself to fit them. For Susanna it is, I have suggested, her illness identity that enables her to keep control over her painful feelings and to derive a sense of wholeness.

Social self-concepts are, of course, an inevitable and necessary part of our immersion in everyday life (Neisser, 1988). But I would suggest that when the psyche is integrated and agentic as a result of being grounded in the body there can be movement between self-concepts: we can find satisfaction in being a teacher or a mother, whilst simultaneously feeling justified in allowing space for our creativity when time allows. When integration is impaired, however, and spontaneous contact with the bodily core self is lost, self-concepts have to provide us with a way of keeping under control the unintegrated parts of the psyche.

They act as an effective capstone on the split psyche, providing a measure of safety and containment, but they limit the amount of the psyche available to us.

Defending the split psyche is also a very time and energy consuming task. By contrast with bodily-based reflexivity, which is both grounded and flexible, the psyche has to be constantly monitored, a form of psychic control that, drawing on Sass (1992), I will call 'hyperreflexivity'.[13] Applied to defensive self-concepts, hyperreflexivity works to maintain tacit awareness of the dominant self-concept so that its rules are always available as a means of shoring up the fragmented psyche. It is a form of self-objectification in the service of an unrelenting top-down self-regulation. This move away from bottom-up bodily-based wholeness towards a top-down ad hoc unity can provide a degree of stability and identity, but it is stability at the expense of growth. For when our cognitive and emotional resources are employed to provide a sense of unity for the split psyche, the possibilities for inner space and psychic movement decrease, so that the cognitive flexibility necessary for learning and creative work is impaired. Control of the fragmented psyche can be seen as a means of halting the reflexivity and change that is intrinsic to a dynamic system; in other words it is a strategy for stopping the flow of time (Siegel, 2003). This is most visible in Susanna's case where her sense of temporal ongoingness has been severely affected, but it is also there implicitly in the blocking or separating off of the creative temperamental part of the personality that afflicts many of the students.

Loosening psychic control and expanding the psyche

The loosening of psychic control and the opening-up of the psyche to inner space and movement, which happens for all the Group 2 students to varying degrees, is quite challenging, as I have shown, with repressed emotions and unintegrated parts of the personality becoming freed up and differentiated. Whilst, as I said in Chapter 6, small changes in the leading edge of the psyche can lead to quick and significant changes across the whole dynamic system, it takes time for the different parts of the personality to move towards integration and for bodily-based regulation of the whole dynamic system to develop. Recall that the other side of openness and stability is (relative) chaos (Siegel, 1999), and not a few students report being significantly at sea at the end of their first year of study (see Chapter 11). The tendency might simply be to close down again, which was certainly the case for Claudia during the latter part of the MA.

In some instances new, holistic mental models can be seen to emerge spontaneously, often at the implicit rather than the explicit level, which indicates a move towards better regulation of the psyche. Simon's metaphor for his sense of self as author – the rancher comfortably surveying the unruly prairie of the imagination – is an example of this, as is Maria's storyteller-self who contains the space of storytelling for her family's history. In both these instances there is also evidence of dialogue rather than conflict between the expansive side of the personality and the managing side. Simon's distinction between his expansive 'writer' self and his managing 'author' self is an apt conceptualisation of the different parts of the psyche involved in writing: 'author' is a social self-concept associated with having produced a piece of writing for an audience, whilst 'writer' implies the embodied process of writing. For other students a more benevolent parental part of the psyche emerges whose role it is to manage the unruly childish part rather than control it. Susanna's experience demonstrates this, as does Claire's, Ruth's, and Harriet's. Lucy is keen to find a self-concept that feels more fitting for her as a single childless woman in her 40s. This is not just a quest for another defence, rather, as she is 'happier to embrace contradictions as to who I am', it is a desire to find an identity in the world that resonates with an important dimension of herself.

Tershakovec suggests that 'mental models only make a good way of thinking if we already have, and can consciously revise, a sound master model of the self and of the world, a model of the self-in-the-world' (2007: 123). That students are beginning to develop new and more flexible mental models of the self-in-the-world, as illustrated above, provides strong evidence that there has been a shift away from the less flexible mental models with which they began their studies and the beginnings of the development of, or a return to, a 'sound master model' informed by the reality-evaluating core self. I say 'return to', because some of the students characterise their experience of change as a sense of *re-finding* themselves. I'm thinking of Susanna's 'I'm easing back into myself', but there is also Maria's 'I am finding my way back to myself', Claudia's 'I feel very much a sense of the true me', and Rhiannon's 'It's ... a *re-awakening* of who I am'. These comments indicate that for some people change is a reconnection with a previously known state. This supports Siegel's (1999) suggestion that traumatic or anxiety-rovoking events at any time across the lifespan can disrupt hemispheric integration.[14]

Having increased access to the bodily core self and to the whole range of the emotions means that there is a bodily basis for agency on which a grounded sense of self-worth can develop. Clearly this is centrally important in being better able to manage relations with others, as some of the students have found. It is also centrally important in a learning context, where it allows *actual* talents and abilities to be valued and therefore developed progressively over time rather than, in instances where idealisation has come to form the leading edge of the psyche, lost sight of in the pursuit of short-term highs. Indeed, one of the most striking developments amongst Group 2 students is how many of them begin to be able to evaluate their creative and academic writing more realistically and to trust their own judgement. This is particularly visible in Susanna's experience, but it is also there in Simon's and Maria's and in that of many of the others. Whilst this is in part the result of sharing their work in small groups and getting feedback from tutors (see Chapter 9), engaging more readily with the felt body for learning and writing is, I suggest, an important factor here.

As I said in the Introduction, the relationship between structure and agency is a key ontological theme in the findings of this research at a number of different levels. What the foregoing discussion leads me to conclude is that genuine self-agency and self-worth can develop only if the psyche has a flexible leading edge, that is, the autobiographical 'I' in spontaneous and reflexive contact with the bodily core self. In other words, a bottom-up or bodily-based reflexive self-structure giving rise to a stable but flexible core state (Fosha, 2005) is the key to the psyche's ability to differentiate and integrate itself in its innate drive towards maximum complexity and agency (Siegel, 2003). How the different elements of the CWPD programme work together to open-up the psyche and generate reflexivity is the subject of Part III.

Notes

1 Kegan's constructive-developmental approach (2000) does distinguish between more or less workable psychic states, but he uses fictional examples only and does not explore the question of why some people do not make the shift from what he calls the 'socialized mind' to the 'self-authoring' or 'self-transforming' mind. Cranton (2000) distinguishes between different learning styles rather than more or less workable psychic states.
2 McGilchrist argues that the tendency towards left hemisphere dominance in Western culture is a consequence of post-Enlightenment thinking with its privileging of reason at the expense of feeling, as well as the progressive atomisation of life since the industrial revolution, as reflected in our art as much as in our scientific and bureaucratic culture. This is not to deride reason, but to highlight the imbalance that has developed between the different views of the world provided by the brain's hemispheres (McGilchrist, 2009: 389–427).
3 Attachment theorist Allan Schore also sees the early response to anxiety in the emergency reactions of fight and flight (Schore, 1994). The biological basis of these moves may account for their tenacity, as we have seen in the case of compliance.
4 For Rowan a sub-personality is 'a semi-permanent and semi-autonomous region of the personality capable of acting as a person' (Rowan, 1990: 8). I see it as a complex of emotions and character traits that can dominate the psyche temporarily or permanently but is not a complete person.
5 Horney identifies different manifestations of the three main solutions, such as perfectionistic, narcissistic, or arrogant-vindictive behaviour in the case of expansiveness (Horney, 1951: 193). However, it has been suggested that some of these tendencies can become combined with any of the three main solutions, so that, for example, perfectionism could just as easily be a feature of compliance or detachment (Riso and Hudson, 1996: 323). In fact Horney implies that perfectionism is a general feature of idealisation (Horney, 1951: 24–5).
6 This is an example of collaboration between perfectionism and compliance rather than conflict between them (see previous note).
7 For McGilchrist boredom results from the dominance of the left hemisphere, which re-presents experience rather than capturing its felt presence as the right hemisphere does (McGilchrist, 2009: 191–2).
8 The idea of 'decentering' the self (Derrida, 1978) as the deconstruction of a singular sense of self can be usefully understood not as a liberation from the self but from a controlling autobiographical 'I', which facilitates a more fluid, bodily-based sense of self. Logically this should be called a 'recentering' rather than a 'decentering', as it involves finding a bodily grounding that allows movement and flexibility of the psyche.

9 Horney's notion of the psychic vicious circle (or positive feedback) is consonant with the notion of 'recursive causality' (Lewis, 2005) in dynamic systems theory.
10 Horney reserves the term 'central inner conflict' for the deeper conflict that occurs later in therapeutic work between the entire pride system and the real self.
11 I am reluctant to call them 'selves', as this makes them too separate and autonomous.
12 It has become fashionable to celebrate the fragmentation of the psyche because it allows us to change our identity at will (e.g. Gergen, 1991), but it seems unlikely that we could function coherently if our personality was intrinsically fragmented, without a sense of wholeness. Indeed, the drive to wholeness, whether this is the intrinsic biological drive that motivates the psyche as a dynamic system, or the drive to construct an alternative holistic self-structure based on idealised images or dominant self-concepts in instances where basic anxiety or trauma initiates a shift away from the bodily core self, indicates that a sense of psychic wholeness is essential for human functioning.
13 Sass uses this term to describe the extreme objectifying of the self-concept in schizophrenia, but he also suggests that there are likely to be less extreme forms of self-objectification. I would suggest that Horneyan life solutions, or self-concepts containing a narrative of 'shoulds' (Hunt, 2000), can be understood as an everyday form of hyperreflexive self-objectification.
14 For Schore (1994), by comparison, lack of hemispheric integration results from inadequate parenting in infancy.

Part III

Facilitating transformative change through creative life writing

For the majority of students in Group 2 the initial opening-up of the psyche occurs in Course 1 (*Writing for Personal Development*), with deepening and/or consolidation taking place across the remainder of the programme. For quite a few of them Course 3 (*Writing and Groups*) is particularly important in taking the process of change further, and for many the two terms of *Independent Study* are a key period of consolidation. But what are the specific elements within these courses that facilitate the shift from top-down left hemisphere control towards a more flexible and bodily-based self-agency?

In my previous attempts to understand students' experience of change I have focused mainly on the role of the creative life writing and have not explored to the same extent other factors in the learning environment. In attempting to do so now, I take as my starting point critical realist Gordon Brown's conceptualisation of the learning environment as 'a semi-permanent, often episodic, complex ensemble of causal mechanisms that enable and constrain learning'.[1] These causal mechanisms are a consequence of the 'layered' or 'laminar' nature of the 'open or quasi-closed system' of the learning environment with its physical, biological, psychological, socio-cultural, and curricular dimensions, with the possibilities for learning emerging from the way these work together for individual learners (Brown, 2009: 31).[2] This conceptualisation is helpful in that it provides a broad, multifaceted way of thinking about the structures or mechanisms at work in a learning environment, although the terms 'layered' and 'laminar' are metaphorically rather too static in a dynamic systems context where the different dimensions are constantly subject to change (ibid.: 19). Nevertheless I use these ideas heuristically in what follows.

I combine with Brown's ideas two psychodynamic concepts: 'holding' and 'containment'. 'Holding' is Donald Winnicott's metaphor for the way the 'good-enough mother', through a combination of attentive, emotional presence and detachment, creates a 'holding environment' for her baby, which enables it to feel 'safe-enough' to explore the 'potential space' between them (Winnicott, 1960). Safely 'held' by the mother's presence, the infant 'is able to become unintegrated, to flounder, to be in a state in which there is no ... external impingement', which means that it can more easily receive its own sensations or impulses and feel real (Winnicott, 1958: 33). This is crucially important for developing independence and the ability to be creative in the 'transitional space' between psychic reality and the outside world (Winnicott, 1971). This idea has been extended to education, where the 'good-enough teacher' creates a safe-enough holding environment for pupils or students to open-up to the state of not-knowing that learning and creativity involve (Wyatt-Brown, 1993; Hunt, 2000: 47–9).[3] 'Containment' is Wilfrid Bion's notion that the mother receives the baby's intolerable emotional states through appropriate caring behaviour, which enables it to reintroject them combined with the mother's containing presence, thus rendering them tolerable (Bion, 1962). Whilst these two ideas clearly have different meanings – 'containment' indicating a wholly inner process and 'holding' a process taking place between inner and outer worlds (Symington and Symington, 1996: 58) – both imply the development of beneficial mental structures, which contribute to the possibility of 'thinking feelings' or 'mentalized affectivity' in Fonagy's sense (Fonagy *et al.*, 2002). I use them here not only in relation to the role of tutors but also in the way that other 'layers' of the learning environment can, in optimal circumstances, generate in students a sense of being 'held' and can then become internalised as a means of self-containment.

Applying the idea of a laminar or layered structure to the CWPD programme, I can easily identify the enabling and constraining role of the physical environment of students' learning. For example, in the period of Group 2 students' studies teaching largely takes place in a temporary, pre-fabricated building, with noise leaking between seminar rooms. When the two student groups taking *Writing and Groups* are located next to each other, the audible laughter of one group is a source of uncomfortable self-questioning for the other, quieter group, but this nevertheless provides a useful opportunity for group reflection, a key element in that course. A less positive example is the difficulty Susanna has in taking proper breaks in the full-day sessions, following her period of hospitalisation, because of the steep hill between the temporary teaching block and the café, which considerably impairs her learning experience.

The curricular dimension[4] can similarly be seen to enable and constrain students' learning. For example, for some students the all-day fortnightly sessions generate a strong sense of being part of a 'community of writers', which contributes to a sense of being 'held' during their studies. For others, particularly for those taking *Writing Practice* and *Projects: Practical and Theoretical* in 2004–06, the gaps between sessions are too long, causing them to lose connection with the programme and their writing. This is also the case for some of the students during the two terms of *Independent Study*. The work for assessment – another curricular aspect – again has enhancing and constraining effects. For many students, the end-of-course essays are an important means of consolidating course learning (see Chapter 10), but for one student in Group 2 the institution's regulations associated with assessment mar her whole experience of the MA (see Chapter 11).

Seeing that the physical and curricular dimensions of the learning environment relate to the programme as a whole, they could be thought of as 'macroscopic' or 'overlying' (Bhaskar and Danermark, 2006: 289), in the sense that they frame students' overall experience, although students will experience their enhancing and constraining effects differently. I would also include in the macroscopic dimensions the organisational role of the programme convener, who holds together the programme, the student body, and the tutor group administratively, managerially, and to an extent pastorally (more than one student refers to the convener as 'the mother of the MA').[5] Similarly, for some students the ethos of the programme generated by the tutor team creates, as one Group 1 student puts it, 'the sense of a vast space encompassed in which to play and explore'. What Bhaskar and Danermark call the 'normative' dimension (ibid.: 288), which can be thought of here as the expectations students will have for how a higher education learning environment operates, that is, the mode of engagement with their learning and with other learners, can also be seen as macroscopic.

By contrast the bio-psycho-social dimensions at work in individual psyches could be said to be less macroscopic, or underlying, in the sense that their enhancing or constraining effects on students' learning will vary considerably between individuals. For example, if the biological dimension relates to bodily matters such as health or sexuality, then Susanna's chronic illness impacts more significantly on her learning experience than that of others. A similar point applies to the psychological dimension, with fears and anxieties from previous learning environments impacting on some individuals more than others; and to the social dimension, with considerable differences in how students conceptualise themselves as writers or learners. But whilst the bio-psycho-social dimensions are more individual, they inevitably influence the environment as a whole in gross or subtle ways. They are also potentially more in process during the actual period of study than the physical, curricular, and organisational dimensions (at least in CWPD), as these latter change as a result of the tutor team's retrospective reflections on the running of the programme and students' feedback. However, in CWPD the macroscopic 'normative' dimension is also set in motion, in the sense that the learning environment is often a hybrid, somewhere between an academic seminar and a play space (Creme and Hunt, 2002) (see Chapter 11) and therefore quite different from what students expect.

Whilst some of the macroscopic dimensions in the CWPD programme – the overarching curricular structure (see Chapter 10), the organisational role of the convener (see Chapter 11), and the sense of being part of a community of learners – can be seen to provide an important element of background structure or 'holding' against which the bio-psycho-social and normative dimensions of the learning environment are set in motion, it is the curricular and pedagogical dimensions at work in individual courses that do the main work of both challenging the dynamic system of the psyche (i.e. opening it up and keeping it in motion) and 'holding' it (i.e. preventing a collapse into chaos). These include not only the creative life writing exercises, but also the collaborative, experiential groups for sharing this writing, and the reflective work students engage in. Although it is quite difficult to separate out the effects of these different elements, as will be obvious from the case studies, Chapter 8 focuses on the creative life writing, Chapter 9 on the collaborative, experiential group work, and Chapter 10 on the role of reflection. Throughout these chapters I relate my discussions to key ideas in the theory and practice of transformative learning. Mezirow's idea of 'disorienting dilemmas', by which he means events in a person's life that trigger the process of transformative learning (Mezirow, 1981), is particularly useful when applied to triggers operating within the learning environment.

Notes

1 Brown uses 'constrain' here in a positive sense to indicate the way a learning environment enhances learning by limiting the range of things to be learned. In this sense it has a similarity with my use of the terms 'holding' and 'containment' (see below). However, the more usual meaning of 'constrain' is to inhibit, and I use it primarily in this sense.

2 The terms 'layered' or 'laminar' to describe the multiplicity of mechanisms at work in open systems derive from Bhaskar and Danermark (2006).
3 I note that Gunnlaugson (2007) also uses this idea in a transformative learning context, drawing on Kegan (1982).
4 Brown defines curriculum as 'what we teach' and pedagogy as 'how we teach' (Brown, 2009: 8). In the CWPD programme I understand curriculum as the structure of courses and sessions within courses, and mandatory course content, including the creative life writing, the reading lists, and the end of course assessments. I understand 'pedagogy' as the facilitation of the learning environment and the tools and practices employed.
5 The research project also acted, for some Group 2 students, as an overarching and containing macrostructure (see Introduction).

Chapter 8

Developing reflexivity through creative life writing

Since my research began there has been an increasing amount of work on the role of fiction and autobiography in transformative learning. Christine Jarvis, for example, focuses on fiction's 'power to engender empathy', as well as its 'ability to enable us to stand back from our own situations [through] distancing techniques' (Jarvis, 2012: 487). Elsewhere she talks about fiction as offering 'the kinds of "disorienting dilemmas" that Mezirow and others have identified as triggers that start the transformative process' (Jarvis, 2006: 76). These ideas resonate strongly with my own findings, as does Rebecca Ruppert Johnson's view that autobiographical writing can help us to 'trust our intuition ... and allow self-reflective processes to increase flow and resonance' for learning (Ruppert Johnson, 2003: 242). Closely related to the experiential approach of the CWPD programme, as will become obvious from this chapter, is John Dirkx's mythopoetic and imaginal approach to learning, where participants are encouraged to become aware of images that arise spontaneously in the mind from immersion in the learning environment. They then use freewriting to explore the images, and the resulting writing is reflected on for themes that emerge (Dirkx, 2008).

Two kinds of writing exercises

In thinking about the role of creative life writing in students' experience of change, I have come to see the exercises they undertake in Course 1 (*Writing for Personal Development*) as falling into two main types, with the first working more significantly with core consciousness and the second with extended consciousness. In 2004 when Group 2 students were studying, the first type included the web of words, freewriting, recalling words or sayings from childhood and using them to create a rhythmic or rhyming poem, and conveying the feel or mood of a remembered place using long Proustian sentences (see Chapter 1). In previous writings I have referred to these as 'semiotic' exercises (Hunt, 2004a; 2010a), following Julia Kristeva's use of the 'Semiotic' to denote the prelinguistic bodily felt experience of early childhood which, she argues, is always present in linguistic meaning-making in dialogue with the structural elements of language, such as grammar and syntax, which constitute the 'Symbolic' (Kristeva, 1984).[1]

The second type of exercise focuses on developing imaginative engagements or dialogues between fictional characters and narrators created out of oneself or significant people in one's life. In 2004 these included writing from old photographs, the 'self as source', 'creating the future self', and 'imagining the reader in the writing process'. I have previously called these exercises 'dialogic', following Mikhail Bakhtin's use of this term to denote fiction writing that gives characters and narrators a voice of their own and allows a dialogue between them as far as possible on equal terms (Bakhtin, 1984). As I said in Chapter 6, Bakhtin's notion of 'dialogue' has strong similarities to reflexivity in my understanding of this term, so these exercises could also be called 'reflexive' (see below).

Subverting left hemisphere control

For many of the students the semiotic exercises are centrally important to what psychotherapist Christopher Bollas calls the 'cracking-up' of the psyche, the dismantling of fixed ways of thinking and being through free association (Bollas, 1995: 221–56) and the loosening of cognitive control.[2] Freewriting is revealed to be one of the most effective for this purpose, challenging conscious intentions with its requirement of letting go of the rules of grammar and syntax and making space for what everyday language keeps at bay. As we have seen in Susanna's story, the initial freewriting exercise on the theme of 'beginnings' subverts her conscious intentions for 'an elegant dance of prose' by evoking a spontaneous expression of rage at her situation. As Stacey says of this subversive exercise: it is 'as if the writer inside has taken command of our fingers and our will is being bypassed'. This echoes Simon's discovery that his inner 'writer' has its own intentions, which are quite at odds with those of his 'author-self'. Not surprisingly, quite a few students resist freewriting at first. Ruth procrastinates about the home exercise until the last minute, then, having done it, rages about the pointlessness of it and the 'complete and utter bollocks' she has written. Later she reflects that: 'I was clearly very cross at having to open up to myself.., of taking my hand out of a by now very obvious mental dam'. But allowing this to happen is an important first step in accessing the source of her creative block: the unresolved pain and rage at her losses.

Similarly effective in subverting cognitive control is the exercise that involves recalling everyday words or sayings from childhood and using them in a rhythmic and/or rhyming poem. Maria's experience of 'listening to' Flemish words from her childhood and the difficult memories of her relationship with her mother that accompany them is a good example of the impact of this exercise: how it enables her to bring the feel of her past self into the present and to experience her lost sensuality and repressed anger. Stella's poem is written in what she calls her 'cockney/posh vernacular ... interspersed with a song or two, a poem, the weather forecast and football scores'. It captures for her the sound or tone of her early environment, including her mother's voice:

> Eat an apple if you're hungry; dinner's at 6
> Go and buy some fags; put it on the tick
> Get a blooming plate; you're dropping all the crumbs
> No you can't have more cake; it's for Peter when he comes.

As with Maria, Stella's recovery of the feel of her childhood brings her into more direct contact with her anger at her mother. Harriet also finds that: 'Once I start looking at my childhood and expressing it through language, my mother emerges more fully because it is *her* language that dominates my childhood, and my memories of it'. In her poem 'Yan, Tan, Tethera, Methera, Pimp' – the ancient way of counting sheep in her ancestral Cumbria – she speaks 'the northern "a's", hard as unripe apples' and listens 'for the curlew', but concludes that the 'language is no longer my own'. And yet this is the language she uses to write her poetry, which leads her to ponder whether 'the fact that I had to use [my mother's] language cause[d] my [20 year writing] block?' Reconnecting with her anger at her mother is like entering a 'toxic sea', but it has to be done, she says, if she is to lay claim to her own voice.

The subversive effect of these exercises comes in part from drawing the past into the present of the writing, where it is possible to 'think' the feeling, but it also comes from the use of imagery and metaphor, literary devices that provide an oblique angle on past experience rather than a head-on encounter, making it more tolerable (Cox and Theilgaard, 1987). In some instances particular genres transgress usual ways of thinking and feeling. As we have seen in Maria's story, spontaneously moving into fairy-tale in her poem from the child's point of view shifts her into a world where the good/bad dichotomy of her childhood environment can be blurred, which frees her to 'transgress' the familiar boundaries of her self-identity. A similar subversive effect is visible in Megan's struggle with the requirements of poetic form. From peer feedback on her poem, 'Speak Properly', which focuses on 'a mother so obsessed with [her child] speaking properly she misses the joys [it] is experiencing', she learns that the rhythm is lost at the end because it is 'told' (i.e. reported) and not 'shown' (i.e. conveyed feelingly through imagery or dramatization) (Booth, 1991; see Hunt, 2000: 92). Through discussion with her reading group she realises that she doesn't actually know how she wants to end the poem, but accepting the not-knowing allows her to feel her way into a new and unexpected ending with 'a little of rebellion about it' that, she says, is directed as much against her own perfectionism as against her mother's:

> I don't know what to say,
> I don't know how to say it,
> Finally I realise, Mum, I ain't never gonna
> Speak properly.

Thus having to sustain the rhythm and 'show' the emotion subverts the rules of the internalised mother, allowing the creative, rebellious self to speak (cf. Hunt, 2000: 18).

Capturing the mood of a remembered place using long Proustian sentences is similarly subversive for Lucy, enabling her to access a more authentic sense of herself beneath her familiar professional identity. When she reads her piece of writing about her native Cornwall, she finds that: 'There is something in the feel of its elongated and crowded sentences and feisty energy that feels like me'. She goes on to say that:

> It could be that having spent years writing predominantly in a business context my current mode of writing owes more to having to get a message across succinctly to a slightly bored audience than to anything else. And that what this exercise did so powerfully was jump me out of this learned way of capturing my thoughts, providing an opportunity to gain insight into what my true voice could sound like.

The value of the Proust exercise for Claire is that 'I can give myself permission "to go on", to "show off" and not to "come to the point" [which] was a novelty for me'. Thus, being required by the course to do the exercise enables her to let herself go in ways her rule-bound psyche would not normally allow.

The semiotic exercises, then, are a powerful means of subverting familiar patterns of thinking and feeling, and increasing awareness of what lies beneath; they are a source of 'disorienting dilemmas', in Mezirow's sense. Freewriting, by switching off left hemisphere functions of language, disrupts linear thinking and the tendency to remain with familiar, often unexamined ways of being. It tricks the psyche into allowing hidden thoughts and feelings to emerge, often in the form of metaphors or images, and meaning to be made from bottom-up rather than top-down. Something similar happens in the poetry and poetic prose exercises: putting the emphasis on sound, rhythm, and mood as starting points effects a shift away from known categories towards the felt but not-yet-known, and the requirement to fulfil the rhythm and show the emotion involves staying with the feeling that wants to express itself.

The self in language

What these exercises highlight is the power of everyday language to constrain thinking and feeling and the power of poetic or free associative language to free it up. As I said earlier, by enabling us to impose patterns on experience language provides us with a powerful tool, but it can also obscure 'the more intricate order' of our experience beyond those patterns (Gendlin, 1991: 21). Gendlin encourages an approach to language that seeks to access what lies beyond the patterns by attending to the 'felt sense', a concept that echoes Damasio's descriptions of the experience of core consciousness. Felt sense is the pre-reflective dimension of meaning-making that comes to us first and foremost as felt images (Johnson's moments of bodily-felt awareness); for example, the way we can walk into a room and sense that people in it have been arguing. Gendlin calls this tacit knowing a 'wholistic, implicit bodily sense of a complex situation' (1996: 58). The term 'wholistic' is particularly relevant here in light of the 'global' nature of the brain's mapping in the protoself that gives rise to a holistic bodily-felt sense of self (Damasio, 2000), and of the holistic functioning of the right hemisphere (McGilchrist, 2009).

Gendlin's most apt example is of the poet in the process of creating a poem, who re-reads the line she has written and knows in an intuitive, bodily-felt way that it has not yet captured what she is trying to say, but does not yet know what will. There is a blank (a '...'), a felt space of experience not yet articulated. In order to find the word or phrase that is appropriate to this blank, the poet must keep the space of not knowing open by 'listening' to it. Only by doing this will it become possible to open the felt sense, differentiate between its different components, and 'carry forward' into the line of the poem the meaning that emerges (Gendlin, 1991: 47–8). A felt sense, Gendlin says, is not an emotion; whilst the feeling of an emotion is readily recognisable, a felt sense is not yet recognisable. But if we reflect on a felt sense, we find that it contains not only emotions but also thoughts, perceptions, memories or desires (Gendlin, 1996: 59).

Gendlin's description of the engagement with the felt sense captures very effectively students' experience of the semiotic exercises at the start of Course 1. The felt sense is experienced when they let go of their familiar ways of being in language and immerse themselves in the feel of the present moment. This shift of attention, which evokes Marion Milner's 'internal gesture' (see Chapter 6), involves a loosening of *intention*, of *will*, accepting a degree of passivity rather than being the active determining force, although intention remains in holding the psychic space open for whatever comes. Milner captures this perfectly with her metaphor of the benevolent policeman:

> I must neither push my thought nor let it drift. I must simply make an internal gesture of standing back and watching, for it was a state in which my will played policeman to the crowd of my thoughts, its business being to stand there and watch that the road might be kept free for whatever was coming.
> (Milner, 1952: 102)

Elsewhere she describes this stance as 'ordered freedom', involving 'reciprocity' between the agency that holds the space open and the sensory impressions that spontaneously appear within it (Milner, 1971: 71–6). This is quite different from day-dreaming, where 'thought is just playing with itself'; rather there is an expressive, active relationship between what she calls 'mind and body' (ibid.), which can be understood as the relationship between the bodily agency of the core self in the right hemisphere and the consciously ordering self-agency of the autobiographical

'I' in the left. Indeed, Milner's benevolent stance is echoed by McGilchrist's description of the kind of will associated with the right hemisphere as 'caring', which he contrasts with the controlling will of the left hemisphere. McGilchrist also uses the term 'reciprocity' as an equivalent of the 'betweenness' he identifies as characteristic of right hemisphere functioning. It involves 'patient openness to whatever is', in order that it can be 'taken further' by the left hemisphere (McGilchrist, 2009: 171–3, 194), which echoes Gendlin's 'carrying forward'.

When students move on to write a poem or prose piece, bringing more directed thought to bear on the felt sense, this begins to open it up and carry it forward into words. Reflecting on the writing and the writing process via their reading groups and in their learning journals and reflective essays provides another level of carrying forward, which helps to consolidate the opening-up (see Chapters 9 and 10). I suggest that it is these various stages of bringing the 'more intricate order of experience' beyond fixed patterns into the light (Gendlin, 1991) and carrying it forward into thought and action that presses students to loosen their dominant self-identities. This view is supported by laboratory research into the effects of felt sense techniques, where participants' experience often involves a 'loosening or even disappearance of the feeling of individual identity' (Petitmengin, 2007: 69). Engaging with the felt sense, then, through freewriting and poetry and poetic prose, facilitates the suspension of tacit self-concepts and immersion in the bodily-felt sense of self. This not only makes more of the psyche available but also opens up the possibility of change.

The self in time

Gallagher and Zahavi suggest that we experience time in two different but complementary ways. The first is what they call the 'dynamic now', which includes 'the retained just-past and the protended just-about-to-occur'. This is not a 'knife-edge present, but a duration-block, having forward and rearward ends, a bow and a stern'. This very short-term but constantly repeated experience of time, estimated at between 0.5 and 3 seconds, provides coherence to our sense of being a body in the world and manifests itself in a sense of 'flow' (Gallagher and Zahavi, 2008: 82–4; Thompson, 2007: 334). This is Damasio's core consciousness with a sense of self. The second experience of time is characterised by:

> a kind of temporal stretch. The past continually serves as the horizon and background of our present experience, and when absorbed in action, our focus, the centre of our concern, is not on the present, but on the future goals that we intend or project.
>
> (Gallagher and Zahavi, 2008: 86)

This is Ricoeur's 'narrated time, a time structured and articulated by the symbolic mediations of [familial, social and cultural] narratives'; it is Damasio's extended self of higher consciousness or the narrative self (ibid.: 86, 200–2; Ricoeur, 1988: 244). As in Damasio's self-schema, narrated time emerges out of the experience of the 'dynamic now', but can also come to obscure the experience of ourselves in the flow of time. I would suggest that engaging in the semiotic exercises with their emphasis on the felt sense and writing in the present tense enables students to experience more closely the feel of themselves in the 'dynamic now'. Capturing the experience of the exercises in the course diary or learning journal when it is still fresh also emphasises the 'dynamic now', as does the experiential nature of the weekly student-led groups (see Chapters 9 and 10). This experiential work is supported by course readings, such as Miroslaw Holub's *The Dimension of the Present Moment* (1990), which explores the idea that poetry works primarily with the 'now phase of consciousness', with poets, even those writing apparently free verse, instinctively making use of the 3-second 'experience parcels' of the present moment.[3]

This emphasis on the bodily-felt movement of the 'dynamic now' seems particularly important in view of what I have referred to in Chapter 7 as the stopping of time accompanying the shift away from core consciousness which, in light of the above, could be understood as the obscuring of the experience of ourselves in the flow of time. This is most visible in Susanna's sense of having no future and perseverating on the past, but it is also there in others. Claudia, for example, who, in response to a tutor's comment that her piece of writing does not stay with the present, becomes aware that the past:

> is where the ground feels more solid beneath my feet. I know the past. I can talk about the things outside, and behind me, all day long, but this piece revealed to me my very real discomfort of being in the present. ... I think this reluctance to inhabit the present or the future comes from a deep-seated insecurity. I have believed my future to be uncertain because my present felt unstable, a house of cards that could be destroyed by one wrong move, so the only safe place was the past.

As we have seen, it is the right hemisphere of the brain that provides the sense of movement in time, whilst the left hemisphere is more focused on fixed points in time (McGilchrist, 2009: 76–7). So where left hemisphere functioning has become dominant, attention is likely either to be hyperreflexively focused on the past, for example because of the need to defend oneself against painful feelings; or, in instances where life solutions have taken hold, on maintaining an idealised mental model of the future self-in-the-world (Tershakovec, 2007: 181–2). In this context Maria's comment that her experience of engaging in the semiotic exercises has helped her to 'transcend' time, as Proust did (see Chapter 4), can be understood as meaning that they have enabled her to transcend the stasis of left hemisphere attention by reconnecting with the temporality of the right. This idea of transcending time via the right hemisphere is present in McGilchrist's discussion of music, a key right hemisphere function: 'Music takes place in time.

Yet music also has the capacity to make us stand outside time', he says, but then qualifies it by saying that 'music does not so much free time from temporality as bring out an aspect that is always present within time, its intersection with a moment which partakes of eternity' (McGilchrist, 2009: 77). This sounds very much like the experience of ongoingness provided by the bodily core self, and this reconnection with the sense of being in process is a central dimension of students' experience of change.

The idea that the self is a process is, of course, central to Damasio's model, but it is present also in Julia Kristeva's notion of the 'subject-in-process' between the Semiotic and the Symbolic (Nicholls, 2006), where the term 'subject' carries two different meanings: the first person *subject* of consciousness who is also *subject* to language and society (Kristeva, 1984). According to Kristeva, where our self-conceptualisations have become fixed in language, stopping time and movement, reading and writing poetry can set us in motion again. It returns us to the earliest phase of life when our sense of self was more immediately in the living present, not yet dependent on self-objectification. This earliest stage is characterised by a gestural and rhythmic form of relating to primary carers – clapping, rocking, babbling – an engagement that may have given rise to the 'temporal arts' as a whole, including poetry and music (Dissanajake, 2001). It is a time when the child's experience is dominated by the right hemisphere, so that its way of making meaning is primarily spatio-temporal and bodily, the language functions of the left hemisphere not yet having developed (Kane, 2004). In other words, the child is still immersed in the bodily-felt sense of self in the 'dynamic now'.

Research in cognitive neuroscience supports Kristeva's view of poetry as providing access to a more process-oriented sense of self. It used to be thought that language was confined to the left hemisphere, but it has now become clear that, whilst the left brain 'possesses the complete lexicon and rules of syntax' (ibid.: 22) and is responsible for linear and clear-cut meanings, the right hemisphere has 'a number of very subtle but intriguing "linguistic" functions', including the processing of images and symbols, metaphor, metonymy and synecdoche, inference and allusion, personification, prosody, assonance and alliteration. All of these are central features of poetry or poetic language, and indeed of creative writing as a whole. Particularly interesting in relation to the semiotic exercises is that the right brain processes 'familiar expressions' such as those dominant in early childhood, such as nursery rhymes, songs, and jingles (ibid.: 44), precisely what students are encouraged to access in the childhood words exercise. Also, many of the right hemisphere linguistic functions feature ambiguity or 'double-voiced' language (Bakhtin, 1981), so that rather than the either/or (black and white) thinking of the left hemisphere, right hemisphere language generates 'betweenness'.

The intense focus, then, on poetry and poetic language in the semiotic exercises can be seen to stimulate the right hemisphere and the functions that are associated with it, such as the holistic bodily sense of ongoingness in time and space, engagement with subtle and tacit dimensions of feeling, and the expression of the emotions. It sets the psyche in motion again, whilst at the same time providing a degree of 'holding' for this challenging process through the cognitive frames that are an intrinsic part of poetic writing and a left hemisphere function (Kane, 2004: 51) (see also Chapters 9 and 10). What, then, do the 'dialogic exercises' contribute to this picture?

Imagining a larger space for the self in time

When Group 2 students were studying, the semiotic exercises occupied the first two sessions of Course 1 and the dialogic exercises the remaining two. The 'future self' exercise in Session 3, 'Past, Present and Future Selves', carries forward the focus on temporality, with students writing about themselves in the future in relation to an imagined new person in their lives (see Chapter 1). As we have seen in Chapter 5, this is a key exercise for Susanna, bringing a sense of space and movement back into her psyche frozen by trauma. Claire's experience is similar. The requirement to imagine the future 'at once gave me an image of standing, poised, at a point on life's continuum with a view to the past and a vision of the future'. This broad, temporal–spatial perspective enables her to imagine a positive future for herself and her troubled sister (see Chapter 2). She imagines her 40th birthday celebration at home with her parents, her sister, and her sister's daughter, and most significantly her own (imagined future) partner and their exuberant daughter Izzy. The detail of the writing is sometimes opaque – Claire has not yet learned to take account of the reader's needs – but what comes across is the joyful intensity of the relationship between the narrator and her daughter, who evokes Claire's playful side, interested in everything. Her relationship with her sister is also playful and loving, indicating that the latter has now achieved a degree of stability. And there is a subtle hint that another child is on its way. Reflecting on this piece, Claire says that:

> I had meditated on my deepest fears for the future and written them out of my life. Its negative depicts my bleakest outlook; I had indirectly focused on what I am most terrified of. And yet the positive felt *joyous* to write.

The sense of 'empowerment' this exercise brings spurs Claire on to 'make two swift changes in my life', one involving the decision to have an operation she had repeatedly been putting off. Like Susanna, being given permission imaginatively to transcend her familiar sense of identity enables her to *experience* what it is she legitimately desires from life, and the impact of this breaks open the psyche, leading to increased agency and action. At the core of this experience is Milner's reflexive shifting of attention from narrow to wide, as is clear from Claire's reflection on it: 'because I wrote the ... piece and could visualise – it was so fantastic to visualise – and I saw myself having had the operation done and I thought I can't put it off any longer...'.

The owning of legitimate desires is the outcome of this exercise for others too. Harriet envisions herself 'as a free woman [free of spouse, offspring, job, home, writing ambitions] totally in control of my life ... but not totally controlled by my mother's voice'. This desire to jettison everything that constrains her seems extreme, a reflection perhaps of the black/white, freedom/control dichotomy that I have highlighted before (it is significant that total freedom here means being totally in her own control), but is not surprising in view of the long years of internal repression. What seems key in these imaginings of the future is being given permission imaginatively to step outside of what one *should* feel according to inner dictates or social conventions and to experience what one *actually* feels. Of course what one actually feels may be extreme or unrealisable, but bringing actual needs and desires more clearly into view means that present dilemmas can be thought about differently. In all three examples new thinking and reflection lead to decision-making and action that forge new life directions. Thus there is a significant step towards self-agency rooted in spontaneous bodily feeling.

The 'future self' exercise is similar to the semiotic exercises in that it can facilitate breaking out of embedded self-concepts and gaining access to authentic feeling and emotion hidden beneath, but the approach is different: rather than focusing on the feel of the 'dynamic now', as in the semiotic exercises, it involves imagining and learning to manage a larger, more fluid space for the self in time, as reflected in Claire's striking image of being able to view past, present, and future simultaneously. Attention is pulled away from current preoccupations or from the task of hyperreflexively defending the split psyche, to form a broad temporal–spatial frame. It is an imaginative distancing that opens up mental space for 'seeing' differently with the mind's eye, but which also begins the process of learning to hold the space open for creativity to occur. A key feature of this process is the development of a narrative stance.

Self-agency and finding a narrative stance

A narrator in fiction can be a character who takes part in the action of the story (autodiegetic or homodiegetic)[4] or a voice that tells the story from outside of the action (heterodiegetic). In an autobiographical context both of these positions involve writers in creative splitting of the self or what Christopher Bollas calls 'generative narcissism' (Bollas, 1995: 155). This is different from the splitting that results from Horney's 'alienation' from self, which is the consequence of trauma or on-going anxiety. It can be understood as the beginnings of reflexivity, an 'intrapsychic rapport' (ibid.) that develops between the autobiographical 'I' and the growing awareness of, and trust in, core consciousness. This is a challenging task, particularly where the psyche is led by top-down control, which is often at the core of students' difficulties with creative writing (Hunt, 2000: 86–91). Stella's struggle to create an autodiegetic narrator out of herself in the future self exercise is a good example. In her first attempt she is too bound up in her current 'psychic drama'[5] to be able to allow creative splitting, but her second attempt is more successful:

> I started to build up my own character and was better able to distance myself from the [difficult present] emotions. At last I had started to use myself as a source and to project the emotions into the future. Perhaps this was the beginning of a greater self-awareness ... .

This is a key moment for Stella, in which she is able to fictionalise herself for the first time. Her reference to drawing on herself as a 'source' (Moskowitz, 1998) captures the 'generative narcissism' involved in creative splitting, with its connotation of a rich store of bodily-felt material that her writer-self can use to create characters. It is also implied by her sense of being able to '[get] inside the characters' she is creating. Similarly, distancing herself from her difficult emotions seems not to indicate that she is blocking them out, rather that she is aware of them and able to use them creatively rather than being overwhelmed by them. It implies a less controlling and more managing stance, a more reflexive, bodily-based agency as opposed to hyperreflexively keeping her vulnerable emotions at bay through her dominant persona of professional carer. It involves relaxing control, trusting the holistic spatiality and temporality of the core self and allowing her 'self-on-the-page' to develop a life of its own.

Developing a narrative stance that facilitates management rather than control of the 'space of composition' (Clark, 1997) is a central feature of all the dialogic exercises. But it is most clearly visible in the 'Self as Source' exercise,[6] which involves creating two self-characters out of different dimensions of the personality and bringing them together in a story where they exchange something of mutual value (see Chapter 1). For Rhiannon this exercise provides, she says, the breakthrough that has not occurred up to this point (Session 3 of Course 1). She has strongly resisted self-expression through the semiotic exercises, although there has been some psychic loosening. Her starting focus for the exercise is what she sees as her split roles of 'good mother' and 'bad mother', out of which she creates, through collage and metaphor, her two characters. She is helped in this by the idea of working in 'the negative space in these experiences', on the analogy of the space left on a canvas when the visual artist draws an object: 'This is how I now see the roles we play out in life. These roles fill the positive space but we also have at our disposal as writers the negative roles that we choose not to play out'. Working with the idea of the writing process as a space of possibility beyond her usual way of thinking about herself enables Rhiannon to project herself into that space and, like Stella, to fictionalise herself for the first time.

Moving on to write the story, Rhiannon feels the need for a narrator 'to breathe more life into the characters', which also suggests to her the possibility of 'a narratee', a character or presence in the text who 'hears' the narrator (Nelles, 1993: 22). She is also 'aware of wanting to produce feelings of unease within the reader'. This she certainly achieves in the writing that emerges. Her autodiegetic male narrator, Clive, is the cocky, upbeat host of a virtual reality game show called 'Wombwomen', in which the audience, whom Clive is addressing, can select options for the encounter between Rhiannon's two mother characters, 'Mrs. Mothermemore' and 'Mrs. Mothermeless'. These two women have been 'cast adrift from the world of reality by their polarised and extreme views of the world', the former being over-solicitous to her offspring and the latter neglectful (in fact they again evoke the control/freedom dichotomy I highlighted above). Whilst the 'differences between them are stark', what they have in common is that their traits – 'insecurity and self-gratification', respectively – lead them to 'perpetrate the ultimate of crimes', the murdering of their children. When I ask Rhiannon how she came up with the idea of the game show, she says:

> I wrote a couple of pieces, it didn't work very well, it didn't flow very well, it wasn't fast enough pace for me, I thought how can I put pace on it, or I could put a narrator to it … It was a whole stumbling process of, you know … and I actually was driving home from school and I thought: *I know*, I could make it into a video game …, that's how it would really work because they are extremes and that's where you find extremes, in these weird video games. And yes so that's where it all came from. But that's where the process also came from for me of being able to write out a plan because I could see my thinking, my thinking was really sort of coming out then.

Rhiannon's new ability to tolerate a chaotic space of creativity is obvious here: she can allow the writing process to be fluid, in transition, so that a structure can emerge spontaneously. From her metaphor of 'see[ing] my thinking' (see Chapter 2) it is also obvious that she is able to distance herself creatively from the material and visualise it, in a similar way to Claire in the 'future self' exercise. Attention is broad and there is 'a patient openness to whatever is', in McGilchrist's words; it implies the ability to hold mental space open for the imagination to get to work. Here is an extract from the finished piece:

> Hi, my name's Clive and I'm here today to update all you hard working *Global World* folk on a few of our 'about to be released' games. It certainly is an exciting time to be working in the virtual reality game business. More particularly, exciting times working at *Global World*, the home of the interactive video game, games that help *you live the reality*. I've got some brilliantly clever overheads for you to interact with, giving you the opportunity to play some of our exciting new software as we move through the morning's programme, sat there in your interactive, top of the range Global World seats. Well, hold on to your hats and we'll get stuck in.

Two things leap out here: first, the narrator's cocky self-assurance and, second, the imagined storyworld[7] opened up by the presence of the audience as narratee.

This is achieved – intuitively rather than by design – through deixis, the way language directs the reader's attention to different locations in time and space; it has been called the 'pointing' function of language (Stockwell, 2002: 41). In the above piece the key deictic features are Clive as the 'internal focaliser' (Bal, 1985),[8] who is '*here* today', and the audience, 'all you hard working Global World folk [over *there*]' whom Clive is addressing, with imagined space opening up between them. As readers, our attention is shifted deictically (Zubin and Hewitt, 1995) back and forth between Clive with his slightly unnerving pitch and the audience who are being invited to make choices in the messy lives of Mrs. Mothermemore and Mrs. Mothermeless, their partners, and offspring. To facilitate this, Rhiannon has had to do two things. First, she has had to create a narrator strong enough to act as focaliser. This is in itself a considerable achievement seeing that this assertive male significantly contravenes Rhiannon's usual sense of herself: there is a slightly malicious, almost misogynistic edge to Clive's monologue, as if he is barely able to contain his anger against mothers. Second, she has had to find a simultaneously stable and flexible, that is reflexive, intentional stance as the 'governing consciousness'[9] of the narrative space in order to allow her narrator freedom to act.

That this piece was a breakthrough for Rhiannon derives, I would suggest, not only from her being able for the first time to use in her writing the more unruly (angry), previously less acceptable part of herself that went underground as a result of the oppressive mothering she experienced as a child, but also from beginning to trust the bodily agency of core consciousness as a flexible grounding for the creative process that enables her to 'hold' the space of the storyworld and, by extension, the space for the imagination more generally. This is supported by what she says at the end of Year 1:

> I really do now give much more voice to the other voices that are inside my head ... but before I didn't know were there. ... if you said how many voices in your head, how many 'yous' are there, well there's one and this is the one you see. But there's not, you know there's lots, and I say that and I don't feel fragmented, I feel more whole.

Rhiannon's sense of being able to give voice to the many different aspects of herself whilst feeling more whole is striking in the context of her previous sense of being confined to one dominant sense of self.

Practising reflexivity in the text

In his discussion of the relationship between structure and agency in critical realist research, Scott says that: 'an undue focus on structures has a tendency to sideline agency, and in particular, the key moment of change, the meeting point between structural forms and agential actions' (2010: 131). Extending the relationship between structure and agency to the bio-psycho-social world of the psyche, I would suggest that the above examples constitute key moments of change, where increased agential action is achieved – at least in part (see also Chapters 9 and 10) – through students' immersion in the demands of the cognitive structural forms of the dialogic exercises.

I say 'demands' because, once writers are transported into, and become immersed in, the storyworld, the cognitive structures at work there are subtly directive of the psyche (Gerrig, 1993).[10] I highlighted earlier how the cognitive requirements of poetry or poetic prose compel writers to 'show' feeling and emotion, that is, to create emotional movement in the text. Movement in time and space is similarly an intrinsic part of the narrative storyworld, with deictic shifts constantly taking place between the time-space locations of narrators and characters involved in the action, as the above examples show. There are also, it has been suggested, two other time-space levels in fictional narrative: the more abstract time-space of the plot, and the abstract time-space of the worldview or overarching theme. These three levels are simultaneously present and there is constant movement between them (Keunen, 2001: 11–38). This is visible, for example, in Claire's 'future self' piece, where the requirement to create a scenario portraying a relationship with a new person in her life simultaneously involves her in devising the action of characters in a specific locale (level 1), constructing a plot within which the action takes place (level 2), and creating an overarching space for the expression of her deepest desires (level 3). Making this multi-levelled, holistic time-space world intelligible to the reader demands that she learns to manage all three levels simultaneously, and to move deictically back and forth between them, even if not fully consciously.

In other words, the structures of the time-space world of the text put subtle pressure on students to develop a relaxed intentional stance that both anchors the time-space of the autofictional storyworld and gives the characters and narrators who embody their different senses of self with their different feelings and emotions the freedom to act within it. In the process, I would suggest, students learn to trust the bodily-felt sense of agency that this involves, and this generates a bodily-felt pattern or 'image schema' (Johnson, 2007: 136) for managing the opened-up psyche in their lives more generally and being more authorial in the re-construction of the narratives in which they are embedded. I call this 'practising reflexivity in the text' (Hunt, 2004a; Hunt and Sampson, 2006) and see it as a method for generating reciprocity between the brain's hemispheres.[11] Apart from the instances I have discussed above, the development of this relaxed intentional stance over the two years of the MA is visible in many of the other Group 2 students, including all three of those featured in the case studies, albeit in different ways. For Maria it is there in her sense of becoming a narrator/storyteller who 'holds' her family's history; for Simon it is implicit in his metaphor of the rancher who manages the unruly prairie of the imagination; for Susanna it manifests in what she calls her new-found 'passivity' as a learner and group facilitator, which enables her to 'hold' the learning space for herself and others.

This development bears a strong relation to the process of thinking feelings or 'mentalised affectivity' in psychotherapy, where clients engage in a 'pretend mode of functioning' in the relationship with the therapist, thus promoting 'fantasy and imagination in the way that [they] regulate [their] affects' (Fonagy *et al.*, 2002: 439). In the CWPD programme the dialogic writing exercises can similarly be seen as a pretend mode of functioning, which promotes fantasy and imagination for learning to manage reflexively the more dynamic and complex psyche opened up by the semiotic exercises. Whilst there is no therapist here to 'hold' this playful but challenging process, the cognitive frames of the exercises, as well as other dimensions of the learning environment (see Chapters 9 and 10), provide a degree of 'holding' which, when the process works well, renders the learning environment 'safe-enough' for this reflexivity work to take place. The contribution of the collaborative, experiential groups to this process is the subject of the next chapter.

Notes

1 Kristeva's distinction between the Semiotic and the Symbolic has strong similarities with Damasio's distinction between core and extended consciousness (Nicholls, 2006). There is also a strong similarity between both of these theories and McGilchrist's view of the relationship between right and left hemispheres.
2 Some students find the dialogic exercises more powerful, although there is evidence that the semiotic exercises loosen up the psyche, thus preparing the ground for changes that take place through the dialogic.
3 Holub draws on Turner and Pöppel (1983).
4 Autodiegetic is used where the narrator is the main protagonist, and homodiegetic where the narrator is one of a number of characters (Genette, 1980). The term 'diegesis' derives from Plato and has come to mean 'the world of the story' (Porter Abbott, 2002: 68).
5 Stella is in the midst of a very painful relationship break-up at this point.
6 It is also visible in other dialogic exercises, such as 'imagining the reader' (see Hunt, 2004b).
7 The term 'storyworld' is used by David Herman to 'suggest something of the world-creating power of narrative', which he feels is not sufficiently implied by the more standard term 'discourse'. Storyworlds are '[mental] models built up on the basis of cues contained in narrative discourse' (Herman, 2002: 14, 17). This is a very useful way of thinking about what is happening cognitively in Rhiannon's story.
8 The term 'focalisation' has come to replace 'point of view' in narrative theory under the influence of Genette's distinction between 'who sees' in the narrative and 'who speaks' (Jahn, 2007). In Genette's view the narrator cannot be a focaliser unless he or she is also a character, that is, inside the storyworld (auto- or homodiegetic) (Genette, 1980). However, in Mieke Bal's re-working of Genette's ideas a narrator who is outside of the storyworld, that is, heterodiegetic, can also be a focaliser. Thus an auto- or homodiegetic narrator is an 'internal focaliser' and a heterodiegetic narrator is an 'external focaliser' (Bal, 1985). Bal's approach supports assumptions I have long been making about cognitive processes in creative life writing.
9 This is a term used to describe the 'implied author' in the literary text, which is regarded by some (e.g. Booth, 1991: 73) as the author's 'second self' and therefore a personal presence in the text, and by others (e.g. Rimmon-Kenan, 1996: 88) as an

impersonal presence. However, there seems to be general agreement that the implied author can be distinguished from the narrator and the characters (Herman *et al.*, 2005: 240), although in heterodiegetic narration this is sometimes difficult (Stockwell, 2002: 42).
10 As they are, of course, of the reader's psyche, which is Gerrig's main concern.
11 Siegel suggests that it is formulating a linear self-narrative that facilitates reciprocity between the hemispheres (Siegel, 2007: 309), but I would argue that the development of a narrative stance and the accompanying sense of feeling whole are more important.

Chapter 9

Reflexivity and group process

The creative life writing exercises, then, with their potential for subverting cognitive control and facilitating the development of the relaxed intentional stance are perfectly suited to what I have called reflexivity work. By this I mean that they can facilitate both the fluidity and the stability of the dynamic system of the psyche; or in critical realist terms they provide a flexible but 'holding' structure for the development of bodily agency. But the effects of the creative life writing cannot be seen in isolation from students' experience of sharing it in groups throughout the programme. Indeed I fully concur now with Simon when he says that: 'without the groups the thing wouldn't have worked'. This supports Brown's suggestion that 'the group is both the condition for and the outcome of human agency' (Brown, 2009: 31). Much transformative learning theory also highlights the key role of group work in the experience of change (e.g. Boyd, 1991; Mezirow, 2000; Dirkx, 2012). Thus in this chapter I discuss the contribution of the collaborative, experiential groups to students' shift to a more reflexive self-experience.

Developing trust in small reading groups

Collaborative group work was a central pedagogical feature of the CWPD programme, with different variants occurring in all courses. In Course 1 (*Writing for Personal Development*) students worked in the full group (maximum of 16) for undertaking the experiential writing exercises and discussing course readings. But they also spent about 80 minutes each session in small student-led reading groups sharing the creative writing they had written at home in response to the exercises.[1] Students remained in the same groups for the whole term. They brought paper copies of their writing for each group member and could either read the work out or let others read it on the page. Whilst the groups were student-led, tutors would (with students' permission) spend a while in each, observing and offering guidance.

For many students the small reading groups are the primary site for beginning to open-up the psyche, for it is here that they bring their creative writing, and their self-on-the-page, into the light for others – and for themselves – to see. For some people this is initially very daunting, but finding that others are similarly daunted is helpful. Stacey's comment is typical: 'Reading groups: initially a terrifying prospect; together we built confidence and trust'. Susanna echoes this: 'The whole of the first year was a development of trust and discovery of each other and that we were all terrified of sharing our work'. The continuity of the groups through the term is an important factor in the development of trust, according to Jill: 'The length of time [we spent together] helped in building up a very close reading group and enabled us to trust each other's responses and to really know each other's voices'. Ruth provides a good example of this: 'the response I received [to my poem] championed what I sensed was the first emergence of my writing voice; the voice I grew up with; the voice of the little girl in the photograph'. I previously defined 'writing voice', from the writer's point of view, as 'a metaphor for a style of writing that contains the author's sense of self' (Hunt, 2000: 17). It will contain rhythms and tones deriving from speech and writing in the writer's social and cultural background, as well as rhythms and tones arising out of his or her individual temperament. The idea of 'finding a voice' is also associated with developing a sense of agency to 'speak' in one's writing (Hunt and Sampson, 2006: 24–39). All these elements are implicit in Ruth's recognition of the authentic sound and feel of herself on the page, and the group's support validates its emergence.

Something similar happens for Miranda:

> I worried that my audience might find my writing absurd or dull. I had included some jokes in the piece. Would they find them funny or was my sense of humour as impenetrable to the rest of the world as my storyteller's voice might prove to be? Reading it to the group, however, I was delighted to find they followed my meaning, laughed at my jokes and that their criticism was positive, valid and honest. I had not written work to be read out loud before. I was experiencing what it was to have a reader, and the experience was exhilarating. Very quickly I was no longer afraid to read to the group, indeed I really came to look forward to our session. I always felt that, even if what I wrote was not what I hoped it would be, that it would be positively received, sympathetically criticised and that the criticism would be useful, not discouraging.

Here we see Miranda becoming more confident to bring her writing out into the open in the relationship with her trusted audience. As she does so, her writing *process* becomes more relational as she anticipates sharing with them what she is writing. In this way the space of the group, both its external reality and its internalisation as a benign structure, becomes a container for growth.

An important part of this development are the guidelines for giving and receiving feedback on creative writing which students receive in Course 1.[2] These suggest that students do not rush in with their comments, but take a few moments to reflect on the piece they have just heard and their felt response to it, trying to identify both the feeling it has evoked and what it was in particular that had that effect. Tutors model this approach for the students at the first session.[3]

The emphasis on listening is not only directed at the readers of the writing, but also at the writers, who are required to listen to the group's responses before saying anything themselves. This helps them to remain open to, and reflect on, what is being said, as Maria points out: 'Receiving feedback and criticism means being open to receive something that is other and use it'. Tutor Christine echoes this. Learning to listen, both to themselves and to others, she says, is a centrally important part of students' learning. It involves them in 'open[ing] up to a variety of voices ... and what yours is'. It also helps them, tutor Sarah adds, to learn 'what their feelings are and ... what it is that they want to say'. If 'finding a voice' is, at least in part, being able to get one's own sound and feel into one's writing, then listening and feeling are key both to developing the writing and developing oneself. As Claudia says, the reading groups give her 'the opportunity to hear how my voice is distinct, not better or worse, just different from others'. This gives her confidence in her writing, but it also helps her sense of agency generally, against the background of 'being the seventh out of eight children [and not wanting] to let my light really shine in case it outshone others ... and incite[d] my siblings' resentment or jealousy', residues of which continue to haunt her learning.

Learning to listen to the writing – both literally if the work is read out loud, and metaphorically with the mind's 'ear' when readers engage with it on the page – and to feel one's way into it cultivates a bottom-up or embodied response in the first instance rather than a top-down, critical one; it is 'receptivity' in Boyd and Myers's sense (1988: 277). Like the writing exercises, receptive listening encourages the relaxing of the strong intentional stance (left hemisphere), the expanding of space for the imagination and the experiencing of the embodied intentional stance (right hemisphere) that holds the space open. It is another way of inhabiting the 'dynamic now' (see Chapter 8). It can also create a collaborative learning environment rather than the primarily competitive one writing groups often are, sometimes undermining participants' already fragile confidence. This is not to suggest that competitiveness is always a bad thing or that it is possible or desirable to eliminate it altogether; rather that in a context where *personal* development is as important as academic or professional development, creating an environment where students can feel safe enough to loosen the personas and strategies they bring to group learning and open up to new ways of thinking and being-in-relation is key.

When they work well – and they do not work well for everyone (see Chapter 11) – the reading groups create a receptive space for students to start bringing the sound and feel of themselves into the open through the creative life writing. But they can also challenge participants to delve deeper into themselves. I highlighted in Chapter 8 how using poetic and fictional techniques in autobiographical writing puts subtle pressure on the writer to go deeper into the feeling of an experience in order to fulfil the requirements of the form, but the group and/or the tutor as audience to the work are, of course, integral to that process. We see this at work in Jill's experience:

> My overriding impression was that the group did not know how to respond or what to say [to my first poem]. I had baffled my readers. ... When I

> submitted [my response to the 'future self' exercise] the group were more explicit. They could do with more about me. 'Doesn't she feel anything?' 'This feels like the bare bones of something ... I want some of her feelings'.

The pressure for a self-character that feels authentically real to the readers pushes Jill to 'dig deeper and revise constantly'. This means 'acknowledging' her fear of self-expression that, she has come to realise, is at the root of her 'frozen writing'. In Susanna's Course 1 reading group we can see some members explicitly challenging others to be more open:

> the third session was a turning point in that the material was more exposing for two of us. In the discussion that followed our work we urged the other two to be more revelatory, and there was a very open dialogue about the content of our work and the way in which we commented on each other's work. The fourth week brought forth a very much changed approach in the writing of the remaining two people and our discussions.

In fact this was Simon's group and, as we have seen in Chapter 3, it is in the fourth session of Course 1 that he breaks through to a deeper and more challenging self-experience, when he realises in the reader exercise that there is no imagined reader in his writing process. In view of his subsequent comments about the centrality of the small groups in his learning, I would suggest that it is the simultaneously challenging and 'holding' relationship with this first group and the feedback he receives from them, which enables him to start experiencing a sense of company in the space of composition that later renders this space more manageable.[4]

The small reading groups in Course 1, then, with their listening- and feeling-led modes of engagement, can be thought of as small, enabling structures – self-organising sub-systems within the larger dynamic system of the learning environment (Davis and Sumara, 2001). By creating 'disorienting dilemmas' they challenge students to be more psychically open and in process but also, where trust and collaboration develop, provide 'holding' for that process. They equip students with a methodology for participating in subsequent courses, which is particularly important for those opting for the more intense relational work of *Writing and Groups*.[5]

Creating a structured space for deep change

Writing and Groups was introduced into the programme specifically to provide training for people who wished to facilitate developmental writing groups in healthcare and the community (see Chapter 1). But we soon found that it was also helpful for those seeking personal development, whether or not they wanted to facilitate groups. As in Course 1, the collaborative group work in *Writing and*

Groups was a mixture of experiential learning and critical reflection, but there were significant differences. Here the working day was divided into two discrete halves, with the mornings taking the form of a tutor-led developmental writing group and the afternoons consisting of a tutor-led seminar for reflecting on the experience of the morning with the aid of course readings. Students worked in one group for all activities (maximum 10 members), rather than dividing into smaller groups. The sessions were designed to imitate the typical stages of a group as suggested by Corey and Corey (2002) – beginning stage, transition stage, working stage, ending – with critical readings appropriate to each stage, and the specially-devised sequence of writing exercises for the morning workshop (see Christine Cohen Park's Appendix) providing a means of responding to these stages experientially. Students were required to keep a learning journal, to capture in the moment their own learning process and that of the group as a whole, and to use the resulting material as a resource for writing the end-of-course essay (see Chapter 10).

Like the experience of entering into the shared space of the reading groups in Course 1, the transition to *Writing and Groups* is daunting for some, as it involves the dismantling of the familiar learning groups of Courses 1 and 2 in order to create new groups for Course 3. Stacey notes in her journal a general 'sense of dismemberment as we said goodbye to friends we had studied with for two terms'. But this 'dismemberment' is another disorienting dilemma, designed to stimulate students' reflection on how a new group takes shape. By contrast there are pedagogical techniques designed to generate cohesion in the group. For example, at the outset the tutor leads the students in drawing up a contract for how they will work together supportively.[6] Claudia finds this particularly helpful:

> I liked the fact that everyone contributed something to [the group contract], we weren't just told by the facilitator [tutor of Group A][7] what was expected of us. We generated ten group norms, which I felt was significant because there were ten group members including the facilitator, who was fully participating in the ice-breaking exercises and felt very much as though she were one of 'us'.

The contract covers matters such as confidentiality, mutual respect and collaboration, the importance of listening and being heard, so is fundamental in generating trust and a sense of safety. Listening is also emphasised by the requirement that group members respond to each other's creative writing just by hearing it being read out rather than having paper copies to look at. This is very demanding, but again is aimed at creating a group that is intensely focused on the 'dynamic now' (see Chapter 8). The writing exercises similarly emphasise this, with their focus on: 'This is who I am, now'; 'This is where I shelter'; 'This is where I risk'; 'This is what I remember' (see Appendix).

The process of intensely listening to, and feeding back on, each other's creative work in the full group can be seen to generate a more cohesive dynamic as the course develops. This is particularly visible where, as Maria notes, students '[link] creative writing assignments with group process, and learning in general, [which helps] produce very original writing pieces'. A good example is Jill's response to the final exercise – 'This is what I remember'. Here she takes as her focus the metaphor of food in the word 'feedback', exploring not only its power to nourish ('... I lick my lips at the thought of/Feedback; a starving audience, eager/To devour my prose, salivate over puns and laugh at alliterations'), but also its more visceral dimension ('... the/ignominy of exposing our open hearts to/ The sharpened butchers' knives'), both necessary parts of the dynamic process of change involved in group learning. In Tess's response to the same exercise the seminar room is her focus ('A stark, staring straight ahead room/with flimsy white walls and a vacant expression ...'), which is given life by the group ('... flexing/its muscles warming up/with games and stretching/exercises'). In fact the room becomes the group in search of itself ('A room reaching for its identity ... a crowd forming and re-forming ...', one moment 'hotting up/flushed with excitement' and the next 'filling up/with tears and disappointment').[8] The writing exercise here provides an opportunity for students to write to and for each other, creating metaphors that bind them together into a dynamic but containing whole, generating for some a strong sense of community.

The receptive learning environment of *Writing and Groups* makes it possible for many of the students to feel more at ease with their newly expanded sense of self and to start exploring it more thoroughly. As we have seen in Chapter 4, it is here that Maria feels most safely 'held' in her fragmented state. This makes it possible for her to start giving shape to the different parts of herself in fragments of poetic prose and to feel more authentically present in the group in all her complexity. By the end of the course she is beginning to learn how to be a more effective container for her own learning, to 'hold' herself open for the change that learning involves, which indicates that she has internalised the 'holding' provided by the group. It is here too that Susanna feels safe enough to disclose her illness identity, although ultimately she does not disclose directly to the group; rather she allows aspects of her story to become visible through the series of connected autobiographical poems she writes. Like Maria, she uses the creative writing here to work at herself in fragments that constitute a whole, which provides another level of 'holding'. *Writing and Groups* is also where Susanna's more open and accepting stance as a learner, which she sees modelled by the tutor, begins to take root, and which has a profound impact on her facilitation of others' learning (see Chapter 5).

In fact, the shift to a bottom-up, embodied learning process, which clearly begins for some students in Course 1, becomes in *Writing and Groups* a central feature of many students' learning. From their essays it is obvious that this is enhanced by discussing the course reading, including John Keats's notion of 'negative capability' in the creative process, a state in which the writer 'is capable of being in uncertainty, mysteries, doubts, without any irritable reaching after fact and reason' (Keats, 1958: 72). But I would suggest that it is putting this into practice through listening intensely, not only to the others in the group but also to themselves through the creative life writing, which enables students to become more deeply aware of processes at work within them: what writing feels like, what learning feels like, what it feels like to be themselves in the moment, what it feels like to be in relation.

Exploring the self-in-relation

Within the more complex 'holding' structures of *Writing and Groups* some of the most significant – and most difficult – learning takes place.[9] With the emphasis on what is happening in the present of the group, the focus of students' attention shifts from relations with parents, siblings, and other significant people in their lives as in Course 1 to relations with their fellow learners. This focus is sharpened by the course readings, including emotionally-laden topics such as the silent person in the group (Coltart, 1996) and the role of the 'shadow' (Jung, 1983). Judging from its presence in students' essays, the latter is one of the most significant of these readings. The 'shadow', in Jung's thinking, is the lower or primitive level of the personality with its 'dark aspects' and 'uncontrolled or scarcely controlled emotions', which can impair moral judgement. Often repressed and projected onto others, these dark aspects have to be recognised 'as present and real' if self-knowledge is to be achieved (ibid.: 91–2). However, the shadow can be thought of more broadly and productively than simply as a primitive area of the personality. In a Horneyan context it can be understood as a part of the personality that conflicts with the dominant life solution and has been repressed, but continues nevertheless to be experienced as a vague, troubling presence in the psyche; or as the Pride System waiting to punish contraventions of its rules, which Horney calls an inner source of danger (Horney, 1951: 153). In a socio-psychological sense the shadow can be those thoughts or tendencies we keep hidden, from ourselves or others, because they are socially disapproved of. In a group it may be unspoken tensions hovering beneath the surface of behaviour, or a particular group member who bears the group's negative transference.

With the 'normative' constraints of the academic learning environment suspended (Bhaskar and Danermark, 2006) through the shift of focus to what is happening in the group, students become more aware of their shadow sides. For example, when the tutor of group B asks students to think about whether everyone is getting their fair share of the talking time, Harriet is challenged to think differently about her disgruntlement with her reading groups in Courses 1 and 2, where she did not get the in-depth critical feedback she needs, and to reflect on how her own behaviour contributes to this:

> I always find it difficult to talk up in groups, I always let noisier ones talk, so I think it was only by objectifying it that I was able to look at myself objectively and realise how I had to change my way of working, otherwise I would

> have been stuck with feeling embarrassed about not being able to cope in a group. ... I'm much more aware [now], and I can also see what sort of group I need and what I need from the group and what I have to give to the group to get back [what I need].

Harriet's learning involves becoming aware of her conflicting needs in the group: on the one hand to be liked and valued by the tutor and the other students and, on the other, to get in-depth feedback on her writing. In other words she sees that she has to 'change [her] passive behaviour and become more assertive' if her needs are to be met. This means breaking out of her tendency to be 'good', whether the good daughter to the tutor or the good mother to the other students; in other words she has to experiment with bringing her assertiveness and anger into her relations with others in the moment.

This is precisely what Megan finds herself doing when there is not enough time left to discuss her writing at the second session and she has a 'sensation of being ignored'. Rather than pocketing her feelings and withdrawing as she would usually, she expresses them forcefully. In response a group decision is made to have a timekeeper to ensure everyone gets equal time. Being 'listened to and heard' enables Megan to feel 'for the first time to be a part of the group'. However, subsequent tensions in the group again evoke her sense of exclusion, but reflecting in her learning journal on this tendency which, her researches reveal, is not shared by many of the other students, she links this feeling to her childhood when she was 'sent away to boarding school whilst my sister remained at home and part of the group'. She also becomes aware that her past learning experiences 'can exaggerate [a present] feeling, taking it out of place and leaving me feeling on the edge'. Opening-up to herself in this way ultimately enables her to feel that she has been 'allowed to be myself and accepted' in this group whereas 'in every other group I have been part of I have felt [that I am] different'.

As noted in Chapter 2, anger is the dominant emotion students unearth in their self-explorations: anger at parents, siblings, partners, teachers, painful life circumstances, themselves. In Course 1 this anger is expressed largely in the writing exercises, but in *Writing and Groups*, with its explicit focus on the self-in-relation, anger becomes a more spontaneous presence, and this has a considerable impact on the dynamic system of the group and individuals within it (Chazan, 2001: 17). Megan's outburst, for example, is significant for Jill, for whom the expression of anger does not come naturally. She is convinced that the group will not go through Corey and Corey's stages, with difficult emotions emerging in the 'working stage':

> I kept thinking well this isn't going to happen, oh no no no, then sure enough ... there was one particular bit where [Megan] came in and started being really angry with how little time she'd been given, and then I immediately felt guilty myself because ... perhaps I'd had an unfair amount of the time, I thought oh no, you know, but I was sympathetic to her and ... but

> I think she was quite belligerent and of course coming from *my* sort of background where I would not be belligerent ... first of all I was a bit shocked and then I thought well good on you, you know, fair enough if you feel this and you can then affect the dynamic of the group.

It is particularly important for Jill that: 'the confrontation *was* allowed and the group didn't fall apart'. Whilst the equilibrium of the dynamic system of the group is disturbed, it proves robust enough to tolerate this and adjust itself accordingly (Davis and Sumara, 2001: 89).

Facilitating difficult learning

A key factor in this is, of course, the way the tutor facilitates the group. Whilst in Course 1 the tutors' role is to facilitate a learning environment within which students will work collaboratively in large and small groups, in *Writing and Groups* they are in addition modelling an approach to facilitating a developmental writing group. We have already seen an example of this in Claudia's mention of the tutor being 'one of us' by contributing to the group contract and sharing her own creative writing in the first session, which is clearly important for Claudia's sense of safety in this new group. A greater degree of personal openness on the tutor's part can in turn encourage students to be more open. But greater openness also means that tutors must be able to manage a potentially more turbulent learning environment. An example of this is tutor A's response when Claudia confronts her angrily about not sharing her creative writing in the second session as she did in the first. This is an important moment for Claudia, her 'old feeling of rebelliousness [from] high school', which got her into trouble with the nuns, re-emerging spontaneously. But this time, rather than being met with disapproval, Claudia's challenge is taken seriously by the tutor, who 'openly examined her decision not to contribute her own writing', according to Stacey, which 'felt very honest and spontaneous, satisfying two of the group norms we had established'. Thus by responding in this way the tutor not only validates Claudia's self-assertion, but also models the reflective process for the students.

A more serious challenge to the tutor occurs in group B when one of the students becomes distressed at the tutor's request that she bring writing for sharing that responds to the exercises rather than extracts from her novel in progress.[10] This upset seems to provide a channel for the unexpressed anger of several other students and becomes a moment of high emotion and disequilibrium for the group as a whole. One student describes it as a 'mini-rebellion' against the tutor. Rather than being defensive, the tutor responds openly and honestly to the confrontation, as one student says, reflecting on her contribution to the events, and subsequently the anger subsides and the group settles down again. By the final session, as another student puts it, 'the group seemed to have rescued itself from the chaos and become cohesive'. This is in part a consequence of the trust that has developed in the group through listening and responding to each other's creative writing: 'patterns of relating having the quality of trust enable people to go on together despite the anxiety they feel' (Stacey, 2006: 278). But the tutor's stance also plays a crucial role here. In Bion's terms one could say that by receiving the students' anger and not being destroyed by it, the tutor not only remains a good-enough container for the group, but she also enables the angry group members to 'reintroject' (psychically re-absorb) the difficult emotion now accompanied by her containing presence, which makes it more manageable (Bion, 1962).

In these examples the tutors are not seeking to control and keep out of sight the expression of difficult emotions for the sake of the comfort of the group, rather they accept them as part of the dynamic process and use them as an opportunity for group members to 'mentalize' the affects (Fonagy *et al.*, 2002), or think their feelings whilst experiencing them. At the same time they model a reflexive approach to facilitation for students who will go on to facilitate their own groups. As Jill says, she is 'amazed' at the way the tutor deals with the mini-rebellion, and this constitutes a 'big learning curve' in her development as a writing group facilitator, in the context of her own lifelong tendency to avoid confrontation.

Modelling reflexive facilitation is a key way in which tutors 'hold' the students. For Christine this involves '[being a mirror for] the very thing that we're trying to teach'. By this she means bringing together in the teaching process 'the way we're thinking of our work and the way we *are* as people', which involves being more emotionally open and present to the students. This echoes the emphasis in transformative learning on establishing authentic relationships with learners (Taylor, 2009: 13–14). Of course, Christine adds, being able to do this will very much depend on the stresses and strains in tutors' lives beyond their teaching. Another important way that 'holding' takes place, in Christine's view, is:

> through hearing and receiving [students'] work …; that was the thing that most deeply connected me to students, the kind of quality of attention, and that sense at its best of being able to be with someone with their work in a very quiet and concentrated way.

Sarah agrees that 'listening and hearing … was one of the most important things we did as tutors' across the whole programme, and she adds that this is one of the key differences between the CWPD programme and standard creative writing MAs where tutors are expected just to give a critique of students' writing. So it is not just hearing the work, but hearing the students as well: being *with* the students *with* their work, as Christine says. It implies that the tutor can be fully present and real, as Cheryl says, but I would also add the ability to get a workable balance between closeness and distance. A good example of this is the tutor's engagement with Susanna's 'Future Self' piece in Course 1, which is a 'turning point' for her (see Chapter 5). Discussing this piece in tutorial, she says it is 'romantic fantasy'. However, '[the tutor's] interpretation was something entirely different ..., he put it in quite different words which gave it a kind of weight. He said it's about desire and it's about future', which enables Susanna to 'begin to read myself in a different way'. Here the tutor 'reads' the work and says what he sees happening in terms of theme and imagery. He is not interpreting *the student* but drawing attention to something important in the work. Of course this involves him in a judgement as to whether the student is ready to hear what he sees (see Chapter 11).

Tara Fenwick, drawing on Davis, Sumara and Luce-Kapler's dynamic systems approach to learning (2000), suggests that educators need to be 'catalysts of "playing" occasions, "planning" occasions, "adapting" and "varying" occasions. The role involves open-ended design but not control: making spaces, removing barriers, introducing and amplifying disturbances' (Fenwick, 2003: 136). This echoes in many respects the tutorial approach of *Writing and Groups* and indeed the experiential work of the CWPD programme as a whole. The idea of 'open-ended design' that is not a form of control captures the optimal reflexive stance of the good-enough tutor, where the structure of facilitation is soft but tangible at the level of bodily feeling. The idea of introducing 'disturbances' into the dynamic system of the group also resonates with the programme's aim of eliciting openness and change, in the context of the individual psyche's or the group's tendency towards inertia or stasis in the quest for safety or comfort. Disturbance – or disorienting dilemmas – comes not only through the writing exercises and sharing them in the group, but by the way the tutor gives individual students different ways of looking at their self-on-the-page, or encourages them to reflect how they engage with each other.[11] At the same time tutors have to be able to 'hold' individual students and the dynamic system of the group as a whole in moments of disequilibrium, as well as the disequilibrium of their own psyche that might result from it. Needless to say this can be very challenging (see Chapter 11). As Dirkx says of his experience of facilitating transformative learning, 'I am challenged on a regular basis by dramatic and potentially disruptive emotional dynamics that occur within and among the learning teams' (Dirkx, 2012: 127).

Reflexivity and group process

It is clear from the above that the collaborative, experiential group work, particularly in *Writing for Personal Development* and *Writing and Groups*, is for many of the students a key factor in their experience of change during the MA programme. In conjunction with the creative life writing, these groups simultaneously challenge participants to be more spontaneously in the moment and are, at their best, safe-enough to 'hold' the often difficult emotions that emerge so that change can take place. Brown's description of the learning environment as 'an open or at most a quasi-closed system' (Brown, 2009: 31) is particularly useful here, with the latter term capturing the 'relative disorder' (Siegel, 2003) of the dynamic system of the group: it is neither completely open and therefore in constant flux, nor is it fully closed and controlled, rather it is open within certain flexibly 'holding' curricular and pedagogical structures. Jill aptly describes these structures as 'soft':

> I think the group structure certainly this term [*Writing and Groups*] and certainly the first term [*Writing for Personal Development*] I was very aware of a very soft structure of the group and again something that I wasn't used to dealing with in business or, I was used to much more fixity, much more goal direct [sic]. Obviously there were goals and obviously there were things to be achieved, but I'm much more aware of fluidity and sort of, you know, watery-type things now rather than something very hard.

Jill's distinction between group structures that are 'goal-directed' and those that are 'softer' or more fluid evokes again the distinction between top-down and bottom-up structures within the framework of dynamic systems theory and my conceptualisation of the experiential groups as bottom-up or embodied in a similar way to the writing exercises. Indeed McGilchrist refers to evidence indicating that 'shared mental states in general activate the right hemisphere' (McGilchrist, 2009: 168). Being 'soft' structures means that, whilst they create a framework for change for those working within them, they are themselves visibly open to change as agency develops in individuals or in the group as a whole. For example, in *Writing for Personal Development* mutual trust in Susanna's reading group facilitates beneficial change in the way the group operates; in group A of *Writing and Groups* Claudia's self-assertion causes the tutor to reflect on her actions; in group B Megan's anger changes the group rules, and the 'mini-rebellion' causes the tutor to open up emotionally to the group. Thus in the reading groups structure and agency are constantly in process, mutually influencing and changing each other. This is consonant with the critical realist idea (morphogenesis) that structure and agency each have their own distinct properties and powers and mutually act on each other, giving rise to constant change (Archer, 1995). In a dynamic systems context this can be thought of as circular causality. This combination of dynamic openness and soft 'holding' structures makes the learning environment a fruitful space for the development of reflexivity.

Notes

1 The student-led reading groups were also a feature of Course 2, *Creative Writing and the Self*, and Course 4 Option 1, *Contexts for Practice*.
2 These were devised by Cheryl Moskowitz and Christina Dunhill.
3 Modelling is highlighted as an important technique in transformative learning (Taylor and Jarecke, 2009: 286–8).
4 This is later enhanced by some of the critical readings (see Chapter 10).
5 12 of the 15 Group 2 students took *Writing and Groups*, with the other 3 taking *Writing Practice* (see Chapter 11).

6 This was introduced initially into *Writing and Groups* and later extended to other courses.
7 I refer to the two groups taking *Writing and Groups* that year as A and B.
8 This is a good example of how the physical space can become internalised as part of the holding environment for students' learning.
9 'Significant learning' is Carl Rogers's term for learning that involves change in the organisation of the self (Rogers, 1951: 390). 'Difficult learning' borrows from Deborah Britzman's idea of 'difficult education', which involves negotiating self-other relations (Britzman, 2003: 1–32).
10 This was in part the consequence of some students' confusion about the nature of the writing group in *Writing and Groups*, arising out of the tension in the CWPD programme between using creative writing for personal development and developing writing skills (see Chapter 11).
11 The idea of actively 'amplifying' disturbances is not so applicable to the work of the CWPD programme, as the work can be disturbing enough without the need for amplification (see Chapter 11).

Chapter 10

Reflection and reflexivity

The picture that emerges from Chapters 8 and 9 is of students' experience as simultaneously set in motion and flexibly 'held' by the combination of the creative life writing exercises and the experiential, collaborative groups where they share their writing. But my researches reveal that there is another key dimension in students' experience of change, which is the reflective work they engage in, whether through diaries or learning journals, or end-of-course reflective essays and academic papers, with the help of course readings. Indeed, what becomes clear is that there is a central dialogue in Group 2 students' experience between the reflective work and the experiential work. Thus in this chapter I take a closer look at the place of reflection in students' experience of change, both at the course and the programme level, and its role in enhancing reflexivity.

The use of course diaries and learning journals

When Group 2 students were studying, a course diary or journal was recommended for use in Course 1 (*Writing for Personal Development*) to enable them to record their experience of the course in the moment, thus creating a resource for writing the end-of-course reflective essay. In Course 3 (*Writing and Groups*) a journal specifically focusing on what students were learning was mandatory, and they were expected to quote from it in the reflective essay (see Chapter 1). As the Course 1 diary was not a formal requirement, not everyone chose to do it. The students who found it most useful were mainly those already in the habit of keeping diaries and journals, such as Maria.

Whilst, as we have seen, Maria doesn't feel 'held' by her reading groups in Courses 1 and 2, keeping a journal provides her with a 'safe space … to gather together fragments of myself, give voice to forgotten, silenced, sometimes conflicting voices'. This gentle gathering together and 'holding' of different fragments of her personality helps sustain her in her period of depression before she finds more significant containment in the 'maternal holding environment' of *Writing and Groups*. Her experience of keeping the mandatory learning journal in this latter course is similarly 'holding' but, by contrast, more active and intentional, providing a space for psychic movement between different sites of learning. It helps her:

> to become more flexible by having to make links between personal feelings, reflection triggered by reading academic texts, and the creative writing process needed to write the home assignments. I see the journal acting like a bridge between the 'MA', the writing group and the 'World'.

Increased psychic movement and flexibility is also indicated in Rhiannon's comments on her *Writing and Groups* journal: it is 'a place to record everything and anything of relevance to *me*, and slowly I began to see a circular almost rhythmic flow of life (my life)'. This greater openness to the flow of experience allows 'difficult issues [that] might otherwise still be floating around in my head as an incomprehensible and unapproachable muddle [to be] uncover[ed] and resolve[d]'. Here the soft structure of the learning journal not only acts as a container for experience in all its guises, but it also allows a more spontaneous and intuitive shaping and ordering of experience.

For Jill the learning journal is a place for letting go of her public persona and giving expression to a more authentic sense of self, in privacy in the first instance. She notes that her writing here is 'much more emotional and serious than the [humorous] tone I adopt in my creative writing', which leads her to wonder whether 'I shelter behind my humour from public exposure'. Stacey can also try out her less public self in the journal: it provides a place for 'writing things that I would never show to others but which sometimes form the basis of future creative work'. Here 'there is no need for the writing to be good or artful, it is held in this space for me to develop as I choose'.

The writing of the learning journal in these examples creates a 'transitional space' (Winnicott, 1971) between inner and outer worlds where learners can become aware, in a relaxed and private way, of thoughts and feelings emerging spontaneously out of the different components of their studies and where the learning self can be more fluid and playful (Creme, 2008). It is another form of 'holding'. But the journal can also be used more consciously and systematically for planning the end-of-course essay, as Claire discovers:

> I included all kinds of things: my reflections on the sessions, on the reading, on my writing, on thoughts I had between sessions. I colour coded these thoughts as suggested and it really clicked! It felt very natural to do, not contrived at all, and made writing the paper for term 3 much easier ... .

Here, there is more critical distance in the process of reflection, a more conscious and willed approach of drawing out and interrogating ideas and insights from the gathered material. Susanna also finds that the journal leads to a more critical, conscious process of reflection, saying that it 'has increased the level of consciousness in my writing and participation in the group and, I hope, in my academic writing'. It helps make her learning more explicit.

Embodied–experiential learning in dialogue with critical reflection

The above examples indicate that there are two different kinds of reflection taking place through the course diary or learning journal: on the one hand there is a spontaneous process of becoming aware of thoughts and feelings experienced in the moment and gathering them together in the diary or journal where they are loosely but safely 'held'; on the other there is a more consciously intentional and retrospective process of developing the material into creative writing or interrogating it for the work for assessment. These sound very much like the two modes of knowing I identified in Chapter 6: *embodied–experiential learning* and *critical reflection*.

The term experiential learning is used in many different ways (Fenwick, 2000). Moon identifies some of its key connotations: it is a kind of learning that is not 'mediated or taught'; it usually involves 'reflection either deliberately or nondeliberately'; there is usually an 'active phase' and a 'formal intention to learn' (Moon, 2004: 120). All of these are certainly present in the students' material, but I would add a further element: whilst there is an active phase and an overall intention to learn, the learning process itself involves relaxed, low level intentionality, the 'listening' mode that is open to the bodily-felt sense of inner and outer worlds, in Gendlin's terms (see Chapter 8). This allows the carrying forward of whatever arises into words, but in a preliminary, receptive way before a more intentional, top-down processing or interrogation of the material takes place. Thus my understanding of experiential learning connects with 'embodied learning', which is described as a process of bringing forth a world via holistic bodily experience (Horn and Wilburn, 2005: 751, quoting Varela *et al.*, 1991; cf. Mathison and Tosey, 2008). It has similarities with Milner's attending with the 'imaginative body' (Milner, 1971: 36) and Siegel's 'receptive awareness' (Siegel, 2007: 127), and is intrinsic to Boyd and Myers's 'receptivity' (1988). It is knowledge derived intuitively from bottom-up rather than top-down, similar to that derived from the creative life writing.

Critical reflection is, of course, Mezirow's term for the process at the heart of transformative learning, where learners 'critically reflect on [their] own assumptions as well as those of others' (Mezirow, 2000: 25). However, what I have in mind is more than just 'premise reflection' (Mezirow, 1991), and critical not just in the sense of 'ideology critique' (Brookfield, 2000), although it might involve that; rather it is a highly focused and intentional (critical) mode of attention to material gathered via the embodied–experiential mode, which aims at clear, reasoned articulation and understanding, often with the help of seminar discussion and conceptualisations derived from course texts. This is Milner's sharply pointed 'thinking mode' (Milner, 1971).

Students' essays show them moving back and forth between embodied–experiential learning and critical reflection, bringing tacit, bodily-felt meanings into the light where they can be explored more consciously, and then re-embodying what they have found into more holistic understandings. This is most clearly visible in the essays for *Writing and Groups* where students discuss their learning through critically reflecting on their own and the group's experience as recorded in their learning journal, drawing also on the creative writing done during the course and conceptual understandings derived from course texts. Claudia's is a particularly good example. Reflecting on her embodied experience of the group that she has recorded in her journal, she notices that she has distanced herself from the other students right up to the final session. She 'desperately want[s] to be seen' by the group and really appreciates that: 'Everyone seemed to really attend when someone was sharing their piece, especially the facilitator'. But at the same time she is 'very afraid of exposure'. This conflict is at work from the start when she reveals more of herself in her creative writing than is comfortable and then '[feels] terrible, as though I just took all my clothes off in a public place', causing her to withdraw. In her isolation she projects her strong tendency to self-criticism onto fellow students, becoming acutely 'self-conscious as I judged my work to be not as good as theirs and that they were "proper writers" whereas I was just an amateur'. Then her anger at the tutor emerges (see Chapter 9). Whilst she understands, through reflections in her journal, that the anger and sense of being judged adversely by the group are, at least in part, the result of being 'angry and disappointed' at herself, this does not relieve her anxiety, and she toys with dropping out.

It is only when writing the home assignment on 'This is where I risk, what I risk' that Claudia is able to distance herself sufficiently from her own struggles and look at her relationship with the group differently. Unable to confront the exercise head-on, she imagines herself as a sea anemone on a coral reef: 'The life of the anemone is difficult. In each moment she must be alert to the changing conditions, choosing always whether to open herself up and risk being vulnerable or close herself in and run the risk of starvation'. Mostly the anemone 'camouflages [herself] in browns and greens like the darkest, dankest, foul-smelling seaweed'. But whilst this protects her, it also deprives her of food, sunlight and the stroke of passing fish, all of which she needs to survive. Aching to be part of the rich life of the reef, 'she begins to unfurl her tentacles' revealing her rainbow colours. Now she can draw plankton and algae deep inside her, the clown fish can 'cavort in and out of her colourful skirts' bringing her companionship. But she also realises that opening-up is not just about what *she* can get from the reef; rather it has a 'positive effect ... on her environment' and that the other creatures have longed for her to open up and be an active part of their 'underwater world'. This extended metaphor enables Claudia to recognise that:

> my contribution in the group could have had a very positive effect and that the group had indeed wanted me to join them in their 'underwater world'

because my personal struggle blocked the group as a whole, not just my own process.

The journal entries she quotes in the essay show her engaging in a difficult dialogue with herself:

Why do I do this to myself? I have paid for this course, and was delighted to be offered a place, because it was something I genuinely wanted to do. Why do I sabotage my own happiness by then not allowing myself to fully participate?

In the final session she is able to recognise:

a deep sadness that I hadn't got to know any of the group members and hadn't dedicated myself to the work of the course, always fitting the reading and writing exercises in at the last minute and seeing them as a chore rather than as something I had chosen to do.

What Claudia learns from writing the paper is 'the damage I can do to myself when I push uncomfortable feelings in the shadow rather than express them'. The 'shadow' here is Jung's concept (see Chapter 9), which Claudia uses to explore the rebellious part of her personality from childhood and which re-emerges strongly in this course. In fact she did try expressing this part of herself when she confronted the tutor – quite legitimately it seems (see Chapter 9) – about her inconsistent participation in the exercises, but at that point she was not yet able to trust and manage it, and it went underground again. Yet her later reflections on the course for the research project, where she notes that she has 'become more authentic and real in my responses even when it is uncomfortable',[1] indicate that there has been progress towards this.

What we see here, then, is a series of soft structures for 'holding' the dialogue between embodied–experiential learning and critical reflection. The learning journal provides a space for Claudia's felt experience of conflict between closeness and distance in her relationship with the writing group to be gathered and processed as it happens. The creative life writing exercise enables her to reflect on her experience obliquely through the metaphor of the coral reef, which captures both her individuality as a learner and her place in the organic whole of the group – this is an example of how the creative life writing exercises can be used as a form of intentional reflection on current dilemmas. Jung's concept of the shadow, interpreted in her own way, gives conceptual shape to the underlying psychic structures at work in her conflict, and the end-of-course essay provides a vehicle for critical reflection on all the other components. In critical realist terms Claudia's learning here emerges out of the 'layered' or 'laminar' nature of the learning environment (Brown, 2009), with the learning group, the journal, the creative writing, and the essay constituting a series of nested layers that both challenge her to greater openness and insight but also 'hold' her in that process.

A framework for thinking feelings

The possibility of engaging in a dialogue between embodied–experiential learning and critical reflection, then, is built into the structure of *Writing and Groups*, but it also becomes visible as a key feature of the MA as a whole. As outlined in Chapter 1, Course 1 (*Writing for Personal Development*) is primarily an experiential course, with creative life writing exercises providing opportunities for embodied–experiential learning. However, some literary and theoretical readings are introduced alongside practice, to enable students to start bringing creative writing and personal development together conceptually through seminar discussion. The end of course essay, which requires students to reflect critically on what they have learned about themselves and their writing practice from the combination of writing exercises, conceptual material, and experiential group work, provides a structured space for bringing these different components together, with the course diary available for capturing experience in the here and now. Course 2 (*Creative Writing and the Self*) reverses this pattern, privileging student- and tutor-led discussion of key concepts over experiential practice, although creative writing arising out of this material and sharing it in small reading groups remains as a means of connecting the two.[2] The academic paper requires students to demonstrate their understanding of one or more of the conceptual frameworks they have engaged with during the course and their relevance for creative writing and personal development.

Courses 1 and 2 constitute the core of the programme, designed to ground students in the experiential and conceptual approach of the MA. In the remaining three courses the experiential work and critical reflection go hand-in-hand, with those students taking the practice-based courses being required to reflect critically on their writing practice via conceptual material (as in *Writing Practice* and the creative writing option of *Independent Study*) and specifically with the aid of a learning journal in *Writing and Groups*. The only exceptions are *Projects: Practical and Theoretical* and the research option of *Independent Study* where students undertake a piece of qualitative or text-based research, although some students also use these to reflect critically on practice.[3]

This interweaving of embodied–experiential learning and critical reflection across the programme is clearly visible in the case studies. As we have seen in Simon's story (Chapter 3), the opening up to a more bodily-felt space for the imagination, which he experiences through creative life writing and small group work in Course 1, is at first distressing, although the trust he develops in his reading group generates a degree of 'holding' for this. At the same time the conceptual material – particularly Chatman's visual representation of multiple textual agents in a narrative – provides additional psychic structuring through the different 'selves' and others that he now sees inhabiting his writing practice. This continues in Course 2, where the ideas of Bakhtin and Bruner enable him to 'erect a three dimensional mental framework or scaffolding on which the narratives, events, metaphors and biographical fictions of my life can be spread out and examined'. That the mental scaffolding is 'three dimensional' indicates that his strong visual imagination is enabling him to embody the conceptual material and to start moulding it creatively in his own way.

In his research project for Course 4 (*Projects: Practical and Theoretical*) his embodied understanding of the conceptual material from previous courses enables him to move away from his sense of himself as unconnected fragments to formulate a metaphor for self as a rope made up of a multitude of strands twisted together and constantly undergoing change whilst giving an outward impression of uniformity. The conceptual framework of stability and fluidity implicit in this metaphor, together with increased trust in his writing process derived from the collaborative group work, subsequently facilitates a more reflexive collaboration in his creative process between his managing 'author' self and his more unruly 'writer' self, resulting in the spontaneous creative pieces he writes for *Independent Study*. The emergence in one of these pieces ('Pencil') of an extended metaphor for the reflexive relationship between stability and fluidity suggests that this conceptual framework has now become embodied.

A similar trajectory is visible in Maria's story (Chapter 4). The experiential work of Course 1 cracks open psychic space, more painfully than for Simon, as Maria does not feel sufficiently 'held' by her reading group and becomes depressed although, as we have seen above, the journal does provide a degree of 'holding'. In Course 2, Kristeva's conceptualisation of the psyche as constantly in process between the bodily-felt Semiotic realm and the language-based Symbolic realm helps Maria to understand her sense of being split between her French and English identities, and exploring this in the critical paper makes her feel more contained and integrated. In her Course 3 option (*Writing and Groups*) she finds 'experiential grounding' for this conceptual understanding through experiencing the all-female group as Kristeva's 'chora' or maternal holding environment that facilitates psychic movement between the Semiotic and Symbolic realms. Again the learning journal is an important means of 'holding'. Feeling more contained internally and 'held' externally, she is able, in Course 4 (*Contexts for Practice*), to start experimenting with capturing her fragmented self-experience in a connected series of writing fragments. This culminates, through the combination of creative writing and reflection in *Independent Study*, in the creation of a multi-voiced personal narrative held together by the transcendent image of herself as a storyteller who 'holds' the space for stories to be told. Thus the sense of containment, which begins to develop through the journal and the internalisation of Kristeva's conceptual framework, and then through its experiential consolidation in *Writing and Groups*, becomes objectified in the creative writing in the form of a self-narrator who contains the more relational space of the self.

Both these examples demonstrate a clear movement from embodied–experiential learning, which brings uncomfortable fragmentation of the psyche into view, to the unpacking of that experience through critical reflection, and then the re-embodying of the new learning into a more holistic sense of self as writer or learner, which can tolerate and begin to manage psychic multiplicity.

However, whilst these different dimensions can be separated out, once set in motion embodied–experiential learning and critical reflection quickly come together into a dynamic recursive process of thinking feelings.

The primacy of bodily experience[4]

From the above examples it is clear that in the dialogue between embodied–experiential learning and critical reflection the former *precedes* the latter, although the two quickly come together into a dynamic bodily or bottom-up process. Some students refer to this explicitly. Miranda finds that: 'as soon as I experience a feeling ... I am reading some literature that helps me understand and assimilate the feeling'. The verb 'assimilate', with its first dictionary meaning of 'taking in and using as nourishment – to absorb into the system' (Merriam-Webster), implies that the dynamic relationship between bodily experience and critical reflection moves from intuitive awareness of the experience to a more conscious understanding and back to embodied, and presumably less conscious, meaning-making. In Ruth's reflections on writing her novel for *Independent Study* the dynamic relationship between bodily-felt experience and critical reflection is just *beginning* to develop, although the conscious nature of it presents some difficulties:

> I began to recognise a feeling of the 'felt self' in my writing, when it was coming from a more authentic sense of place. This was difficult to keep up sometimes, but I learnt to identify when it was there, and not to keep on writing when it had gone. This was a progression from *Projects: Practical and Theoretical*, when I looked into the notion of the felt self, and how to access it.

Here the concept appears to come first, through Ruth's engagement with Gendlin's concept of 'felt sense' in her academic paper for Course 4. But as she has been engaging deeply with her feelings through the creative writing exercises in earlier courses, when she becomes consciously aware of her 'felt self' in her writing in *Independent Study* she is in all likelihood naming something she has already started experiencing at a deeper, less conscious level. By becoming more aware of it and giving it a name, she is able consciously to practice using it as a way into her writing. That, in the writing of the novel, she is able to start giving fictional shape to her painful obsession with her former boyfriend (see Chapter 7), indicates again that, whilst this process goes through a fully conscious stage, it is gradually becoming embodied into lower level consciousness where it becomes an intuitive part of the creative process.

The potential tension between embodied–experiential learning and critical reflection is also visible in Harriet's experience. Theoretical material from Course 2 on the bodily-felt self facilitates conceptual understanding of a psychic mechanism she discovered intuitively during a previous creative writing course of 'shutting-off some controlling bit of my mind and going straight into some other place and writing from that and trusting what I write ...'. She had noticed that: 'if I went for a swim in the morning and then came back and did my [writing] exercise it would come'. But at that time 'I hadn't got the underpinning, whereas now I know after Damasio etc. why it is that that works. So it means I can do it more consciously'.

Making an intuitive process conscious can, of course, inhibit it, at least in the short term, as it increases the potential for cognitive control, which is a danger for strongly intellectual Harriet: 'I like having the theoretical underpinning, which gives me, well it gives me arguments I suppose, but it also allows me to justify myself that I am doing what's right. I feel it is a healthy thing to do'. However, there is an indication in her more relaxed sense of where she will go next with her writing that understanding the mechanism intellectually gives her greater confidence and trust in the writing process: 'I haven't got definite plans, I've just got sort of feelings really, intuitions if you like, directions I want to go, so I'm just sort of pursuing things at the moment and hoping things will sort out'. Here conscious critical reflection does not seem to be inhibiting the writing process, rather it is again becoming assimilated into the less conscious context of her writing practice.

Whilst these examples show an awareness of distinct stages of bodily experiencing and conceptualising and their re-embodiment, Lucy who engages with the MA in a more intuitive way (see Chapter 2), becomes aware only of the consequences of embodying the dialogue: 'one of the things that the theory and writing together has helped me with is knowing when things are OK and not OK for me and my identity, for my sense of who I am ...'. Here the two sides of the process have become integrated into an intuitive, bodily way of knowing.[5]

Developing reflexivity through the learning process

Students' learning, then, could be described as becoming more aware of what their experience of writing or learning or being in relation *feels* like, through the experiential work of engaging in creative life writing, sharing it in the collaborative groups, and recording it in course diaries or learning journals, then reflecting critically on this experience for the end-of-course essays and papers with the aid of course readings, and then allowing the new knowledge to become embodied into intuitive writing, learning, or interpersonal processes. As the examples show, this happens more consciously for some than for others. Also whilst learning from bodily-felt experience and critical reflection might start off being separate and potentially in conflict in some instances, there is evidence that they are becoming assimilated into a dynamic process. This sounds very much like McGilchrist's 'reciprocity' between the brain's hemispheres.

As discussed in Chapter 6, the hemispheres give rise to two different ways of seeing the world: the right rendering a holistic, bodily, and largely unconscious engagement with the world, and the left a narrowly focused, fragmenting, analytic, and largely conscious engagement with what it receives from the right. For optimal functioning there needs to be constant collaboration between the two, for whilst the right hemisphere sees things whole, it cannot describe them; and whilst the left hemisphere can powerfully analyse parts of the whole, its analyses on their own are devoid of felt life and cannot generate personal meaning. For creative thinking to occur, there needs to be a fluid, recursive flow from the right hemisphere's embodied engagement with experience to the left hemisphere's unpacking of that experience, and then the re-embodying of it by the right hemisphere, which brings 'a new, enhanced intuitive understanding of this whole' (McGilchrist, 2009: 176–206). This is precisely what we see happening in the above examples. The potential tension between the two modes, also visible in some of the examples, is intelligible in light of the intrinsic conflict between the hemispheres' different world views and their need to inhibit each other for optimal functioning (ibid.: 208). So for some people there is a need to practice the working together of the two modes consciously and with intent or, as I have called it, practising reflexivity.

This picture of reflexivity as involving a fluid, recursive flow between right hemisphere embodied–experiential learning and left hemisphere critical reflection finds considerable resonance in Yorks and Kasl's understanding of transformative change as taking place through 'multiple ways of knowing'. Drawing on the work of Heron (1992), they identify four different ways of knowing: experiential (affective), presentational (imaginal or expressive), propositional (conceptual), and practical. Combining this 'whole-person epistemology' with insights from transformative learning, they construct a 'pathway to knowing' that moves from 'tacit and subconscious forms of knowing' to 'expressive ways of knowing', and only then to 'critical reflection' (Yorks and Kasl, 2006: 60–1), with interpersonal learning-within-relationship and intrapersonal whole-person learning taking place in parallel, as in Figure 10.1.

I find this a very helpful model, but in light of my bio-psycho-social conceptual framework I would suggest developing it as in Figure 10.2:

Level 1 – *Pre-reflective Bodily Self-awareness* – is Damasio's core consciousness with a sense of self. It is the 'source of thoughts' (Petitmengin, 2007) emerging out of the body's constant relationship with internal and external environments via bodily processes including, most significantly, the emotions, which provides a sense of ongoingness and a holistic sense of bodily agency. It is the primary level of engagement with reality as mediated by the body. Whilst Yorks and Kasl refer to 'tacit and subconscious forms of knowing', the centrality of this dimension of the whole is not sufficiently articulated in their model.

Level 2 – *Embodied–experiential Learning* – is reflective awareness of Level 1 at low level consciousness and with low level intentionality. It is right hemisphere knowing, in the form of moments of bodily-felt awareness emerging as bodily cognition (Johnson, 2007) and being 'carried forward' (Gendlin, 1991) into spoken or written words or aesthetic images. This may happen via individual or

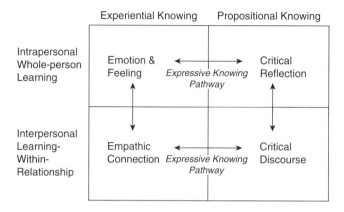

Figure 10.1 Expressive knowing is a pathway.
Source: Yorks and Kasl, 2006.

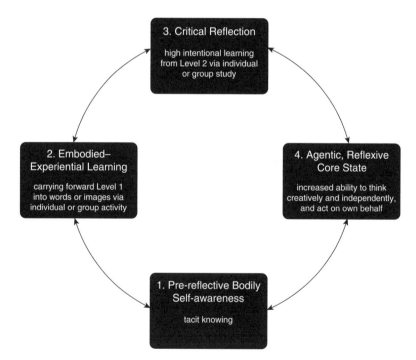

Figure 10.2 Cycle of transformation.

group learning activities. I prefer the term 'embodied–experiential knowing' to Yorks and Kasl's 'expressive knowing', as the latter implies active expression of the emotions rather than the more organic emergence of 'felt sense' from pre-reflective bodily self-awareness, although this will often give rise to emotional expression. The threshold between Levels 1 and 2 can be thought of as the 'liminal space' (Green, 2012) or the 'growing edge' (Berger, 2004).

Level 3 – *Critical Reflection* – is left hemisphere attention to, and processing of, what emerges from Level 2. It takes place at the level of extended consciousness and with high intentionality. It involves critical reflection undertaken either individually or through group learning. Reflexivity emerges spontaneously when there is reciprocity between Levels 2 and 3, or between right and left hemispheres, i.e. when the autobiographical 'I' of the left hemisphere is flexible enough to retract and become part of the frame for the engagement with core consciousness. This often needs to be 'practised' consciously in order for reflexivity to become a more automatic and less conscious psychic process.

Level 4 – *Agentic, Reflexive Core State* – emerges out of the psychic stability and flexibility that is the consequence of reciprocity between levels 2 and 3. It involves an increased sense of agency and trust in bodily processes for learning and being and increased ability to think creatively and independently. The reflexive core state facilitates constant openness to memory and pre-reflective bodily self-awareness of the engagement with the world at Level 1, thus keeping the dynamic system of the psyche both grounded and open to change. This echoes Kegan's idea of the 'self-transforming mind' (Kegan, 2000). It is a picture of circular causality (Lewis, 2005), where negative feedback from individual and group learning activities keeps the system constantly in motion and open to change, as opposed to the positive feedback of vicious circles that reinforces stuckness (hyperreflexivity) (Chapter 7).

Applying the above schema to the work of the CWPD programme, I suggest that what I have called the semiotic creative writing exercises and the work of the experiential, collaborative groups, as well as the more embodied use of learning journals and diaries, connect Levels 1 and 2, bringing greater openness to, and awareness of, pre-reflective bodily self-awareness and carrying this new knowledge forward. The dialogic creative writing exercises connect Levels 2 and 3, as do the reflective essays and learning journals in their more intentional usage. All of these, however, are closer to Level 2 than 3, with the academic papers, seminars, and discussion groups closer to Level 3. Creative life writing can also be used nearer to Level 3 as an intentional reflective tool for exploring conceptual material or self-experience, as in the example of Claudia. The cycle is kept in motion by negative feedback, in the form of disorienting dilemmas provided by the creative life writing, the group work, and material from course readings, but the inherent structures in these curricular and pedagogical tools simultaneously provide a degree of 'holding', as do other more overarching elements in the learning environment, such as the relationship with tutors and the convener, and the sense of being part of a community of learners. As the arrows indicate, the cycle of transformation is by no means uni-directional. Indeed it is a much messier, less ordered process than might appear from the diagram. Jill's comment on it was that in her experience it was more like a spiral, 'a DNA helix wrapping continuously around us, with us being at different stages of the model all at the same time'. This captures effectively what I was trying to convey.

Many of the problems for Group 2 students can be understood as a consequence of the stiffness or 'stickiness' between Levels 2 and 3 when Level 3 becomes the dominant, hyperreflexive (defensive) mode of cognition (see Chapter 7), which results in an imbalance between psychic freedom and control. The more reciprocal functioning between these levels and the shift towards Level 4 happens for students in different ways and at different stages of the programme, as we have seen, but for quite a few of those in Group 2 it only starts to become a more intuitive, spontaneous process in the two terms of *Independent Study*. Jill, for example, describes her more reflexive state as having 'two senses of yourself. I don't find I'm analysing while I'm doing, but quite quickly now I can analyse afterwards, whereas I wouldn't have done that before'. This demonstrates her ability, as she says elsewhere, 'to trust myself and my instincts'. In fact students' ability to *trust the process* of writing, which is a key theme in their reflections on their learning at the end of the two years, seems to be a key component of Level 4. This implies that they are much better able to tolerate the 'not knowing' intrinsic to the creative process between Levels 1 and 2, which means that reflexivity can function more intuitively. This development comes in part, as tutor Sarah suggests, from having to sustain a piece of critical-creative writing over two terms in *Independent Study*, that is, working intensively across Levels 1–3 in one piece of work, but the opening-up to a more bodily-felt learning process in previous terms has prepared the ground, as we see in Megan's reflections on the place of *Independent Study* in her learning:

> I managed to look more in depth at myself and my writing, but in a much more subjective way. This term and the first term seemed to teach me the most. Or it may be that this last term has brought all the learning together in a more complete form?

That it is the first and last terms from which she has learned most provides a picture of the programme as starting with opening-up and finishing with consolidation. This mirrors the process of differentiation and integration intrinsic to the dynamic system of the psyche. That her learning feels 'much more subjective' implies that her sense of self in the learning process is now more tangible, so that the results of her analyses and conceptualising make sense to her in a more experiential, holistic way. The spontaneous emergence of holistic and reflexive images in the creative writing during this final stage, as evidenced in the case studies and visible in other students too, also supports this.

My aim in this chapter was to understand better the contribution to students' shift to a more reflexive self-experience of the different kinds of reflective work they engage in during their studies. What I have found is that, by virtue of its role in both experiential–embodied and critically reflective forms of learning, it is the only curricular tool to span Levels 1 to 3 in my model and could therefore be seen as a crucial connector between all the other elements in the transformative cycle. This suggests that it is a more 'macroscopic' than 'underlying' dimension of the learning environment (Bhaskar and Danermark, 2006), potentially 'holding' the whole learning process, whilst also, in its critical guise, keeping it open and alive (cf. Taylor, 2006). This is in line with some Group 2 students' view that it would have been beneficial to keep learning journals in all courses. It also supports Mezirow's view of the importance of reflection in transformative learning, although, as we have seen, it is not just reflection in its critical guise, and ultimately critical reflection is secondary to the experiential work.

Notes

1 This is an example of how the research creates another level of reflection (see Introduction).
2 Some Group 2 students found Course 2 rather overloaded with theory and, whilst they found it interesting and relevant, particularly later when they had had time to process it more thoroughly, many of them said that it was not possible to maintain their writing practice meaningfully during this course. A better balance between theory and practice would have improved this course.
3 Most MA students took the creative writing option in *Independent Study*. In the earlier Diploma all students undertook a research project, the creative writing option not then being available, although again some used the research project to reflect critically on their writing practice.
4 This echoes Margaret Archer's argument for the 'primacy of practice', by which she means the primacy of bodily engagement with the material environment out of which emerges the 'sense of self' with its 'continuity of consciousness' (Archer, 2000). As I said in Chapter 6, I see the bodily-felt sense of self as innate but developed through the relationship with the material environment and other people.
5 This links with Taylor's (2001) discussion of transformative learning taking place out of conscious awareness.

Part IV

Implications for adult learning

As Part III has shown, whilst the curricular and pedagogical dimensions of the CWPD programme have the potential to disrupt students' psyches and set them in motion, there are many different ways in which the learning environment can provide 'holding' for that difficult process, both at the macroscopic and underlying levels. However, that 'holding' is possible within the programme at many different levels and in many different ways does not mean that students and tutors always feel adequately supported by it, as we have seen throughout my discussions, or that they do not sometimes need additional 'holding' outside the programme. Thus in Part IV I look in more detail at the challenges of a programme of study that aims to facilitate students' self-learning at a deep level, as well as the implications for teaching and learning of working on the education–therapy borderline.

Chapter 11

Challenges of transformative learning through creative life writing

The challenges of transformative learning for both students and tutors are well recognised in the literature. Mezirow says that:

> Transformative learning, especially when it involves subjective reframing, is often an intensely threatening emotional experience in which we have to become aware of both the assumptions undergirding our ideas and those supporting our emotional responses to the need to change.
>
> (Mezirow, 2000: 6–7)

As usual, Mezirow makes 'subjective reframing' too conscious and rational, but the description of it as 'an intensely threatening emotional experience' certainly resonates with some of the examples in my study. Boyd and Myers's description of the transformative process of 'discernment' as involving a period of 'grieving' in response to the 'involuntary disruption of order [and collapse of] previous assurances and predictable ways of interpreting reality and of making meaning' (Boyd and Myers, 1988: 276–8), also echoes the experience of some CWPD students. Their suggestion, however, that mourning is a *necessary* part of transformative change is not borne out by my study.

The challenges involved in students' emotional opening-up – for the students themselves, for the tutor team, and for the university – have become more visible through the research, as have the challenges of combining personal development with the development of an arts-specific skill. In this chapter I discuss these various challenges, drawing out what might be important for others to bear in mind when pursuing similar approaches.

Challenges for students of opening-up emotionally

CWPD students' reactions to the experience of greater emotional openness vary considerably. Whilst for some there are transitory moments of sadness or distress, as in Simon's tearfulness when he is unable to imagine a reader in his writing process in Course 1, this is sometimes just a small part of a larger experience of excitement, even exhilaration, at what they are learning about themselves.[1] However, for others increased emotional openness triggers longer periods of distress or depression, as is the case for Maria during Courses 1 and 2, because of having to '[go] back to a place where I wasn't held' and the mourning this involves. The dismantling of Stella's familiar sense of identity leaves her, at the end of Year 1, feeling 'more deconstructed and insecure now than I have for years' and on one occasion she has 'suicidal thoughts'. However, she finds it difficult to separate the effects of her studies from those resulting from her relationship break-up. Jill's relinquishing of her dominant sense of identity also leads to a period of insecurity early on in the programme: 'The fragile container, the identity I have manufactured, I now see is cracked into many shards, yet I still fear to move away from playing parts I know by heart'. If identity is a cognitive-emotional container that provides familiarity and safety, even though potentially constraining, then relinquishing it at the start of a two-year programme of study requires being able to tolerate a more vulnerable state for quite a long period. For some people, as we have seen, it also involves being able to tolerate the emergence of challenging dimensions of the personality. This necessitates having a safe-enough holding environment to bridge the gap before a more grounded, embodied sense of agency develops.

Whilst the different opportunities for 'holding' in the learning environment can be seen to sustain many Group 2 students, the research highlights some significant gaps. For example, the summer vacation between the two years of study is particularly difficult for some people, not surprisingly perhaps in view of the three-month period at a distance from the programme and its community of learners. This is the case for two of the three students who take the craft-based *Writing Practice* in the summer term rather than *Writing and Groups*. Lucy, for example, feels adrift during the vacation with an angry sense that none of the option courses for the start of Year 2 is right for her. The dismantling of her familiar sense of identity means that her reasons for taking the MA are no longer relevant, and she does not know what she should do next. Serendipitously the first research interview late in the vacation provides an opportunity for her to explore this. Together we determine that undertaking, for *Projects: Practical and Theoretical*, a text-based research project on the personal development potential of science fiction will enable her to build on her experience of using this genre to explore her dominant theme of absent males in *Writing Practice*. Normally this opportunity to discuss Year 2 would not have been available unless she had specifically requested it,[2] and this highlights the need for on-going support for transformative learning students across the longer gaps in their studies. This might be achieved, for example, via a scheduled meeting with the convener for all students during the summer vacation to reflect on their experience of Year 1 and prepare for Year 2. Online contact between students as a group or in supportive pairs would also be useful here.[3]

Ruth, who similarly takes *Writing Practice*, also runs into difficulties at this time, although this only comes to a head at the start of Year 2 when she undertakes, for *Projects: Practical and Theoretical*, an extremely challenging but ultimately beneficial exploration of the value of Gendlin's 'felt sense' technique for engaging with her painful feelings about her father. In this instance additional support via the University's counselling services is necessary to help contain her distress, which highlights the importance of having this available as back-up when required. At Sussex, as will be the case elsewhere, students can refer themselves to these services without going via the convener, but it is also useful for the convener to suggest to students in distress that they might benefit from some counselling sessions. In fact, from a certain point we recommended in our publicity that students might wish to consider having therapeutic support in place for the period of their studies, and some 50 per cent of Group 2 students were in counselling or therapy either throughout or for some of the time (see Chapter 12).

The experience of Lucy and Ruth indicates that, paradoxically, what we were calling the 'creative writing and personal development' route through the MA involving *Writing Practice* and *Projects: Practical and Theoretical* was, at that time at least, less 'holding' than the 'professional development' route involving *Writing and Groups* and *Contexts for Practice*. A big factor in this was that the option courses in the former route were structured that year[4] as independent study, with one-to-one supervision and monthly tutor-led reading groups for sharing work-in-progress. In view of the depth of some students' self-explorations in these courses, this was clearly a mistake, and the following year they were brought into line with the standard pattern of fortnightly tutor-led meetings. It is worth noting, though, that all three Group 2 students who took this route – Lucy, Ruth, and Simon – did benefit in personal development terms from undertaking the craft-focused creative writing and the small research project, as we saw particularly in Simon's story (Chapter 3). This indicates that this route is potentially as beneficial from a transformative learning point of view as the professional development route, but 'holding' needs to be more significantly in place than it was at the time of the research.

Another significant gap in 'holding' is in the two terms of *Independent Study* at the conclusion of the MA. For many years – and the research material reflects this – students were saying that the monthly gaps between the tutor-led group meetings during *Independent Study* were too long, causing them to lose connection with the programme. My response was always that individual supervision plus three half-day tutor-led feedback sessions was all we could provide per term, particularly as for most other MAs at the University independent study meant individual supervision only. However, the research leads me to the view that, if we are expecting students to engage in deep emotional learning of the kind under discussion here, providing 'holding' across the two years needs to involve more frequent support during the final stages when consolidation is usually taking place.

Challenges for students of the failure of transformative learning

Of course there are also people for whom the CWPD programme was not transformative, or opened them up but did not enable them to consolidate their learning. One woman from Group 1 who dropped out after Course 2 says: 'I felt I lacked inner creativity, and floundered between depression at the blankness inside my head and irritation at the self-indulgence of it all'. It sounds from this as if she experienced a degree of opening-up but the psychic state that resulted was too difficult to manage. She also indicates difficulties fitting her studies into her busy life: 'I lacked the necessary ruthlessness to complete [the coursework requirements] in the context of my own circumstances'. 'Undertaking the course', she says, 'was a poor decision on my part. Failing to complete it undermined my self-esteem' and 'had a very negative effect on [my sense of self as a learner]'.

There are several different things happening here. She is clearly trying to juggle a demanding programme of study with a demanding home life – a full-time caring role, if I remember correctly – but her reference to the 'self-indulgence' of the learning process hints at a strong reluctance to reflect on herself, which is in tension with her decision to join a personal development programme. Her mention of lacking creativity is also in tension with the gently lyrical creative writing she produced in Course 1, which hints at a strong tendency to self-criticism. It may be that, like some Group 2 students I have discussed, what she was *actually* able to achieve as a learner and writer in the short time she was with us compared unfavourably with her expectations, and that engaging with this was too difficult in the context of her busy life beyond her studies.

Another woman who dropped out after Course 2 also indicates that this was, in part, because her writing did not live up to her expectations. 'I have not made the transition from being "a dabbler" to being "a writer"', she says, which, combined with ill health and her struggle with the academic work, undermined her 'confidence in [her] abilities to learn'. That something similar happened again in a subsequent writing course indicates an ingrained difficulty with learning, and the respondent acknowledges this when, in reply to a question about what she learned from the programme, says: 'there are areas of personal development for me to pursue – to increase my confidence and commitment as a writer – to believe that the small talent I have is worthwhile pursuing'.

What we see in both these instances is the coming together of difficult external factors (heavy family commitments, ill health) with the challenge of opening-up to painful insights about problems with learning or creativity. In both instances failure to complete the programme undermines what in all likelihood is an already shaky confidence. This is not to suggest that there were not shortcomings in the programme in their year that contributed to their difficulties. Some of the responses from Group 1 indicate that our ability to provide a safe-enough environment for this work was not as well developed in the Diploma period as it was later, with one person referring to the personal development work in Course 1 as 'badly boundaried' in her year. Also quite a few Group 2 respondents found the reading for Course 2 both too much and too diverse. But implicit in both of the above instances is the challenge of opening-up to problems with learning and creativity in a context where there is also an emphasis on developing creative writing skills. As another Group 1 respondent says when reflecting on why she stopped writing creatively after the Diploma: 'I wonder if exposure to more able/creative writers did affect my confidence in some way. I think I had a sense of my writing being rather "ordinary"'. Of course, feeling overshadowed by others with more experience can be a problem in any creative writing course – indeed in any group learning – but it is likely to be particularly acute in a personal development context where novice and more experienced writers are working alongside each other, and where there may well be a greater proportion of students who lack confidence as learners. One way to address this would be for tutors to be more aware that it is a possibility and to bring it into the open for discussion. There *were* opportunities for students to reflect on the operation of their small groups in plenary discussions, but more could be done to draw out issues that are known to arise for some learners.

The above highlights the problem of undertaking creative writing for personal development alongside the development of creative writing skills, which I explore in more detail in the next section. But it also highlights the importance of ensuring that students are aware of the personal challenges of transformative learning. At Sussex this usually occurred at interview, where the convener's task was to try and get a sense of applicants' level of self-awareness, so that she could make a judgement about their suitability for the programme. In the first of the two examples discussed above this process does not seem to have been successful. Of course, an interview is not a perfect vehicle for this, as people can appear to be robust and self-reflective at first and then turn out to be less so. But the point remains that with a programme of study that attracts people who have difficulties with learning and whose level of self-confidence may already be shaky, every effort should be made to help them decide whether or not exploring these difficulties in an educational context is appropriate for them. Inevitably, all programmes of study lose students and, to my recollection, the CWPD programme did not lose more than was average in the department. But as tutor Sarah points out, because of the nature of the CWPD programme it is easier for tutors to feel that they are to blame, and it is important to be aware that there are often other factors at work in students' departures not connected with the programme. In a transformative learning context an exit interview can be beneficial, although in my experience students are not always willing or able to talk about their reasons for leaving.

Challenges for tutors of students' emotional learning

As we have seen in Chapter 9, the main challenge for tutors is how to 'hold' the students whilst also helping them to keep the dynamic system of the psyche or of the group open and in process, which implies the ability to be more personally present – more 'real', as tutor Cheryl puts it – to students. This echoes Boyd and

Myers's view that tutors need to be 'actively involved in the inner dialogue of their own personal journeys. They must have travelled a similar road and speak from their own experience' (Boyd and Myers, 1988: 282).

One of the consequences of being more present and real to the students is that the transference, which is of course present in all learning situations, can be more intense. For tutor Cheryl the relationships students form with the tutors in the CWPD programme is a key part of their emotional learning. As the programme progresses, she says, they will have 'both negative and positive encounters' with different tutors, which will evoke previous experiences of 'good parenting or bad parenting or something in the middle', and she suggests that students' negotiation of that can lead them, when it works well, 'to a place where they can become utterly themselves'. Thus students may become 'attached and dependent on a tutor' and want to please them, which may create tensions for them in getting their learning needs met, as we have seen in Harriet's experience; or they may take 'a particular dislike to a tutor' or their teaching approach, but find that not only can they 'voice their criticism', but they can also 'have it listened to', as Claudia found. Becoming more aware of tension in the relationship with the tutor and being required to reflect on it, in *Writing and Groups* for example, opens it up for students to explore, so that they can carry forward the resulting learning into their lives beyond the programme. Horney's suggestion that transference is a defence against anxiety rather than a repetition of infantile patterns offers another way of thinking about students' attachment to tutors, and of their hostility towards them when these defences are challenged (Horney, 1939a: 154–67). This is not to suggest, however, that students cannot have legitimate affection for, or anger at, tutors.

In light of her experience of *Writing and Groups*, Christine thinks that all tutors teaching CWPD need a better understanding of how negative and positive transferences impact the tutor–student relationship, so that they know how to respond to groups or individuals when difficulties arise. Tutors also need to be able to share with the tutor group when this is happening, so that they can learn from each other and feel supported. Of course, tutors also need to understand the phenomenon of countertransference which, in a Horneyan sense, could also be a defence against anxiety. Needing students to like us, for example, may be a way of defending ourselves against less worthy traits, such as destructive competitiveness or self-glorifying tendencies. Or it may protect us against a sense of not being good enough or not knowing enough about our topics. Interestingly, Sarah notices that: 'We've all been really open to learning more about what we're doing and changing'. This connects for her with being open to not knowing all the answers as teachers, which supports the idea that a greater degree of openness is a necessary characteristic of tutors who engage in this kind of work. Cheryl concurs:

> I've drawn a lot of support from that sense that we're all finding things out as we go, and it's that process of discovery that has felt very supportive and enabling because it means that our role as tutors is to enable that process to

continue in the best possible way, but not necessarily to be doling out something that we should have rehearsed very well and have all packaged up.

What the tutors are saying here is that teaching on this programme requires them to be in process in a similar way to the students, and certainly my own experience of it over many years has been a sense of constantly having to open-up to new – and sometimes quite painful – learning about myself. Cheryl's view is that in work of this kind tutors ideally need to be:

> required to be in some kind of facilitated group ... where we are modelling for ourselves, and having modelled for us by a facilitator, some of that holding [that we provide for students], and that we have a shared experience of each other in our more vulnerable states as well as in our more strengthened ones.

In such a setting tutors could explore both transference and countertransference issues, not only those at work in their relations with students, but also with each other. This kind of support is difficult in a context where, as was the case at Sussex, the teaching was primarily carried out by associate, hourly-paid teaching staff and where resources were always an issue. What was possible was a termly tutor group meeting to discuss administrative matters and the development of courses. Tutors teaching *Writing and Groups* also acted as mentors to each other, which some found invaluable, whilst others needed to find support beyond the tutor team. Because the bulk of teaching took place on the same Saturday once a fortnight tutors were also able to support each other informally during breaks. But more formal support is needed for tutors engaged in transformative learning of this kind, and higher education institutions offering it need to recognise that.

Another challenge highlighted by tutors is the necessity of having not only the expertise to hold students in their emotional learning, but also the relevant academic expertise. Cheryl says:

> I think the major breakthroughs that are made in the students' development happen when they have an experience of themselves and of their writing that doesn't fit neatly into an academic framework. I think there are also academic breakthroughs that they make ..., but I think it's when the two come together that the most significant changes [occur]. That's the single most exciting thing about the course, and I do think that presents a huge challenge to the tutors individually and as a tutor group as to how you hold both those areas of expertise in balance and whether or not we come necessarily with both ... .

Having two tutors teaching alongside each other, which was possible in some courses over the years, was a very effective means of developing their expertise across the different aspects of the programme. Occasionally tutors also sat in on a course as a participant–observer, but both these options have significant resource implications, for the institution and for tutors. Apart from appropriate academic and personal development skills, tutors also need, of course, to be experienced creative writers and teachers of writing, so in all they need three different areas of expertise, and it was challenging over the years to find tutors with all of these. Ideally, tutors wishing to teach CWPD in higher education need to have a Master's degree in a relevant subject and some kind of basic therapeutic training, as recommended by *Lapidus* for people wishing to work with creative writing in health and social care, in addition to writing and teaching experience.

Challenges arising from the hybrid nature of the CWPD programme

The challenges both for students and tutors arising from the hybrid nature of the CWPD programme stem from its origins in a more standard creative writing programme. As discussed in Chapter 1, the programme set out to cater for a wide range of people, including those seeking to develop or free up their creative writing through self-reflection, those seeking deeper insight into themselves through creative writing, and those seeking to acquire skills for working with creative writing in the community. Consequently people came to the programme with very different needs and expectations, creating a number of tensions.

Tensions around giving feedback on creative writing

One of the main tensions was around giving and receiving feedback on creative work. Some Group 2 students, like Maria, who experienced significant opening-up in the early stages, needed more opportunities for personal sharing in the reading groups, whilst others, like Harriet, who were more focused on developing their creative writing, were seeking in-depth constructive critical feedback on work-in-progress. This was also a problem for some people in *Writing and Groups*. As discussed in Chapter 9, the feedback hand-out students received in Course 1 suggested engaging with each other's writing by focusing on their own felt response to it. This worked well for some, but less well for those with specific needs, such as Maria and Harriet. To try and remedy this, we suggested that when writers discussed their work they should indicate what kind of response they were seeking, whether a personal or a literary critical one, or both if time allowed, and students received an additional hand-out on how to respond in a more literary critical way. But we did not provide explicit guidance on how to respond when people were seeking a more personal kind of sharing, which clearly was an omission. Claire gives us a good picture of the frustrations of the feedback process in Course 1:

> As a four we gelled superficially, but were not adept at offering the depth of feedback we clearly all craved. I repeatedly wanted to know more about the

circumstances of each piece read out. The questions I asked were of the emotions and outcome created by a piece, and less of its style, structure and content. I realised that I was using the work as bridges into the writers more than as a basis on which to learn from and develop my fellow students. I was doing what I feared the others might do to me.

Whilst it was, of course, desirable that students got to know each other better through their writing, focusing on their own felt response in the first instance prevented what might have been experienced by some as intrusive probing at this early stage, and it is interesting to see this at work here. However, when the discussion *did* move away from the text into personal development issues in Claire's Course 2 reading group, she did not feel equipped to deal with it:

> Sometimes what is revealed in the writing is *big stuff*. It's easy for discussion to move away from the actual writing and towards the impact of the events revealed and the personal development that may have followed. But I haven't always felt adept enough about having those conversations and closing them as a group in a safe and supportive way.

Obviously we were not encouraging students to psychoanalyse each other, and we were also trying to discourage lengthy offloading of individuals' painful material, hence the starting guidelines, but these comments highlight the need for broader guidance on how to respond when challenging personal development issues emerge in a context where sufficient trust has developed. In fact, students need guidance on three different kinds of feedback: (a) their felt personal response to others' writing; (b) their suggestions for how that writing might be developed; and (c) ways of responding when the writer is seeking personal development through their writing. Whilst learning how to do (a) and (b) is fairly straightforward, although not necessarily easy, the third might well require students to undertake some person-centred reading and tutors to model the process. Indeed all three approaches would benefit from more tutor modelling.

With regard to (b), some Group 2 students report frustration that the level of feedback did not gain critical depth until *Independent Study*. Ideally, all students needed to take a *Writing Practice* course where they could focus on developing their creative writing and learning how to give in-depth constructive critical feedback, but this was difficult to achieve within an already crowded two-year programme. Students could, of course, be expected to take a creative writing course as a prerequisite. Conversely, in some of the craft-focused courses such as *Writing Practice* and *Independent Study* the personal development dimension seems to have got lost, with groups becoming more like a standard Master's in creative writing, with their associated competitiveness and sometimes very challenging levels of criticism.

These various points highlight the importance for this work of helping students to gain confidence in giving different kinds of feedback, whether through hand-outs, or reading and discussion, or modelling by tutors. They also highlight again the importance for tutors of having all three areas of expertise mentioned above, for even within a craft-focused course the personal development process does need to be kept in view for those students for whom it is ongoing. As Christine says, the tutor group needed to be able to hold 'the emotional arc of each student's journey' through the programme, in the way that she felt we had come to hold the 'intellectual arc'.

Tensions around assessment

Another significant tension at the heart of the CWPD programme was how to balance the needs of students engaged in sometimes very challenging personal development work with the needs of the institution for them to demonstrate their learning through formal assessment. This is something we struggled with as a tutor team and, whilst some progress was made, more could be done. Because the CWPD programme evolved out of the Certificate in Creative Writing with its focus on developing the writing, assessment in the early years included assessing the creative writing produced in Course 1 alongside the reflective essay. This inevitably created a conflict, which was quite acute for some Group 1 students. One says:

> I felt strongly (and voiced this at the time) that there was a strong conflict within the course between personal writing and using writing as a therapeutic tool. The exercises were based around the latter yet the unformed products of this were 'judged' as the former, and of course they weren't written as such: this 'product' was poor artistically, and tutor feedback underlined this.

As a consequence, she goes on to say, the Diploma 'sapped all confidence in my own writing, and I stopped'.[5] In light of students' feedback we subsequently stopped assessing the creative writing in *Writing for Personal Development* and *Writing and Groups*, and focused instead on assessing students' reflections on the writing and the writing process in the end-of-course essays. This worked much better. However, the creative writing continued to be assessed in *Contexts for Practice* in Year 2, which was a problem for students with little or no experience of engaging in creative writing, and with little opportunity in Year 1 for direct work on the craft, as discussed above. One solution to this might be to give students the *option* in all Year 2 courses of having their creative writing assessed, rather than it being mandatory. Cheryl disagrees with this, saying that 'for writing to work in a personal development context there needs to be an emphasis on quality, as this is what allows the writing to reach and communicate beyond the individual'. This is an important point. However, it may be that group sharing can already achieve this. In light of the effectiveness of having just such a range of assessment options in *Independent Study* (see Chapter 1), a flexible approach of this kind across the programme as a whole could make assessment more beneficial.

Linked to the above is the challenge of running this kind of programme in the context of the less 'soft' structures of academic exam boards and associated committees where submission dates, at least at Sussex, are absolute and extensions only granted for significant mitigating circumstances. Claire's experience of trying to get an extension for the submission of her *Independent Study* on the grounds of an unexpected increase in her professional workload ran into serious problems, causing her extreme stress at a time when she was already feeling fragile as a result of opening-up to painful personal insights. Her view is that:

> the university authorities were unwilling or unable to understand how the content and requirements of this course might impact a student in my position. ... [They] showed absolutely no evidence of understanding *how* people learn and the differences that exist across the range of subjects offered by the university.

Whilst I am obviously not privy to the University's version of events here, Claire's point that universities need to understand the kind of learning taking place in programmes such as CWPD is important. Where much of the work is carried out with the aid of 'soft' curricular and pedagogical structures, the necessarily 'harder' institutional macrostructures need to have sufficient flexibility to take account of the sometimes fragile states of the learners involved. Clearly there is work here for the convener to make sure university authorities are adequately briefed.

Implications for adult learning

The above discussions carry a number of important implications for a transformative learning approach of this kind:

- It is not suitable for everyone, and it is crucial that students are made aware of the challenges at the interview stage;
- Tutors need to have therapeutic as well as subject-specific training for facilitating the multiple modes of learning taking place in this context;
- Students need to be supported across the whole period of study, including the long vacation and periods of independent study, and need to be fully aware of the possibility of extra support via in-house counselling services;
- Tutors also need to be supported, for example through peer mentoring and/or a facilitated group, and need to be able to share information about students' experience as they progress through the programme;
- Careful consideration needs to be given to the question of whether assessment should be flexible to cater for the needs of students pursuing different pathways through the programme;

- Students need more explicit training, within the programme, on how to engage with each other via their creative work in a personal development context;
- Academic institutions need to be aware of the challenges for students of transformative learning.

In sum, a transformative learning programme of this kind needs more support than is usual, whether from the convener, the tutors, or the institution generally. One way of facilitating this, of course, is to locate it not in adult education, as was the case at Sussex, but in a counselling or psychotherapy context. This is, in fact, what has been done with the MSc in Creative Writing for Therapeutic Purposes at The Metanoia Institute in Bristol. Here the emphasis is less on the development of the creative writing and more on personal and professional development for people wishing to augment existing skills or to start working in this new field, with participants having some therapeutic support within the programme. This is a useful approach, but whilst it might have alleviated some of the tensions in the Sussex format, it would have meant losing some of the clear advantages in a personal development context of combining multiple modes of learning. Focusing on personal development via the development of an arts-specific skill in an educational context clearly enables learners to engage deeply with their learning and 'selfing' processes, and problems they might be having with them. This is a different kind of learning from developing professional skills, although it can be combined with it.

Further, as I said in Chapter 1, the programme attracted a very varied and interesting group of learners, making for a rich and stimulating learning environment. For many of the people who participated, the combination of developing creative writing skills and engaging in a degree of self-exploration and studying the connection between the two brought their interests together in a unique way. And some of those who benefitted most would not have applied if it had been located in a counselling context or had been more directly focused on personal development. Indeed at least two Group 2 students applied to the MA as an alternative to therapy, saying they did not want just to explore their psyche, but to produce a significant piece of creative work in the process. This brings me full-circle to the question of the identity of the programme which I discussed in a preliminary way in Chapter 1. Whilst I have come to think of it as a form of transformative learning, is it perhaps more appropriately thought of as a form of therapeutic education? And if so, what does this have to say about the relationship between transformative learning and psychotherapy? This is the subject of the final chapter.

Notes

1 An example of this beyond my study is Jane Mathison's experience of learning to ride a horse through a body-focused method (Mathison and Tosey, 2008).

2 This is a further example of how the research project provides another level of reflection and containment.
3 MA students sometimes spontaneously extended their reading groups into email groups outside the programme. This was before contact via online groups became more generally available at Sussex.
4 This was the first year these courses became available as options for students not wishing to follow the 'professional development' route.
5 This student subsequently returned to creative writing, and to the programme to complete her MA.

Chapter 12

Is transformative learning a form of therapeutic education?

The connection between transformative learning and psychotherapy is occasionally mentioned in the literature, but rarely explored in depth. Illeris classifies transformative learning as a kind of learning that involves 'personality change and is characterised by simultaneous restructuring in the cognitive, the emotional, and the social dimensions', which resonates with the Sussex model. He points out that: 'Such processes have traditionally not been conceived of as learning, but they are well known in the field of psychotherapy', and he points to Carl Rogers's concept of 'significant learning' (1951) as the first attempt to 'connect such processes to learning theory' (Illeris, 2004b: 84). As noted previously, for Rogers significant learning takes place when the organisation of the self undergoes change (Illeris, 2004a: 94).

For Mezirow the difference between transformative learning and psychotherapy lies in the nature of the reflective work taking place:

> Critical reflection in the context of psychotherapy focuses on assumptions regarding feelings pertaining to interpersonal relationships; in adult education its focus is on an infinitely wider range of concepts and their accompanying cognitive, affective, and conative[1] dimensions.
>
> (Mezirow, 2000: 23)

In fact psychotherapy can also focus on more than just interpersonal relationships, so this distinction does not get us very far. Also identifying critical reflection as the main feature in common between psychotherapy and adult learning misses the important role of embodied–experiential learning in both these activities. Patricia Cranton's suggestion, at a transformative learning conference, that the only difference between what she does and psychotherapy is that she is not a therapist is equally limited. It implies that transformative learning *is* psychotherapy but can be carried out by people who do not have the qualifications to do it. Yet, as Yorks and Kasl point out, tutors often shy away from whole-person learning because they feel ill-prepared (Yorks and Kasl, 2006: 46). Clearly there is a need for a deeper exploration of this relationship.

Linden West's description of psychotherapy as a form of adult learning made a deep impression on me when we were writing a paper a few years ago. In fact it triggered in me a perspective shift (although I would not call this transformative learning), causing me to reflect on the similarities between my experience of psychotherapy, in which I was engaged for the second time during the period of the research, and students' experience of the CWPD programme. I went into therapy with a well-defended self-concept, which was quite quickly dismantled through my therapist's gentle drawing attention to my obvious need to justify myself to her. This opened me up to a much more challenging sense of self, with anger and loss emerging, and the recognition of two 'sub-personalities' (see Chapter 7) in conflict with each other. My learning in the ensuing period could be described as becoming more aware of bodily-felt cognition, bringing this into the light and exploring its meanings, sometimes symbolically through dream images and metaphors, or poems I had written, and then allowing the new knowledge to sink back into the less conscious context of my everyday functioning. This is very similar to some Group 2 students' trajectories through the CWPD programme.

Of course, I always knew that there were similarities between the programme and psychotherapy. When interviewing applicants I would say that the programme had a therapeutic dimension but was not therapy. But it was only during the research that I was able to explore the connection more deeply, by asking the tutors and Group 2 students to reflect on it in interview. This chapter presents what I found and draws some conclusions.

The connection between CWPD and psychotherapy

Several students describe the creative and reflective writing of the MA as a form of gentle *self*-therapy. Jill feels that:

> it's self-administered ..., in my control. If I'm at all worried about where I'm going with it I can ... do further writing. I'm not exposing myself if I don't [want] to; I'm exposing myself for me to understand.

This implies that she is taking greater responsibility for herself in the MA than would be the case in working with a therapist. What enables her to do this, she says, is the company of others undergoing the same process. For Susanna the writing approach is: 'A very gentle and focused way of doing all the things I had been trying to do for myself and with a therapist', and it is particularly *Writing and Groups* where the group work and sense of community 'allowed an individual confidence and ability to write in safety ..., very much in the way that a good therapeutic relationship operates'.

Several students indicate that the MA has something that psychotherapy lacks. Megan is surprised that she learns so much about herself through the writing in spite of her time in therapy. Susanna's therapy, which she has been having for several years before she starts the MA, has 'moved along at a much quicker speed than before'. This is because: 'Writing allows me to be with myself, and the MA has enabled that by *requiring* me to be with myself – something that was totally impossible for me prior to the course'. Elsewhere she articulates this 'requirement' as 'an incredible sort of permissiveness ... for me to be myself'. Claudia also highlights the value of being given permission to focus on herself in a context where this is not normally the case: '[normally] you go and do the course and get the mark and *you* don't go there, you just take the bits of you that are required to do that course. But this course requires all of me'.

Claire's comment that her *Independent Study* project is 'a form of therapy, to bring many issues full circle through the creative writing and the critical introduction' also highlights the therapeutic value of being required to engage in a range of different learning tasks. In psychotherapy the task is to think one's feelings through the dialogue with the therapist, but in the MA the multiple ways of knowing – embodied–experiential, reflective, critically reflective, collaborative – provide a holistic way of learning about oneself. In fact the desire for holistic self-learning is precisely why some students choose the MA rather than psychotherapy. For Ruth, having a creative end-product is crucial:

> it's not like going to hours and hours of counselling and, you know, all you've got to show at the end of it is hopefully your improved psyche. You'd actually have the whole thing on paper whether it's, I don't know, in the form of fiction, or autobiography, or whatever, so there's something of artistic merit as the end of it. So I could sort of recycle it into something.

Stella feels that producing a substantial piece of creative writing 'is much more constructive and positive and ultimately cathartic' than endlessly analysing her 'issues' with her mother, as might be the case in therapy. The play she writes for *Independent Study* on her difficult relationship with her partner provides, as she indicates in her Critical Introduction, a therapeutic vehicle for engaging with who she is in the here and now. It facilitates spontaneity of voice and has scope for creating action, which enables her to bring her struggles alive. In this sense it could be described as a kind of drama therapy, but through writing rather than acting.

For several students who are in therapy alongside the MA, exploring the self simultaneously in two different but closely related contexts is particularly valuable. Susanna says that when material arises through the writing or course work that is too difficult or personal to share with her fellow students, she can take it into her therapy session. Conversely, being involved in writing about herself for the MA 'made me sort of put down [on paper] what I was learning [in therapy, which] allowed me to concretise [it] in different ways, and then together [these two activities] seem to have a great energy'. Claire takes her creative writing into therapy, where her therapist has been 'very good in picking out things that I've talked about that I've learned about from the course and ... threading that through'. For Tess, having the therapy for the more direct self-exploration means that 'the writing then became much more a place where I could just express ideas in a more artistic way', thus freeing-up her creativity.

What this tells me about the relationship between psychotherapy and the transformative learning approach of the MA is that both provide opportunities for a form of deep self-learning, but whereas the former is a one-to-one relationship with a therapist or a group facilitated by a therapist, the MA is what one might call supported or accompanied self-therapy, with writing as the core focus. The support or company is provided by the collaborative community of others engaged in the same process, as well as by tutors who understand the mechanisms of, and are experienced in facilitating, deep psychological change.[2] Further, whilst psychotherapy operates through a combination of embodied–experiential learning, involving engaging with bodily feeling via dream images and metaphors, and reflecting on them, the MA utilises multiple ways of knowing including embodied–experiential learning, reflection, and critical reflection via the study and discussion of course readings and the writing of reflective and academic papers. This creates the possibility of a multi-dimensional experience and understanding of the self in the learning process.[3] There are, as we have seen, tensions for some people between the personal and the academic sides of the work, and the possibility of using the latter to reinforce psychological defences. However, this needs to be seen in the context of how easy it is to spend years in psychotherapy without dismantling one's defences. This is not to suggest that the MA is superior to psychotherapy, but that both have strengths and weaknesses.

The evidence for the deep nature of learning taking place in the CWPD programme and the speed at which change can happen for some people highlights the very powerful nature of its multi-dimensional learning approach with creative life writing at its heart, and this resonates with the increasing focus on the arts in transformative learning (e.g. Leonard and Willis, 2008). For tutor Christine the power of this approach lies in its ability to generate 'a particular kind of challenge', which she calls 'an edge'. The ways people come up against this 'edge', she says, are very varied:

> it may be through text, it may be through the writing exercises, the different kinds of writing, but it also may be coming up against sharing something very personal or all sorts of barriers, a barrier of persona perhaps, a way in which the persona that a person comes with simply cracks under the strain of the great change, and it may happen at any time … . And if they can go through that, that seems to be a very significant moment, and I think the [MA] is strange in offering so many different ways you come at that.

Cheryl takes this idea further. The power of this challenge or 'edge', she says, comes from students:

> being put in situations in which their defences and their resistances come into play and working through those. It feels that when they're taken out of

their safety zone, there's a sort of closing-up and then there's a corresponding opening-up, which is a much more significant opening-up than would have happened without that initial resistance really.

This very much supports my findings. It also again echoes Mezirow's idea, which has been important throughout my discussions, that transformative learning necessarily involves disorienting dilemmas. Whilst his original use of this term refers to events in people's lives that lead them consciously to seek out an environment for change – for which there is plenty of evidence in my study – it can also be seen, as others have pointed out (e.g. Jarvis, 2006), as a jolt or a push that comes from within the learning process itself. As we have seen, the CWPD programme creates these in a variety of ways.

The case for and against therapeutic education with adults

It might seem strange to be suggesting that the CWPD programme should be thought of as a form of therapeutic education when this term is being used – at least in the UK – primarily as a negative, to critique an approach to learning that, it is argued, privileges the emotions at the expense of the development of reason:

> no matter how we are emotionally involved, or not, in intellectual work, we pursue that work in a disinterested way. We are not and must not be intellectually or emotionally biased in the pursuit of knowledge. Emphasis on the emotions in higher education is irrelevant, a time wasting activity based on a generalised notion of personal vulnerability.
> (Ecclestone and Hayes, 2008: 97)

The argument that emotional expression in education encourages people to think of themselves as 'vulnerable' is very much at odds with the findings of my own and others' research (e.g. Taylor, 2001) that engaging with feeling and emotion in a learning context can actually *enhance* learners' inner strength although, as I have found, it may *temporarily* involve them in feeling more fragile. It also ignores a considerable amount of research in the cognitive and neurosciences that highlights the origins of thinking in emotional feeling. According to Damasio's somatic marker hypothesis, human experience is always marked neurally by emotion, so that when we engage in reasoning and decision-making, we are always drawing on emotionally-marked prior learning. Thinking and creativity always involve a 'merging of intuition and reason', where intuition comes from the way the emotions facilitate bodily-felt cognition (Salk, 1985, quoted in Damasio, 1994: 189) (see Chapter 6). This is important knowledge that can be used to help students to attend to their 'felt sense' for learning, rather than thinking of learning as disembodied cognition.

Of course, an approach to learning that *only* focuses on the emotions is likely to be as limiting as one that only focuses on disembodied cognition. The model of learning discussed in Chapter 11 takes into account both feeling-based and critically reflective approaches. As I have said, this follows McGilchrist's picture of the working together of the brain's hemispheres where knowledge of the world comes to us first as bodily-felt experience via the right hemisphere, is then transferred to the more conscious and willed left hemisphere for exploration and clarification, and is then returned to the right hemisphere where it becomes a living and growing body of intuitive knowledge. This is not about championing a vulnerable, diminished subjectivity, as critics suggest, but trying to understand more deeply how learning takes place. It is an approach to learning that is particularly important for people whose thinking or creativity have become blocked for emotional reasons.

In fact there seems to be a great deal of left hemisphere thinking amongst critics of 'therapeutic education', with binaries everywhere. All work highlighting the important role of feeling and emotion in education is indiscriminately gathered into one disapproved of category, and this is opposed to the approved of traditional approach to education that privileges the development of reason and focuses 'on knowledge organised into subject disciplines' (Ecclestone, 2010: 71). There is no middle ground where reason and emotion might be seen to work productively together. Another binary is that between a vulnerable, 'diminished self' resulting from an emotion-informed approach to education and an 'empowered, autonomous and resilient self' (Ecclestone, 2007: 466) resulting from traditional subject-based teaching methods. Conceptualising the psyche as a dynamic system where there is movement and collaboration between the right and left hemispheres is, I would suggest, much more useful. It provides a picture of the psyche as grounded and robust whilst also open and in process. It implies the ability to engage with the full range of the emotions for learning, whilst also having a sufficiently grounded sense of agency from which to manage the engagement with learning and other people. It entails a more *challenging* sense of self than a top-down model, but that does not imply a diminished self.

In the versions of transformative learning that advocate a whole person approach, there is an understanding of the place of feeling and emotion in a multi-dimensional learning process. As Dirkx says:

> The imaginal is not intended to take the place of more analytic, reflective, and rational processes that have been associated with transformative learning. Rather, it is intended to provide a more holistic and integrated way of framing the meaning-making that occurs in contemporary contexts for adult learning.
>
> (Dirkx, 2012: 127)

Similarly in the CWPD programme we were at pains to integrate the experiential dimensions of the programme with the more traditionally academic dimensions,

170 Implications for adult learning

as shown in Chapter 11, and the whole was framed by a series of assessments through which students could demonstrate their different kinds of learning. In fact, Ecclestone denies that she wants to disregard the 'emotional aspects of learning and experience' and that she is primarily concerned about what she sees as the high-profile vulnerability discourse in education and the negative effects of this on education policy (Ecclestone, 2007: 467). If this is the case, then she needs to be rather more discriminating in her analyses of the kinds of learning that explicitly engage the emotions. When seen as a form of deep learning that engages the whole person in careful and well-thought-out ways and involves 'self-work, self-change, and transformation' (Dirkx, 2009: 64), therapeutic education is positive and highly appropriate in a world where the ability to think creatively and independently is more needed than ever. As Terry Hyland says: 'The world can only be changed by people, and often the reflective capacity to change ourselves is precisely what is required before any wider social change is possible' (2010: 528–9).

Implications for transformative learning

If, then, the CWPD programme is both a form of transformative learning and a form of therapeutic education, does this mean that transformative learning is itself a form of therapeutic education? As I have made my way through the literature, it has become obvious that there is much disagreement about what transformative learning actually is, with some commentators suggesting that so many different kinds of learning are now being referred to as transformative that the term has lost its value. Thus Newman suggests that much of what goes under this banner does not involve the 'dramatic,[4] fundamental change' (Merriam *et al.*, 2007: 130) that is said to be its characteristic feature; rather it would be better described as 'good learning', of the kind you might expect in much adult learning. The term 'transformative learning', he concludes, is therefore redundant and should be abolished (Newman, 2011: 37). Clearly I do not agree with this conclusion or I would not have written this book, but I do concur with Kegan (2000) and others that it is important to use the term only where it is fully warranted.

The extensive and unwarranted use of the term transformative learning may be a consequence of the limitations of the field's constructivist paradigm, which I have noted before. Putting the emphasis, as Mezirow's more recent work does, on transformative learning as *discourse*, focuses attention on being able to think outside of external 'frames of reference' such as political orientations, cultural biases, religious doctrines, etc. (Mezirow, 2003: 59). And indeed a great deal of transformative learning focuses on this. Yet this sounds very much like learning to think critically, which any adult or higher education worthy of the name is likely to involve. This is not to say that being able to think outside of existing frames of reference is not part of transformative learning, but my research leads me to the view that the change is first and foremost in the way the self functions and only secondarily in the ability to think outside of existing frames of reference.

To summarise my understanding of transformative change, it involves the relaxing of the autobiographical 'I' in the left hemisphere so that it provides a robust but flexible frame for the mind. This facilitates a shift in the leading edge of the psyche from left hemisphere control to right hemisphere bodily agency, which enhances creativity and independent thinking; and it is this shift from top-down to bottom-up cognition that makes it possible to evaluate with a greater degree of independence – that is, from the perspective of the right hemisphere which, it has been argued, brings us closer to the real – the frames of reference in which we are embedded. Thus it is both an ontological shift, in that it entails increased bodily-felt awareness (and, in a programme such as CWPD, a more explicit understanding) of the operation of innate cognitive mechanisms, and an epistemological shift in awareness and understanding that knowledge emerges out of the dialogue between bodily-felt experience of the world at a low level of consciousness and intentionality and more conscious and intentional language-based thinking. This extends Dirkx's idea of transformative change as a shift in ego consciousness and the generation of a dialogue between the ego and the deeper, unconscious aspects of the psyche, and provides an understanding of Boyd's expansion of consciousness as the larger sense of psychic space and movement that accompanies these ontological and epistemological shifts.

If, then, transformative learning involves a fundamental change in the functioning of the self, it is arguably a kind of therapeutic education, as this is precisely what psychotherapy aims to achieve. This description is apt in light of transformative learning's origins in psychodynamic psychotherapies (see Chapter 7) and of the utilisation, by a number of current approaches, of techniques from a range of psychological therapies, from psychodynamic (Jungian, Horneyan, humanistic) to cognitive (neuro-linguistic programming and mindfulness). As outlined in the previous chapter, this has implications for the way it is taught, the sort of training required by tutors or facilitators, the kinds of people we encourage to participate in it, and the learning environment it needs.

Notes

1 Conative means pertaining to the will (Merriam Webster).
2 Of course, it students are simultaneously in psychotherapy, then the MA functions as an accompaniment to therapy, as in the example of Susanna.
3 Constructivist therapies are more multi-dimensional in that they encourage journal and autobiographical work, and some therapists recommend self-help books to read (McLeod, 1997: 76–80), but there is obviously no explicit study of theory or opportunities for articulating theoretical understandings in essays.
4 Actually Mezirow (1978) says that transformative change can be dramatic or gradual, and my study supports this.

Conclusion

I began this book by suggesting that the changes I saw taking place amongst students of the CWPD programme represented an increase in their sense of agency: their ability to be more self-directed and self-determining in their writing and learning processes and in their relations with others. And indeed agency has been a central concept throughout my explorations. By focusing on underlying structures of students' experience and attempting to understand them within a bio-psycho-social conceptual framework I have learned that agency emerges in the context of structures that are simultaneously robust and flexible and that these structures are both in the psyche and in the learning environment.

It turns out that agency is about having psychic space, but also being able to 'hold' that space so that the imagination can move freely. We learn to do this 'holding' when we let go of trying to control our thinking; when we allow our thoughts to emerge spontaneously out of the feelings that are constantly being generated by our bodily engagement with the environment and only then bring to bear more focused, critical thinking. Learning to do this in an educational context requires that the 'holding' is provided in the first instance by the learning environment. This is because loosening control over our thinking often involves confronting difficult feelings about ourselves and our relations with others. It involves confronting who we *actually* are rather than how we have come to think about ourselves, which can be uncomfortable or painful.

It turns out that creative life writing is a particularly helpful tool for engaging in this process because its flexible cognitive structures press us to relinquish our familiar, sometimes defensive ways of thinking and being and to get closer to what experience feels like. At the same time these structures help us to trust the not-knowing that is intrinsic to creativity and independent thinking, and in that process we begin to learn how to 'hold' the space for the imagination and manage the emotions. It turns out that collaborative, experiential group work similarly challenges us to be more in the moment, but can also provide safe-enough transitional spaces for bringing who we actually are into the open and trying out new ways of being-in-relation. Reflecting on this experience through diaries and learning journals can provide us with further opportunities for 'holding' whatever arises into the space for the imagination, and critical reflection can bring clarity and conceptual understanding to our bodily-felt experience. Engaging in these multiple modes of learning within a containing community of learners can generate a sense of the learning environment as 'a vast space encompassed in which to play and explore'.

The question that remains is to whether the approach discussed here is easily transferable to other adult learning contexts. After all, whilst the people who participated in the CWPD programme were in some ways quite diverse, in other ways they were a very specific group, which arguably made change more likely. Not only were many of them explicitly seeking personal development, but many also had some knowledge of the workings of the literary text, were highly self-reflective and familiar with the therapeutic process. Whilst further research will be needed to answer this question fully, what I can say at this stage is that it *has* proved possible to use some elements of this approach, with care, outside of the creative writing context. For example, I and others have successfully adapted some of the writing exercises for use in professional development workshops (Hunt, 2010b) and in short courses aimed at helping university students to be more creative in their academic writing (e.g. Creme and Hunt, 2002). And others have been developing similar work (e.g. Bolton, 2010). But it is crucially important, particularly in short workshops, for the facilitator to ensure that participants are aware of the challenges, and to create an environment that is sufficiently 'held'. This can be done by making a group contract at the outset and using group writing activities, such as the 'web of words', which can quickly generate cohesion. In short workshops it can also be helpful for participants to share their *reflections* on doing the exercises, rather than sharing the creative writing itself. Letting participants know at the outset that there is no pressure to share the creative writing unless they choose to do so can help reduce tensions. It should not be underestimated how powerful these exercises can be in opening people up to thoughts and feelings normally out of conscious awareness, so great care does need to be taken, and facilitators would be well advised to have some basic therapeutic training.

Ultimately this work is about developing a robust but flexible sense of self that frees up the mind for engaging more creatively in learning and participating more fully in the world. Through the research I have become more acutely aware of how difficult thinking is. Of course I already knew this from my own experience: much of my life has been a painful struggle with not being able to think, and I am clearly not alone in this. How paradoxical that the thing that makes us most human is the thing we find most difficult! And yet perhaps it is not surprising in the context of the vicissitudes of extended consciousness – the fragility of early relationships, the anxieties of upbringing, the consequences of trauma across the lifespan, and the power of language to embed us in its concepts. But I have been particularly struck in exploring students' material by how often formal education has instilled an unhelpful top-down model of thinking. This may be a consequence of what McGilchrist sees as the dominance of the left hemisphere in Western culture, the legacy of post-Enlightenment thinking with its privileging of disembodied reason at the expense of feeling. Discussing the source of thinking in core consciousness, Claire Petitmengin says: 'If our ideas draw their meaning from the preverbal dimension of our experience, then there is no real understanding which does not attain such depth'. And yet:

> at present, teaching consists in most cases of transmitting conceptual and discursive contents of knowledge. The intention is to fix a meaning, not to initiate a movement. Which teaching methods, instead of *transmitting* contents, could elicit the gestures which allow access to the source experience that gives these contents coherence and meaning? Such a teaching approach, based more on initiation than transmission, by enabling children and students to come into contact with the depth of their experience, could re-enchant the classroom.
>
> (Petitmengin, 2007: 79)

At its best the approach we developed at Sussex *both* elicited the inner gestures that allowed access to the source experience *and* transmitted ideas, but not so much in the attempt to 'fix a meaning', rather in the attempt to enable students to think for themselves about the meanings of those gestures. For many – although not for all – it did re-enchant the learning environment. As I was completing this book, a former student from the post-research period emailed to say that the radio play she had written for *Independent Study* was shortly to be broadcast by the BBC. She also said, without knowledge of my findings, that 'the MA changed my life and my internal framework'. Having completed the research, I have a better understanding of what that means. Despite the discontinuation of the MA, I very much hope that the approach we pioneered at Sussex will be taken up by others and, if it is, I would very much like to hear about it. I can be contacted at www.celiahunt.com.

Appendix

The Cohen Park Exercises

Christine Cohen Park

In envisioning the *Writing and Groups* course, I had in mind something close to a groups course on a counselling programme, combining both experiential and theoretical learning, while incorporating the additional experience of being part of a writing group that mirrored as closely as possible those which students might lead in the future. To this end, the writing exercises were focused on exploring aspects of the self.

The writing group needed to have its own integrity and unique self-sufficient sequence of exercises, and yet, because it was situated half-way through the Masters, there were particular considerations to take into account. The students had already done a fair amount of self-reflective writing by the time they reached *Writing and Groups*, and so needed new ways to be stretched in their writing. They were also going to be doing these exercises in an environment involving formal assessment, but this was later removed, so the experience of being in a therapeutic writing group would at best be only partial.

The writing exercises I devised were therefore uniquely tailored to the Masters. They are not exercises I would transpose, per se, to a therapeutic environment proper, because of the element of challenge involved, which in the MA learning environment could be contained and was appropriate. But individual elements of the sequence might be used to good effect in other contexts, and I pinpoint below those I think appropriate for general use with a vulnerable or potentially vulnerable client group.

Two kinds of exercises were employed: those undertaken at home between each meeting of the writing group; and those undertaken in class. I have found, over many years of running writing groups that there will be some participants who benefit from the solitude and time for reflection that writing outside the class allows, whilst others may be too distracted to get much down on paper between classes but surprise themselves by what they can achieve, when prompted, in a spontaneous class situation. My aim, therefore, was to provide a variety of opening prompts, in response to which students could harness and experience their creativity at their own pace and in their own way. The home exercises and the class exercises were linked, so that the longer home exercises were informed by further class work. Thus, if a student felt they had not captured what they were trying to in the work done at home, they might get nearer to it impromptu in the class setting.

Though all the exercises were focused on exploring the self, they were devised in such a way as to provide the maximum writing freedom to students half way through a creative writing Masters. For example, if a student was preoccupied with a novel she was writing and reluctant to engage in further self-reflection, she could approach the exercises as if from one of her characters' perspectives. Students could give the exercise titles the broadest possible interpretation, taking them literally or metaphorically. Prose, poetry, drama – any form of writing was acceptable.

There were five fortnightly sessions and thus four assignments (the first given on the first group meeting) as follows:

- *This is who I am, now*
- *This is where I shelter, how I shelter*
- *This is where I risk, what I risk*
- *This is what I remember*

Ideas in the first three of these furthered the intention to broaden the scope and possibilities. The 'now' in the first exercise was there to allow the students to think about themselves in a time perspective, and also for their writing about themselves to allow for the possibility for change that the statement suggests, which softens it perhaps and makes it slightly less threatening. The second and third exercises are extended by a second phrase, again with the idea that students had the choice of engaging with one or the other. The final exercise was a prompt to come up with one strong memory of being in the group, to fill out the details as a novelist might, bringing the moment alive so that it could become a shared memory.

The shorter, in-class exercises, which dovetailed with, and informed, the first three of the primary exercises, were as follows:

- *This is who I am to ...*
   and then a list of possibilities, some playful or fanciful (with students being encouraged to make up their own):

   ... the sheets on my bed when I left it this morning
   ... the cyclamens I watered yesterday
   ... the women next to me on the bus
   ... the receptionist at work/the doctor's surgery
   ... the pavements I walked along

- **Finding shelter** – *imagining a place of shelter, and then the experience of being in it when it is assailed, and then of ultimately finding it strong enough to provide protection*
- **Risking** – *looking at two poems, one by John Fox and one by Martin Jude Farawell, addressing the topic of risking being listened to, as a prompt for*

students to write about when they had been truly listened to and what it had felt like, and to provide inspiration for taking the risk of being heard in their writing.

In the sequence of exercises, reflection on 'who I am' came first, because for our students an exploration of who the self is at the moment of writing was key. The exercise concerning shelter was placed second to enable students to be in contact with their internal home base during the inevitable emotional buffeting of the group situation, especially in its formative phase, before trust was established and relationships formed. The invitation to consider risks could be interpreted in many ways, including risks in their writing, both in content and form, or personal risks they might take; for some this became a prompt to 'dig deeper'. Consequently this exercise was situated in the fourth of the five sessions, only after the group was established and in its working phase. The final exercise provided the opportunity to bring a scene to life, in other words to be a practitioner of the writing craft, while creating an offering that might enable others to relive the moment, thus contributing to consolidation as the course moved towards its close.

This sequence of exercises was used by all tutors teaching *Writing and Groups*. It had sufficient elasticity and yet containment to fit the unique format of the creative writing and personal development programme, and yielded rich results, in terms of students' personal development and the creativity and quality of writing, year on year.

Outside of a teaching environment such as the one described, these exercises would need to be used with caution, and with modifications. In health care environments the first exercise may well feel too intimidating, though not in all instances. The short in-class version provides a softer option, though any such direct focus on the self may be too intrusive, and even inappropriate in certain circumstances. The shelter exercise has a broader application and could help participants feel more at ease in the group, in writing about their own capacity to create safety. The risk exercise – germane to the Masters – may be not so central to a different client group, and once again the group leader would need to exercise caution in considering its use. The 'remembering' exercise may provide creative consolidation, as a group draws to its close and its participants mourn its impending demise, though not all client groups have the capacity, or in some cases energy for this type of recall. And whilst consolidation and closure are important to any writing group drawing to its close – particularly with vulnerable participants – there are many alternative ways to approach this: memories may be verbal, for example; or they may be 'scribed' by the leader; or they may take the form of a poem in the writing of which everyone has participated.

The sequence outlined above constitutes the Cohen Park Exercises, copyrighted by me, Christine Cohen Park. Should you have any queries concerning their use, please contact me via www.celiahunt.com.

© Christine Cohen Park

References

Abbs, P. (1974) *Autobiography in Education*, London: Heinemann.
Alhadeff-Jones, M. (2012) 'Transformative learning and the challenges of complexity', in E.W. Taylor and E. Cranton (eds), *The Handbook of Transformative Learning: Theory, Research, and Practice*, San Francisco, CA: Jossey-Bass.
Anzieu, D. (1984) *The Group and the Unconscious*, London and Boston, MA: Routledge and Kegan Paul.
Archer, M.S. (1995) *Realist Social Theory: The Morphogenetic Approach*, Cambridge: Cambridge University Press.
——(2000) *Being Human: The Problem of Agency*, Cambridge: Cambridge University Press.
——(2003) 'The private life of the social agent: what difference does it make?', in J. Cruickshank (ed.), *Critical Realism: The Difference it Makes*, New York and London: Routledge.
Bakhtin, M. (1981) 'Discourse in the novel', in M. Holquist (ed.), *The Dialogic Imagination: Four Essays by M.M. Bakhtin*, Austin, TX: University of Texas Press.
——(1984) *Problems of Dostoevsky's Poetics*, Manchester: Manchester University Press.
Bal, M. (1985) *Narratology: Introduction to the Theory of Narrative*, Toronto: University of Toronto Press.
Bazeley, P. (2007) *Qualitative Data Analysis with NVivo*, London: Sage.
Beahrs, J.O. (1982) *Unity and Multiplicity: Multilevel Consciousness of Self in Hypnosis, Psychiatric Disorder and Mental Health*, New York: Brunner/Mazel.
Berger, J.G. (2004) 'Dancing on the threshold of meaning: recognizing and understanding the growing edge', *Journal of Transformative Education*, 2: 336–51.
Bertalanffy, L. von (1968) *General System Theory: Foundations, Developments, Applications*, New York: George Braziller.
Bhaskar, R. and Danermark, B. (2006) 'Metatheory, interdisciplinary and disability research: a critical realist perspective', *Scandinavian Journal of Disability Research*, 8: 278–97.
Bion, W.R. (1962) *Learning from Experience*, London: Heinemann.
Bollas, C. (1995) *Cracking Up: The Work of Unconscious Experience*, London: Routledge.
Bolton, G. (2010) *Reflective Practice: Writing and Professional Development*, 3rd edition. London: Sage.
Booth, W. (1991) *The Rhetoric of Fiction*, 2nd edition, Harmondsworth: Penguin.
Bowden, E.M., Jung-Beeman, M., Fleck, J. and Kounios, J. (2005) 'New approaches to demystifying insight', *Trends in Cognitive Sciences*, 9: 322–8.
Boyd, R.D. (1991) *Personal Transformations in Small Groups: A Jungian Perspective*, London and New York: Tavistock/Routledge.

Boyd, R.D. and Myers, J.G. (1988) 'Transformative education', *International Journal of Lifelong Education*, 7: 261–84.
Britzman, D. (2003) *After-Education: Anna Freud, Melanie Klein, and Psychoanalytic Histories of Learning*, Albany, NY: State University of New York Press.
Brookfield, S. (2000) 'Transformative learning as ideology critique', in J. Mezirow and Associates, *Learning as Transformation: Critical Perspectives on a Theory in Progress*, San Francisco, CA: Jossey-Bass.
Brown, G. (2009) 'The ontological turn in education: the place of the learning environment', *Journal of Critical Realism*, 8: 5–34.
Bruner, J.S. (1990) *Acts of Meaning*, Cambridge, MA and London: Harvard University Press.
Carter, B. and New, N. (2004) *Making Realism Work: Realist Social Theory and Empirical Research*, London and New York: Routledge.
Chatman, S. (1978) *Story and Discourse: Narrative Structure in Fiction and Film*, Ithaca, NY and London: Cornell University Press.
Chazan, R. (2001) *The Group as Therapist*, London and Philadelphia, PA: Jessica Kingsley.
Clark, T. (1997) *The Theory of Inspiration*, Manchester: Manchester University Press.
Coltart, N. (1996) *Slouching Towards Bethlehem and Further Psychoanalytic Explorations*, London: Free Association Books.
Corey, M.S. and Corey, G. (2002) *Groups: Process and Practice*, 6th edition, Pacific Grove, CA: Brooks/Cole.
Cox, M. and Theilgaard, A. (1987) *Mutative Metaphors in Psychotherapy: The Aeolian Mode*, London: Tavistock.
Cozolino, L. (2002) *The Neuroscience of Psychotherapy: Building and Rebuilding the Human Brain*, New York: Norton.
Cranton, P. (2000) 'Individual differences and transformative learning', in J. Mezirow and Associates, *Learning as Transformation: Critical Perspectives on a Theory in Progress*, San Francisco, CA: Jossey-Bass.
Cranton, P. and Taylor, E.W. (2012) 'Transformative learning theory', in E.W. Taylor and E. Cranton (eds), *The Handbook of Transformative Learning: Theory, Research, and Practice*, San Francisco, CA: Jossey-Bass.
Creme, P. (2008) 'A space for academic play: student learning journals as transitional writing', *Arts and Humanities in Higher Education*, 7: 49–64.
Creme, P. and Hunt, C. (2002) 'Creative participation in the essay writing process', *Arts and Humanities in Higher Education*, 1: 145–66.
Damasio, A. (1994) *Descartes' Error: Emotion, Reason and the Human Brain*, New York: Harper Collins.
——(2000) *The Feeling of What Happens: Body, Emotion and the Making of Consciousness*, London: Vintage.
——(2003) *Looking for Spinoza: Joy, Sorrow and the Feeling Brain*, London: Heinemann.
——(2010) *Self Comes to Mind: Constructing the Conscious Brain*, London: Heinemann.
Danielian, J. (2010) 'Meta-realization in Horney and the teaching of psychoanalysis', *American Journal of Psychoanalysis*, 70: 10–22.
Davis, B. and Sumara, D.J. (2001) 'Learning communities: understanding the workplace as a complex system', *New Directions for Adult and Continuing Education*, 92: 85–95.
Davis, B., Sumara, D.J. and Luce-Kapler, R. (2000) *Engaging Minds: Learning and Teaching in a Complex World*, Hillsdale, NJ: Lawrence Erlbaum.

Derrida, J. (1978) *Writing and Difference*, trans. A. Bass, London: Routledge and Kegan Paul.

Devinsky, O. (2000) 'Right cerebral hemisphere dominance for a sense of corporeal and emotional self', *Epilepsy and Behavior*, 1: 60–73.

Dirkx, J. M. (1997) 'Nurturing soul in adult learning', in P. Cranton (ed.), *Transformative Learning in Action: Insights from Practice*, New Directions for Adult and Continuing Education, No. 74, San Francisco, CA: Jossey-Bass.

——(2006) 'Engaging emotions in adult learning: a Jungian perspective on emotion and transformative learning', in E.W. Taylor (ed.), *Teaching for Change*, New Directions for Adult and Continuing Education, No. 109, San Francisco, CA: Jossey-Bass.

——(2008) 'Care of the self: mythopoetic dimensions of professional preparation and development', in T. Leonard and P. Willis (eds), *Pedagogies of the Imagination: Mythopoetic Curriculum in Educational Practice*, Heidelberg: Springer.

——(2009) 'Facilitating transformative learning: engaging emotions in an online context', in J. Mezirow and E.W. Taylor (eds), *Transformative Learning in Practice: Insights from Community, Workplace, and Higher Education*, San Francisco, CA: Jossey-Bass.

——(2012) 'Nurturing soul work', in E.W. Taylor and E. Cranton (eds), *The Handbook of Transformative Learning: Theory, Research, and Practice*, San Francisco, CA: Jossey-Bass.

Dissanajake, E. (2001) 'Antecedents of the temporal arts in early mother–infant interaction', in N. Wallin, B. Merker and S. Brown (eds), *The Origins of Music*, Cambridge, MA: MIT Press.

Ecclestone, K. (2007) 'Resisting images of the "diminished self": the implications of emotional well-being and emotional engagement in education policy', *Journal of Education Policy*, 22: 455–70.

——(2010) 'Promoting emotionally vulnerable subjects: the educational implications of an "epistemology of the emotions"', *Journal of the Pacific Circle Consortium for Education*, 22: 57–76.

Ecclestone, K. and Hayes, D. (2008) *The Dangerous Rise of Therapeutic Education*, New York and London: Routledge.

Elbow, P. (1998) *Writing with Power: Techniques for Mastering the Writing Process*, 2nd edition, New York and Oxford: Oxford University Press.

Fenwick, T. (2000) 'Expanding conceptions of experiential learning: a review of the five contemporary perspectives on cognition', *Adult Education Quarterly*, 50: 243–72.

Fenwick, T. (2003) 'Reclaiming and re-embodying experiential learning through complexity science', *Studies in the Education of Adults*, 35: 123–41.

Finger, M. and Asun, J.M. (2001) *Adult Education at the Crossroads: Learning Our Way Out*, London and New York: Zed Books.

Fonagy, P., Gergely, G., Jurist, E.L. and Target, M. (2002) *Affect Regulation, Mentalization, and the Development of the Self*, London and New York: Karnac Books.

Fosha, D. (2005) 'Emotion, true self, true other, core state: toward a clinical theory of affective change process', *Psychoanalytic Review*, 92: 513–52.

Foucault, M. (1971) *Madness and Civilization: A History of Insanity in the Age of Reason*, London and New York: Routledge.

Fox, E. (2008) *Emotion Science: Cognitive and Neuroscientific Approaches to Understanding Human Emotions*, Basingstoke: Palgrave Macmillan.

Froggett, L. and Richards, B. (2002) 'Exploring the bio-psycho-social', *European Journal of Psychotherapy and Counselling*, 5: 321–6.

Gallagher, S. (2008) 'How to undress the effective mind: an interview with Jaak Panksepp', *Journal of Consciousness Studies,* 15: 89–119.

Gallagher, S. and Zahavi, D. (2008) *The Phenomenological Mind: An Introduction to Philosophy of Mind and Cognitive Science,* London and New York: Routledge.

Gendlin, E. (1991) 'Thinking beyond patterns: body, language and situations', in B. Den Ouden and M. Moen (eds), *The Presence of Feeling in Thought,* New York: Peter Lang.

——(1996) *Focusing-Oriented Psychotherapy: A Manual of the Experiential Method,* New York and London: Guilford Press.

Genette, G. (1980) *Narrative Discourse,* trans. J.E. Lewin, Ithaca, NY: Cornell University Press.

Gergen, K. (1991) *The Saturated Self: Dilemmas of Identity in Modern Life,* New York: Basic Books.

Gerrig, R.J. (1993) *Experiencing Narrative Worlds: On the Psychological Activities of Reading,* New Haven. CT: Yale University Press.

Giddens, A. (1990) *The Consequences of Modernity,* Cambridge: Polity Press.

Green, L. (2012) 'Transformative learning: a passage through the liminal zone', in A. Bainbridge and L. West (eds), *Psychoanalysis and Education: Minding a Gap,* London: Karnac.

Greenberg, J.R. and Mitchell, S.A. (1983) *Object Relations in Psychoanalytic Theory,* Cambridge, MA: Harvard University Press.

Gunnlaugson, O. (2007) 'Shedding light on the underlying forms of transformative learning theory: introducing three distinct categories of consciousness', *Journal of Transformative Education,* 5: 134–47.

Hartill, G. (1998) 'The web of words: collaborative writing and mental health', in C. Hunt and F. Sampson (eds), *The Self on the Page: Theory and Practice of Creative Writing in Personal Development,* London and Philadelphia, PA: Jessica Kingsley.

Herman, D. (2002) *Story Logic: Problems and Possibilities of Narrative,* Lincoln, NE: University of Nebraska Press.

Herman, D., Jahn, M. and Ryan M.L. (eds) (2005) *Routledge Encyclopedia of Narrative Theory,* London and New York: Routledge.

Hermans, H.J.M. (2002) 'The dialogical self as a society of mind: introduction', *Theory and Psychology,* 12: 147–60.

Heron, J. (1992) *Feeling and Personhood: Psychology in Another Key,* London: Sage.

Hollway, W. and Jefferson, T. (2000) *Doing Qualitative Research Differently: Free Association, Narrative and the Interview Method,* London: Sage.

Holub, M. (1990) *The Dimension of the Present Moment,* London: Faber.

Horn, J. and Wilburn, D. (2005) 'The embodiment of learning', *Educational Philosophy and Theory,* 37: 745–60.

Horney, K. (1937) *The Neurotic Personality of Our Time,* New York: Norton.

——(1939a) *New Ways in Psychoanalysis,* London: Kegan, Paul, Trench, Trubner.

——(1939b) 'Can you take a stand?', *Journal of Adult Education,* 11: 129–32.

——(1942) *Self-Analysis,* New York: Norton.

——(1946) *Our Inner Conflicts,* New York: Norton.

——(1951) *Neurosis and Human Growth: The Struggle Toward Self-Realisation,* New York: Norton.

——(1987) *Final Lectures,* D.H. Ingram (ed.), New York and London: Norton.

——(1999) *The Therapeutic Process: Essays and Lectures,* B.J. Paris (ed.), New Haven, CT and London: Yale University Press.

——(2000) *The Unknown Karen Horney: Essays on Gender, Culture, and Psychoanalysis*, B.J. Paris (ed. and introductions), New Haven, CT and London: Yale University Press.

Hunt, C. (2000) *Therapeutic Dimensions of Autobiography in Creative Writing*, London: Jessica Kingsley.

——(2001) 'Assessing personal writing', *Auto/Biography*, 9: 89–94.

——(2004a) 'Writing and reflexivity: training to facilitate writing for personal development', in F. Sampson (ed.), *Creative Writing in Health and Social Care*, London: Jessica Kingsley.

——(2004b) 'Reading ourselves: imagining the reader in the writing process', in G. Bolton, S. Howlett, C. Lago and J.K. Wright (eds), *Writing Cures: An Introductory Handbook of Writing in Counselling and Therapy*, Hove: Brunner Routledge.

——(2010a) 'Therapeutic effects of writing fictional autobiography', *Life Writing*, 7: 231–44.

——(2010b) 'Exploring career identities through creative writing', *NICEC Journal*, 23: 18–19.

Hunt C. and Sampson, F. (1998) *The Self on the Page: Theory and Practice of Creative Writing in Personal Development*, London: Jessica Kingsley.

——(2006) *Writing: Self and Reflexivity*, Basingstoke: Palgrave Macmillan.

Hunt, C. and West, L. (2006) 'Learning in a border country: using psychodynamic ideas in teaching and research', *Studies in the Education of Adults*, 38: 160–77.

——(2009) 'Salvaging the self in adult learning', *Studies in the Education of Adults*, 41: 68–82.

Hyland, T. (2010) 'Mindfulness, adult learning and therapeutic education: integrating the cognitive and affective domains of learning', *International Journal of Lifelong Education*, 29: 517–32.

Illeris, K. (2004a) *The Three Dimensions of Learning: Contemporary Learning Theory in the Tension Field between the Cognitive, the Emotional and the Social*, 2nd edition, Leicester: Niace.

——(2004b) 'Transformative learning in the perspective of a comprehensive learning theory', *Journal of Transformative Education*, 2: 79–89.

Jahn, M. (2007) 'Focalization', in D. Herman (ed.), *The Cambridge Companion to Narrative*, Cambridge: Cambridge University Press.

James, W. (1901) *Principles of Psychology*, London: Macmillan.

Jarvis, C. (2006) 'Using fiction for transformation', *New Directions for Adult and Continuing Education*, 109: 69–77.

——(2012) 'Fiction and film and transformative learning', in E.W. Taylor and E. Cranton (eds), *The Handbook of Transformative Learning: Theory, Research, and Practice*, San Francisco, CA: Jossey-Bass.

Johnson, M. (2007) *The Meaning of the Body: Aesthetics of Human Understanding*, Chicago, IL and London: University of Chicago Press.

Johnson-Laird, P.N. (1983) *Mental Models: Toward a Cognitive Science of Language, Inference, and Consciousness*, Cambridge, MA: Harvard University Press.

Jung, C.G. (1983) 'The Shadow', in A. Storr (ed.), *The Essential Jung*, Princeton, NJ: Princeton University Press.

Kane, J. (2004) 'Poetry as right-hemispheric language', *Journal of Consciousness Studies*, 11: 21–59.

Keats, J. (1958) *The Letters of John Keats*, M.B. Forman (ed.), London and New York: Oxford University Press.

Kegan, R. (1982) *The Evolving Self: Problem and Process in Human Development*, Cambridge, MA and London: Harvard University Press.

—— (2000) 'What "form" transforms? A constructive–developmental approach to transformative learning', in J. Mezirow and Associates, *Learning as Transformation: Critical Perspectives on a Theory in Progress*, San Francisco, CA: Jossey-Bass.

Keunen, B. (2011) *Time and Imagination: Chronotopes in Western Narrative Culture*, Evanston, IL: Northwestern University Press.

Kitchenham, A. (2008) 'The evolution of John Mezirow's transformative learning theory', *Journal of Transformative Education*, 6: 104–23.

Knights, B. (1992) *From Reader to Reader: Theory, Text and Practice in the Study Group*, New York and London: Harvester Wheatsheaf.

Koriat, A. (2007) 'Metacognition and consciousness', in P.D. Zelazo, M. Moskovitch and E. Thompson (eds), *The Cambridge Handbook of Consciousness*, Cambridge: Cambridge University Press.

Kristeva, J. (1984) *Revolution in Poetic Language*, trans. L.S. Roudiez, New York: Columbia University Press.

Kuhn, T. (1962) *The Structure of Scientific Revolutions*, Chicago, IL: University of Chicago Press.

Lakoff, G. and Johnson, M. (1980) *Metaphors We Live By*, Chicago, IL: Chicago University Press.

—— (1999) *Philosophy in the Flesh: The Embodied Mind and Its Challenge to Western Thought*, New York: Basic Books.

Laplanche, J. and Pontalis, J.B. (2004) *The Language of Psychoanalysis*, London: Hogarth.

Leiper, R. and Maltby, M. (2004) *The Psychodynamic Approach to Therapeutic Change*, London: Sage.

Leonard, T. and Willis, P. (2008) *Pedagogies of the Imagination: Mythopoetic Curriculum in Educational Practice*, Heidelberg: Springer.

Lewis, M.D. (2002) 'The dialogical brain: contributions of emotional neurobiology to understanding the dialogical self', *Theory and Psychology*, 12: 175–90.

—— (2005) 'Bridging emotion theory and neurobiology through dynamic systems modeling', *Behavioral and Brain Sciences*, 28: 169–245.

Luria, A.R. (1973) *The Working Brain*, trans. B. Haigh, Harmondsworth, Middlesex: Penguin.

McDougall, J. (1985) *Theatres of the Mind: Illusion and Truth on the Psychoanalytic Stage*, London: Free Association Books.

McGilchrist, I. (2009) *The Master and his Emissary: The Divided Brain and the Making of the Western World*, New Haven, CT and London: Yale University Press.

McLeod, J. (1997) *Narrative and Psychotherapy*, London: Sage.

Mantel, H. (2004) *Giving Up the Ghost*, London: Harper Collins.

Mathison, J. and Tosey, P. (2008) 'Riding into transformative learning', *Journal of Consciousness Studies*, 15: 67–88.

—— (2009) 'Exploring moments of knowing', in C. Petitmengin (ed.), *Ten Years of Viewing from Within: The Legacy of Francisco Varela*, Exeter: Imprint Academic.

Merriam, S.B., Caffarella, R.S. and Baumgartner, L.M. (2007) *Learning in Adulthood: A Comprehensive Guide*, 3rd edition, San Francisco, CA: John Wiley.

Merrill, B. and West, L. (2009) *Using Biographical Methods in Social Research*, London: Sage.

Mezirow, J. (1978) 'Perspective transformation', *Adult Education Quarterly*, 28: 100–10.

——(1981) 'A critical theory of adult learning and education', *Adult Education Quarterly*, 32: 3–24.
——(1991) *Transformative Dimensions of Adult Learning*. San Francisco, CA: Jossey-Bass, Kindle edition.
——(1998) 'On critical reflection', *Adult Education Quarterly*, 48: 185–98.
——(2000) 'Learning to think like an adult', in J. Mezirow and Associates (eds), *Learning as Transformation*. San Francisco, CA: Jossey-Bass.
——(2003) 'Transformative learning as discourse', *Journal of Transformative Education*, 1: 58–63.
Milner, M. (1952) *A Life of One's Own*, Harmondsworth: Penguin Books.
——(1971) *On Not Being Able to Paint*, Oxford: Heinemann.
Moon, J. (2004) *A Handbook of Reflective and Experiential Learning: Theory and Practice*, London and New York: Routledge Falmer.
Moskowitz, C. (1998) 'The self as source: creative writing generated from personal reflection', in C. Hunt and F. Sampson (eds), *The Self on the Page: Theory and Practice of Creative Writing in Personal Development*, London: Jessica Kingsley.
—— (2009) 'Life writing the future', paper presented to *The Work of Life Writing* conference at Kings College, London, downloadable at www.cherylmoskowitz.com
Neisser, U. (1988) 'Five modes of self-knowledge', *Philosophical Psychology*, 1: 35–58.
Neisser, U. and Fivush, R. (eds) (1994) *The Remembering Self: Construction and Accuracy in the Self-Narrative*, Cambridge: Cambridge University Press.
Nelles, W. (1993) 'Historical and implied authors and readers', *Comparative Literature*, 45: 22–46.
Nellhaus, T. (2004) 'From embodiment to agency: cognitive science, critical realism, and communication frameworks', *Journal of Critical Realism*, 3: 103–32.
Newman, M. (2011) 'Calling transformative learning into question: some mutinous thoughts', *Adult Education Quarterly*, 62: 36–55.
Nicholls, S. (2006) *Writing the Body: Ways in Which Creative Writing can Facilitate a Felt Bodily Sense of Self*, unpublished Doctoral thesis, University of Sussex.
Oatley, K. (2007) 'Narrative modes of consciousness and selfhood', in P.D. Zelazo, M. Moskovitch and E. Thompson (eds), *The Cambridge Handbook of Consciousness*, Cambridge: Cambridge University Press.
Panksepp, J. (1998) *Affective Neuroscience: The Foundations of Human and Animal Emotions*, Oxford: Oxford University Press.
Paris, B. (1994) *Karen Horney: A Psychoanalyst's Search for Self-Understanding*, New Haven, CT and London: Yale University Press.
Petitmengin, C. (2007) 'Towards the source of thoughts: the gestural and transmodal dimension of lived experience', *Journal of Consciousness Studies*, 14: 54–82.
Platt, C.B. (2010) 'Voices from the other side: neuroscience, attachment theory, and the creative self', *The Jaynesian*, Winter: 11–14.
Porter Abbott, H. (2002) *The Cambridge Introduction to Narrative*, Cambridge: Cambridge University Press.
Qualley, D. (1997) *Turns of Thought: Teaching Composition as Reflexive Inquiry*, London: Heinemann.
Raz, A. and Buhle, J. (2006) 'Typologies of attentional networks', *Nature Neuroscience*, 7: 367–79.
Ricoeur, P. (1988) *Time as Narrative III*, trans. K. Blamey and D. Pellauer, Chicago, IL: Chicago University Press.

Rimmon-Kenan, S. (1996) *Narrative Fiction: Contemporary Poetics*, London and New York: Routledge.
Riso, D.R. and Hudson, R. (1996) *Personality Types*, New York: Houghton Mifflin.
Rochat, P. (2011) 'What is it like to be a newborn?', in S. Gallagher (ed.), *The Oxford Handbook of the Self*, Oxford: Oxford University Press.
Rogers, C. (1951) *Client-Centered Therapy*, Boston, MA: Houghton-Mifflin.
——(1989) 'The interpersonal relationship in the facilitation of learning', in H. Kirshenbaum and V.L. Henderson (eds), *The Carl Rogers Reader*, New York: Houghton-Mifflin.
Rose, G. (1978) 'The creativity of everyday life', in S.G. Grolnick and L. Barkin (eds), *Between Fantasy and Reality: Winnicott's Concepts of Transitional Objects and Phenomena*, Northvale, NJ: Jacob Aronson.
Ross, C.A. (1999) 'Subpersonalities and multiple personalities: a dissociative continuum?', in J. Rowan and M. Cooper (eds), *The Plural Self: Multiplicity in Everyday Life*, London: Sage.
Rothschild, B. (2000) *The Body Remembers: The Psychophysiology of Trauma and Trauma Treatment*, New York and London: W.W. Norton.
Rowan, J. (1990) *Sub-Personalities: The People Inside Us*, London: Routledge.
——(1999) 'The normal development of sub-personalities', in J. Rowan and M. Cooper (eds), *The Plural Self: Multiplicity in Everyday Life*, London: Sage.
Ruppert Johnson, R. (2003) 'Autobiography and transformative learning: narrative in search of self', *Journal of Transformative Education*, 1: 227–44.
Salk, J. (1985) *The Anatomy of Reality*, New York: Praeger.
Samuels, A. (1985) *Jung and the Post-Jungians*, London: Routledge and Kegan Paul.
Sass, L.A. (1992) *Madness and Modernism: Insanity in the Light of Modern Art, Literature and Thought*, Cambridge, MA: Harvard University Press.
Sayer, A. (2000) *Realism and Social Science*, London: Sage.
Schore, A. (1994) *Affect Regulation and the Origin of the Self*, Hillsdale, NJ and Hove, UK: Lawrence Erlbaum Associates.
Scott, D. (2010) *Education, Epistemology and Critical Realism*, London and New York: Routledge.
Sheets-Johnstone, M. (2009) *The Corporeal Turn*, Exeter: Imprint-Academic.
Shuttleworth, A. (2002) 'Turning towards a bio-psycho-social way of thinking', *European Journal of Psychotherapy and Counselling*, 5: 205–23.
Siegel, D. J. (1999) *The Developing Mind: How Relationships and the Brain Interact to Shape Who We Are*, New York and London: Guilford Press.
——(2003) 'An interpersonal neurobiology of psychotherapy: the developing mind and the resolution of trauma', in M.F. Solomon and D.J. Siegel (eds) *Healing Trauma: Attachment, Mind, Body and Brain*, New York and London: W.W. Norton.
——(2007) *The Mindful Brain: Reflection and Attunement in the Cultivation of Well-Being*, New York and London: W.W. Norton.
Siegel, J. (2005) *The Idea of the Self: Thought and Experience in Western Europe since the Seventeenth Century*, Cambridge: Cambridge University Press.
Smith, J.A., Flowers, P. and Larkin, M. (2009) *Interpretative Phenomenological Analysis: Theory, Method and Research*, London: Sage.
Solms, M. and Turnbull, O. (2000) *The Brain and the Inner World: An Introduction to the Neuroscience of Subjective Experience*, New York: Other Press.
Stacey, R. (2006) *Complexity and Group Processes: A Radically Social Understanding of Individuals*, Hove and New York: Brunner-Routledge.

Stern, D. (1998) *The Interpersonal World of the Infant*, London: Karnac Books.
Stockwell, P. (2002) *Cognitive Poetics*, London and New York: Routledge.
Suzuki, D. (1959) *Zen and Japanese Culture*, Princeton, NJ: Princeton University Press.
Symington, J. and Symington, N. (1996) *The Clinical Thinking of Wilfred Bion*, London and New York: Routledge.
Symonds, A. (1978) 'The psychodynamics of expansiveness in the success-oriented woman', *American Journal of Psychoanalysis*, 38: 195–205.
Taylor, E.W. (2001) 'Transformative learning theory: a neurobiological perspective of the role of emotions and unconscious ways of knowing', *International Journal of Lifelong Education*, 20: 218–36.
——(2007) 'An update of transformative learning theory: a critical review of the empirical research (1999–2005)', *International Journal of Lifelong Education*, 26(2): 173–91.
——(2009) 'Fostering transformative learning', in J. Mezirow and E.W. Taylor (eds), *Transformative Learning in Practice: Insights from Community, Workplace, and Higher Education*, San Francisco, CA: Jossey-Bass.
Taylor, E.W. and Jarecke, J. (2009) 'Looking forward by looking back: reflections on the practice of transformative learning', in J. Mezirow and E.W. Taylor (eds), *Transformative Learning in Practice: Insights from Community, Workplace, and Higher Education*, San Francisco, CA: Jossey-Bass.
Taylor, K. (2000) 'Teaching with developmental intention', in J. Mezirow and Associates, *Learning as Transformation: Critical Perspectives on a Theory in Progress*, San Francisco, CA: Jossey-Bass.
——(2006) 'Brain function and adult learning: implications for practice', in S. Johnson and K. Taylor (eds), *The Neuroscience of Adult Learning*, San Francisco, CA: Jossey-Bass.
Tershakovec, A. (2007) *The Mind: The Power that Changed the Planet*, Bloomington, IN and Milton Keynes: Authorhouse.
Thomas, A. and Chess, S. (1977) *Temperament and Development*, New York: Brunner.
Thompson, E. (2007) *Mind in Life: Biology, Phenomenology and the Sciences of Mind*, Cambridge, MA: Harvard University Press.
Todres, L. (2007) *Embodied Enquiry: Phenomenological Touchstones for Research, Psychotherapy, and Spirituality*, Basingstoke and New York: Palgrave.
Trevarthen, C. (2009) 'Commissurotomy and consciousness', in T. Bayner, A. Cleeremans and P. Wilken (eds), *The Oxford Companion to Consciousness*, Oxford: Oxford University Press.
Turner, F. and Pöppel, E. (1983) 'The neural lyre: poetic meter, the brain, and time', *Poetry*, 142: 277–309.
Varela, F., Rosch, E. and Thompson, E. (1991) *The Embodied Mind: Cognitive Science and Human Experience*, Cambridge, MA: MIT Press.
Ward, L.M. (2001) *Dynamical Cognitive Science*, Cambridge, MA: MIT Press.
Wegner, D. (2002) *The Illusion of Conscious Will*, Cambridge, MA and London: MIT Press.
Westkott, M. (1998) 'Horney, Zen and the real self', *American Journal of Psychoanalysis*, 58: 287–301.
Winnicott, D.W. (1958) 'The capacity to be alone', in *The Maturational Processes and the Facilitating Environment*, London: Hogarth, 1965.
——(1960) 'The parent–infant relationship', in *The Maturational Processes and the Facilitating Environment*, London: Hogarth, 1965.

—— (1971) *Playing and Reality*, London and New York: Routledge.

Wyatt-Brown, A.M. (1993) 'From the clinic to the classroom: D.W. Winnicott, James Britton, and the revolution in writing theory', in P.L. Rudnytsky (ed.), *Transitional Objects and Potential Spaces: Literary Uses of D.W. Winnicott*, New York: Columbia University Press.

Yorks, L. and Kasl, E. (2002) 'Toward a theory and practice for whole-person learning: reconceptualizing experience and the role of affect', *Adult Education Quarterly*, 52: 176–92.

—— (2006) 'I know more than I can say: a taxonomy for using expressive ways of knowing to foster transformative learning', *Journal of Transformative Education*, 4: 43–64.

Zelazo, P.D. and Cunningham, W.A. (2007) 'Executive function: mechanisms underlying emotion regulation', in P.P. Gross (ed.), *Handbook of Emotion Regulation*, New York and London: Guilford Press.

Zubin, D.A. and Hewitt, L.E. (1995) 'The deictic center: a theory of deixis in narrative', in J.F. Duchan, L.E. Hewitt. and G.A. Bruder (eds), *Deixis in Narrative: A Cognitive Science Perspective*, Hillsdale, NJ and Hove, UK: Lawrence Erlbaum.

Index

Locators in **bold** refer to figures/diagrams

Abbs, Peter 8
acceptance, self 70
accessing and objectifying the material 87
active/passive distinction, reflexivity 66–7
actual self 71, 88
adult learning: challenges 161–2; and therapeutic education 164–5
affective: core 68; ways of knowing 141, **142**
affectivity, mentalised 72, 100, 117, 128; *see also* emotion
agelessness imagery 45, 49
agency x, xiii, 26, 27, 80, 111, 172; autobiographical self 71–3; bodily-felt perspective 67–8, 69, 87–9, 93; change 63; learning 49; narrative stance 112–15; reflexivity 73–5; relationship with structure 115–16; Susanna 57; ways of knowing **142**, 143
Alhadeff-Jones, Michel 10
alienation from self 87, 112
anger: defences 84; freewriting exercise 104, 105; group work 126, 127–8; psychotherapy 165; reflection 135; repressed 21–3, 24, 26, 27, 86; towards tutors 156
anxiety 40; and compliance 84–5; defences 82–4, 156
Anzieu, D. 55
Archer, Margaret 67, 77, 78, 130, 145
arts, role in transformative learning 167
assertion, self 85, 86, 126, 127, 130
assessment, CWPD programme 160–1, 170
assimilation 139

attachment to tutors 156
attention: selective 73; shifts 74–5, 76, 107, 111
authenticity 16, 63; group work 120, 122, 124, 128; Maria 45; psychodynamic theory 78, 86, 89; reflection 133, 136; reflexivity 106, 112; Simon 35; self-expression 19
author-self: *see* writer-self
autobiographical 'I' 68, 70–4, 78; and core self 80, 94, 107–8; fragmentation vs. multiple self 89–90; and reflexivity 74–5; and transformative learning 171
autobiography, fictional: *see* creative life writing
awareness: receptive 134; self 113

bad mother 113
Bakhtin, Mikhail 32, 65, 104, 110, 137
'Beginnings' (Susanna) 5, 52, 58, 104
being in the present 55
being oneself 25; *see also* self-expression
benevolent policeman metaphor 107
Bertalanffy, L. von 76
betweenness 77
Bion, Wilfred xi, 44, 99, 128
bio-psycho-social framework xi, 64, 101, 141, 172
black and white thinking 77
blank slate metaphor 67
blocks, writing 16, 19–21, 30, 40; freewriting exercise 104, 105
bodily-felt perspective 49, 50, 69–70; agency 67–70, 87–9, 93, 116; and autobiographical self 72–4, 80, 107–8;

Index 189

awareness 171; creative life writing 113; disconnection from 91; neuroscience of 76; psychotherapy 165; reflection 139; reflexivity 74–5; self in language 107; Susanna 59; trauma 80–2; trusting 112; *see also* embodied self-experience; felt sense
Bollas, Christopher xi, 104, 112
bottom-up processes 92; dynamic systems theory 76–7; group work 121; learning 124, 171; meaning-making 106; *see also* bodily-felt perspective
boundaries: CWPD course 154; self-identity 41–3
Boyd, Robert 10, 63, 64, 66, 67, 79, 119, 121, 134, 151, 155, 156, 171
brain hemispheres 173; and agency 88; creative life writing 104–10; dissociative identity disorder 90; dynamic systems theory 75–8; group work 121, 130; integration, self 93; and reflexivity 116, 140–1; therapeutic education 169; and transformative learning 171; and trauma 80–2; ways of knowing 143
Brookfield, Stephen 134
Brown, Gordon (critical realist) 9, 10, 99, 117, 119, 129, 136
Bruner, J. S. 32, 137

case studies: *see* student perspectives
Catholic upbringing 24, 40, 48, 83
change trajectories 77; *see also* transformative learning
chaotic space 114
childhood memories, Maria 40, 42
childhood words/sayings writing exercise 6
chora, semiotic 43, 138
Cixous, Hélène 46
Claire (student) 17–22, 26; psychodynamic theory 82, 83, 86, 91; reflexivity/reflection 111–12, 116, 133; transformative learning challenges 158–9, 161; therapeutic education 166
Claudia (student) 18, 21, 24–7; psychodynamic theory 83, 86, 92, 93; reflexivity/reflection 109, 121, 123, 127, 130, 135–6, 143; therapeutic education 166
closing down of psyche: and anxiety 83; control 86–7; and fixity 38; trauma 80–2; *see also* opening-up
cognitive constructions 63

cognitive neuroscience: *see* neuroscience
Cohen Park, Christine (tutor) xiv, xvi, 2, 4, 7, 121, 123, 128, 156, 160, 167; writing exercises 175–7
collaboration: *see* group work
Coltart, Nina 55
community of writers 100, 101
competitiveness 121
compliance 83, 84–5, 86, 88, 89
concepts of self: *see* self-concepts
conceptual frameworks 32
confabulation 77, 90–1
confidence: *see* self confidence
conflicts, inner 27; role in creativity 34–5, 39
consciousness: dynamic systems theory 75–8; expansion 63–4, 66; studies 11; *see also* autobiographical 'I'; bodily-felt perspective; expanded psyche
constructivism 79
containment/holding 136, 149, 173; and agency 172; bodily-felt-self 49; definitions 99–100; diaries/journals 132–3, 133; group work 120, 122, 124, 129–30; learning environments 101; Maria 40–1, 43–4, 138; reflection 134; reflexivity 143; self in time 111; Simon 137; sub-personalities 91–2; Susanna 55, 57; transformative learning challenges 152–3, 155
Contexts for Practice course 4, 57, 138, 153, 160
control, psychic 15, 16–19, 20, 21; and creativity 86–7; creative life writing 104–6; and freedom dynamic 38; Simon 30, 34; sub-personalities 91–2; *see also* opening-up
cooking metaphor 16, 17
core self: *see* bodily-felt perspective; felt sense
core states, ways of knowing **142**, 143
counselling 153, 161
counter transference 156–7
cracking-up of the psyche 104, 138
Cranton, Patricia 10, 79, 164
creating the future self 104
creative life writing xvi, 1–3, 103; brain hemispheres 104–6, 107–8, 109–10; definition ix; narrative stance 112–15; practising reflexivity in the text 115–17; self in language 106–8; self in time 108–12, 116; *see also* writing exercises

Index

Creative Writing and Personal Development (CWPD) programme ix–x, 1–3; admissions interviews 155; course structure 3–5; diaries/journals 132–4; identity 7–11; and psychoanalysis/psychotherapy 162, 165–8; *see also* writing exercises

Creative Writing and Personal Development courses: *see Contexts for Practice*; *Creative Writing and the Self*; *Independent Study*; *Projects: Practical and Theoretical*; *Writing and Groups*; *Writing for Personal Development*; *Writing Practice*

Creative Writing and the Self course xv, 3, 32, 137

creativity 21; chaotic space 114; closing down of psyche 80; embodied 33, 40; playfulness 86; role of conflicts 34–5

Creme, Phyllis xvii, 101, 133, 173

critical realism xii–xiii

critical reflection: *see* reflection/reflectivity

criticism, self 155

crossdisciplinary approaches xi

cultural self-concepts 82

CWPD programme: *see* Creative Writing and Personal Development programme

cycles of transformation 77, **142**, 144

Damasio, Antonio xii, 32, 68, 71, 73, 74, 106–9

dance metaphor 45, 51–2, 65

Danielian, Jack xvii, 70

dark material 125; Maria 42; Simon 33, 34, 35, 36, 86; Susanna 52; *see also* shadow

daydreaming 73, 107

death metaphor 46

decentering of the ego 64

deep change, group work 122–5

deep learning 167

defences, psychic 172; anger 84; anxiety 82–4, 85, 156; and psychotherapy 165, 167; to self-expression 113; splitting 92; trauma 80–2; *see also* hyperreflexivity

definitions: containment/holding 99–100; creative life writing ix; embodied-experiential learning 134; reflectivity 67; reflexivity 66–8; therapeutic education 164

deixis (pointing function of language) 115

dependence on tutors 156

depression 40, 43, 47, 152

depth psychology 9, 79

development, personal 24, 30, 39, 45

developmental creative writing 1

dialogic writing exercises 104, 117

dialogic relationships 65; *see also* reflexivity

dialogues: embodied experiential learning/critical reflection 134–6; fictional 30–1, 35–6; internal 67, 93

diaries/journals 132–4, 136, 172; containment/holding 138; and reflexivity 143

'Dictionary Pieces' (Simon) 38

Dirkx, John 9, 10, 64, 65, 67, 79, 103, 129, 169, 170, 171

discernment 67, 151; and change 63; *see also* reflexivity

disclosure, illness 50–1, 54, 56, 59, 65, 124

discourse, transformative learning as 170

disembodied cognition 168–9

disorienting dilemmas 101, 103, 106, 143, 168; in group work 122, 123, 129

displacement of painful feelings 81

dissociative identity disorder 90

distancing 103

DNA helix metaphor 144

dominant self-concept 20, 27–8, 115, 144; psychodynamic theory 91–2; shadow 125

drama therapy 166

drum imagery 51–2

Duet (The Development of University English Teaching Project) 8

dynamic now 108–9, 112, 121, 123

dynamic systems theory xii; learning environments 129–30; psyche as dynamic system 75–8; *see also* psychodynamic theory

Ecclestone, Kathryn xii, 168, 169, 170

edge, the 167

ego: and autobiographical self 71; decentering 64, 67

Elbow, Peter 6

embodied creativity 33, 40

embodied-experiential learning 77; critical reflection dialogue 134–6, 139–40; Maria 43–5; and therapeutic education 164; ways of knowing 141–3, **142**; writing exercises 109

embodied realism xii–xiii, xv, 11

embodied self-experience 15, 16, 19, 28; fluidity 44; reflexivity 57; *see also* bodily-felt perspective; felt sense
emergent properties xiii
'Emily's Gift' (Maria) 46–9
emotion 9; and change 63; neuroscience of 76; regulation 72–3, 74; repressed 21–8, 92, 111; role in learning 168–70; *see also* bodily-felt perspective; mentalised affectivity
emotional opening-up 151–3; *see also* opening-up of the psyche
empirical self 71
empowerment 111
equilibrium 46
ethics xv
executive function 73, 74
exercises, writing: *see* writing exercises
exile 41, 42
expanded psyche 63–4, 66, 70, 73, 108–9; group work 124; managing 26–7; and reflexivity 74–5
expansiveness 89, 92–4; and splitting 85, 86–7
expectations of the course 154
experiential grounding 43–5
experiential knowing 141, **142**
experiential writing exercises 109; *see also* embodied-experiential learning
expertise, tutors 157–8, 160
exposure: *see* self-exposure
expressive knowing pathway **142**
extended consciousness: *see* expanded psyche
extensive research xiii–xiv

facilitation of learning: group work 127–9; modelling 157
fantasy, and imagination 117
fear: of exposure 19–21, 59, 89, 133, 135; of self-expression 122
feasting symbolism 42–3
feedback 124, 158–60
feeling 9; mode 73–4; of knowing 69, 74
feelings, thinking 137–9
felt sense 139; dynamic now 109; learning 134, 153, 168–9; meaning 80; self in language 106–8; ways of knowing 143; wholeness 88, 107; *see also* bodily-felt perspective; embodied self-experience
Fenwick, Tara 129, 134
fiction, value of 103
fictional autobiography: *see* creative life writing
fictional dialogues 30–1
first-person body: *see* bodily-felt perspective
'Five Years On' (Susanna) 53
fluidity/flexibility 16, 18, 21, 28; diaries/journals 133; group work 130; leading edge of the psyche 93–4; metaphors 36–9; psychodynamic theory 80; reflection 138; reflexivity 70, 73, 77; self-experience 44; self sense 173; Susanna 56–7, 59, 65
Fonagy, Peter xi, 72, 75, 100, 117, 128
food: metaphor 124; symbolism 42–3
forms, concepts, definitions, categories, distinctions rules 80
fragmentation of personality: grieving/insecurity 152; Maria 44, 45, 46; vs. multiple self 89–91; role in creativity 34–5, 38, 39; *see also* splitting
frames of reference 10, 63, 64, 170–1
free indirect style 36, 47
freedom 17, 27
Freewriting writing exercise 6, 104, 105, 106
freezing of the psyche 81
frozen identity 50–1
Future Self exercise 6, 7, 53, 104, 111, 112, 114, 116, 122, 128

game show, virtual reality 114–15
gender differences, transformative change 29
Gendlin, Eugene 80, 106, 107, 108, 134, 139, 141, 153
generative narcissism 112, 113
genomic unconscious 70
'Ghost Writer' (Simon) 31, 33
Giddens, Anthony 66
goal-directed group structures 130
going with the flow 16
good child narrative 21–2, 47, 82, 88
good mother 113
good-enough: mother 99; teacher 99, 129
grasshopper mind metaphor 29, 30, 38
grieving 63, 151, 152; expression 23–4
groundedness 78
group work xvi, 119; developing trust 119–22; facilitation of learning 127–9; reflexivity 129–30, 143; relationality 125–7; structured space for deep change 122–5

growing edge 143
Gunnlaugson, Olen 11, 74
gypsy imagery 44, 45, 86

Harriet (student) 18, 22; psychodynamic theory 83, 84, 91; reflexivity 105, 111, 125–6; transformative learning 156, 158
Hartill, Graham 5–6
Hayes, Dennis xii, 168
hemispheres, brain: *see* brain hemispheres
higher consciousness: *see* autobiographical 'I'
holding, definition 99–100; *see also* containment/holding
holism/wholeness: bodily-felt sense 88, 107; brain hemispheres 107–8; creative life writing 115; dominant self-concepts 91–2; dynamic systems theory 76; learning 9; Maria 42; mental models 92, 93; self 49
Horney, Karen xi, xii, xiii, xvii, 28, 69–70, 71, 73, 84, 112, 156, 171; life solutions 85–91, 125
humour 35–6
hyperreflexivity 92, 109, 112, 113, 143, 144; *see also* defences

'I' *see* autobiographical 'I'
idealisation 88–9, 109
identity/identity shifts 64, 67; bodily-felt perspective 69; boundary transgressions 41–3; compliance 82–5; frozen 50–1; grieving/insecurity 152; new personal typography 54; professional 20, 91, 113; Simon 34–5; social 67; *see also* dominant self-concept
Illeris, K. 66, 164
illness: disclosure 50–1, 54, 56, 59, 65, 124; identity 81
image schemas 116
imagery 9; agelessness 45, 49; drum 51–2; gypsy 44, 45, 86; Mongolian yurt dwellers 44; music 51–2; ocean 55; self in language 107; shelter 54–5; snake 51–2
imaginal approach to learning 103
imagination: and fantasy 117; space for 30–4
imaginative body 74, 134
Imagined Reader writing exercise 7, 31, 33

implicit bodily sense: *see* bodily-felt perspective; felt sense
implied author 28, 32, 118
Independent Study course 5, 16, 18, 22, 174; assessment 160–1; learning environments 100; Maria 46; opening-up of the psyche 99; reflection 137, 138, 139; and reflexivity 144; Simon 32, 37; Susanna 58; therapeutic education 166; transformative learning challenges 153, 159
individuation 79
integration, self 16, 35–6, 63, 93; dynamic systems theory 76; real self 70; and trauma 82
integrity 63
intensive research xiii–xiv
internal gesture 107
interpersonal learning-within-relationship **142**
interpersonal school xi; *see also* group work; relationality
interpretative phenomenology (IPA) xiv–xv
interviews: course applicants 155; interactive xiv
intrapersonal whole-person learning **142**
intrapsychic rapport 112
intuition 16, 19; psychodynamic theory 80, 82, 83; and reflectivity 133, 134, 139–40; and reflexivity 67, 77, 103, 107, 115

James, William 70, 71, 72
Jarvis, Christine 103, 168
Jill (student) 17, 20, 22; psychodynamic theory 82, 91; reflection 133, 144; reflexivity 120, 121–2, 124, 126–7, 130; transformative learning 152, 165
Johnson, Mark xii, xiii, 69, 74, 107, 116, 141
Johnson, Rebecca 103
journals. *see* diaries/journals
Jungian perspectives 9, 10, 64, 125, 136

Kasl, Elizabeth xvii, 9, 141, **142**, 143, 164
Keats, John 124
Kegan, Robert 143, 170
kinaesthetic melodies 69
Kristeva, Julia 43, 46, 110, 138
Kuhn, T. 79

Lakoff, George xii, xiii, xv
laminar/layered structures 99, 100, 136
language 43; autobiographical self 68, 70; Harriet 105; Maria 48; self in 106–8
language-based autobiographical 'I': *see* autobiographical 'I'
Lapidus organisation 1, 158
leading edge of psyche 76, 77, 88, 92, 93–4
learning 27; agency 49; consequences of splitting 40–1; diaries/journals 132–4; embodied experiential 134–6; environments 99–101, 124, 129–30; group facilitation 127–9; from mistakes 57; reconceptualising 55–6; and reflexivity 140–5, **142**; *see also* transformative learning
left hemisphere: *see* brain hemispheres
levels, ways of knowing 141–5, **142**
liberating lost parts of the personality 24–6
life changes, Susanna 50
life solutions 85, 87–8, 90, 125
liminal space 143
listening 121, 123, 128, 134
loosening of psychic control: *see* opening-up
loss 24, 50–1, 165
Lucy (student) 20–1, 24, 106; psychodynamic theory 84, 87, 91, 93; transformative learning 152–3

macroscopic dimensions, learning environments 100–1
magpie metaphor 17
managing the expanded psyche 26–7
Mantel, Hilary 54
mapping, brain 68, 76
Maria (student) xv, 40, 83, 116, 152; bodily-felt-self 49; diaries/journals 132–3; experiential grounding 43–5; feedback 158; freewriting exercise 104–5; group work 121, 124; identity boundary transgressions 41–3; imagery 45–6, 86; integration 93; narrator self 46–9; psychodynamic theory 91; reflection 138; self as process 43; splitting 40–1; writer self 92
McGilchrist, Iain xii, 76, 80, 90, 91, 94, 107, 108, 110, 114, 117, 130, 140, 141, 169, 173
Mathison, Jane 11, 134

meaning-making 174; bottom-up 106; felt sense 80; personal 10; self in language 107
Megan (student) 20, 86, 87, 105, 126
memory, working 73
mental frameworks, scaffolding 32, 137–8
mental models 77; holistic 92, 93; idealisation 109; top-down control 173–4
mentalised affectivity 72, 100, 117, 128
metacognition 66, 73
Metanoia Institute, Bristol 162
metaphor xv, 9; benevolent policeman 107; cooking 16, 17; dance 45, 51–2, 65; DNA helix 144; food 124; grasshopper mind 29, 30, 38; magpie 17; music 69; prairie/ranch 33, 38, 65, 92, 116; reflexivity 38; sea anemone 135; seeing my thinking 114; self 32, 35; self as writer 33–4; Simon's use of 36–9; stunned fog 23, 81; visual 27; water 37–8; writing 46
Mezirow, Jack 63–5, 79, 101, 134, 144, 151, 164, 168
Milner, Marion xi, 73–4, 107–8, 111, 134–5
mind-body relationality 107; *see also* bodily-felt perspective; embodied self-experience; felt sense
mindfulness 74, 171
Miranda (student) 19–20, 22–3, 81–2, 120, 139
mistakes: learning from 57; making 18
modelling: facilitation of learning 128, 157; ways of knowing 141–5, **142**; *see also* mental models
Mongolian yurt dwellers imagery 44
Moskowitz, Cheryl (tutor) xiv, xvi, 2, 6–7, 128, 130, 155, 156–7, 160, 167–8
'Mother-Food' (Maria) 42
mourning: *see* grieving
multi-dimensional learning 167, 173
multiple personality disorder (dissociative identity disorder) 90
multiple self 54–5; vs. fragmentation of personality 89–91; reflection 138–9; *see also* splitting
multiple ways of knowing 141, **142**
'Murder' (Simon) 36, 38, 54, 65
music 109–10; imagery 51–2; metaphor 69

Myers, J. G. 10, 63, 66, 67, 79, 121, 134, 151, 156
mythopoetic approach to learning 103

narrated time 108–9
narrative self 70, 109; Maria 46–9; *see also* autobiographical self
narrative stance, creative life writing 112–15
need to be right 77
negative capability 124
Neisser, U. 32
neuroscience of the self xi, xii, 11, 64, 68–9, 110; *see also* brain hemispheres
new personal typography 54
Newman, Michael 170
Nicholls, Sophie xvii, 1, 33, 74, 110
non-learning 79–80, 154–5
normal polypsychism 90
normative dimension, learning environments 100–1

object relations theory xi
objectifying the material 87
objective reframing 63
ocean imagery 55
open-ended design, course 129
opening-up of the psyche 15–16, 28, 92–4, 99; attention shifts 74–5; diaries/journals 133; fear of 89; learning environments 129–30; reflection 135; and reflexivity 77; Susanna 50, 51, 52, 55, 56, 58; transformative learning challenges 151–3
ordered freedom 107
Ostrelande (Land of the Other) 42
otherness 42, 44
ownership, bodily-felt perspective 69

paradigm shifts 64, 79
passive/active distinction, reflexivity 66–7
pathologisation 79
'Pencil' (Simon) 37, 53, 65, 138
perfectionism 86–7
perseveration 77
personal development 24, 30, 39, 45
personal identity: *see* identity/identity shifts
personality, fragmentation 34–5; integration 35–6
perspectives, transformation 66

Petitmengin, Claire 69, 108, 141, 174
photography, Maria 45, 46–7
playfulness 35, 38, 86, 117
poetry 6, 41–2, 105, 107, 110
practical ways of knowing 141, **142**
prairie metaphor 33, 38, 65, 92, 116
pre-reflective bodily self-awareness 141, **142**
presentational (imaginal or expressive) ways of knowing 141, **142**
pretend modes of functioning 117
pride system 88, 125
primordial feelings 68
professional identity 20, 91, 113
projections, self-criticism 135
propositional (conceptual) ways of knowing 141, **142**
protoself 68, 71, 76
Proust writing exercises 42, 106
psyche as dynamic system 75–8; *see also* expanded psyche
psychic control: *see* control, psychic
psychic multiplicity: *see* multiple self
psychic shifts 34; *see also* attention shifts; identity/identity shifts
psychodynamic theory xv, 71, 79–80; agency and core self 87–9; anxiety defences 82–4; compliance 83, 84–5, 86, 88, 89; dominant self-concepts 91–2; fragmentation vs. multiple self 89–91; loosening of psychic control 92–4; splitting 86–7; trauma 80–2; *see also* dynamic systems theory
psychotherapy 117, 149, 159, 161, 164–5; and CWPD programme 162, 165–8; *see also* therapeutic education

Qualley, Donna 66
quasi-closed systems 129–30

rage: *see* anger
ranch metaphor 33, 38, 92, 116
real self 69–70
realism 77
reality constructions 10
reanimation, Susanna 51–2
rebellion: childhood 24–5, 105; student mini-rebellion 127, 128, 130
receptive awareness 134
receptive listening 121, 123, 128, 134
receptivity 63, 121, 134
recognition 63

Index   195

reconnection, with subconscious/unconscious mind 64
reflection/reflectivity xvi, 63, 65, 67, 77, 172–3; definition 67; diaries/journals 132–4; and embodied experiential learning 134–6, 137, 139–40, 144; and reflexivity 67, 140–5, **142**; and therapeutic education 164; thinking feelings 137–9; ways of knowing **142**
reflective function 72
reflexivity xv–xvi, 28, 65–6; and agency 68–70, 73–5; creative life writing 115–17; definition 66–8; dynamic systems theory 75–8; group facilitation 128–30; higher consciousness 70–3; metaphor 38; and reflection/reflectivity 67, 140–5, **142**; self-experience 57; writing exercises 104
relationality: and compliance 84–5; group work 125–7; Susanna 58–9; writing process 120; *see also* group work
repressed emotions: anger 86; childhood 40, 48; expression 21–8, 92, 111; and transformative learning 65
resistance, to self-expression 113; *see also* defences
responsibility for self 165
Rhiannon (student) 17, 20, 21, 25, 27; psychodynamic theory 83, 91, 93; reflexivity 113–15, 133
right hemisphere: *see* brain hemispheres
Rogers, Carl 55, 164
rule-bound perfectionism 86–7
Ruth (student) 18, 20, 21; psychodynamic theory 81, 91; reflexivity 104, 120, 139; transformative learning 153

sadness, expression 23
safe spaces xvi, 20, 92, 99, 109, 117, 172; group work 121, 124, 127, 129; Maria 44; psychodynamic theory 81, 84, 85, 87, 89; reflection 132; Susanna 51–5, 59; transformative learning 154; *see also* containment/holding
Salway, Sarah (tutor) xiv, xvi, 121, 128, 144, 155, 156
Sampson, Fiona 1
Sass, Louis 92
scaffolding, mental frameworks 32, 137–8
sea anemone metaphor 135
see[ing] my thinking metaphor 114
selective attention 73

self xiii; actual 71, 88; affective core 68; constructions 10; formation 79; in language 106–8; metaphors 32–5; as process 43, 54–5, 70, 110; sense/concept of 67; as source 104; in time 108–12, 116; validation 93; *see also* autobiographical 'I'; dominant self-concept; embodied self-experience; identity/identity shifts
self-acceptance 70
self-agency: *see* agency
self-assertion 85, 86, 126, 127, 130
self-awareness 113
self-belief 21
self-concepts 67; defensive 92; dominant 20, 27–8; identity shifts 64; and psychotherapy 165; social 64, 71, 91, 93
self-confidence 16, 17, 19, 21, 25, 26; Maria 40, 49; psychodynamic theory 83, 84, 86, 87; reflexivity 120, 121; Simon 39; Susanna 50, 58; transformative learning challenges 154–5, 159, 160, 165
self-criticism 155
self-dialogues 31
self-exposure through creative writing 65, 87; fear of 19–21, 59, 89, 133, 135
self-expression: authenticity 19; fear of 122; repressed emotions, expression 21–4, 25; resistance 113
self-identity: *see* identity/identity shifts
Self as Source writing exercise 7, 26, 85, 113
self-on-the-page 112–15
self-punishment 89, 90
self-regulation 72–3, 74
self-reliance 58
self-respect 56
self-therapy, therapeutic education as 167
self-transforming mind 143
self-work 9
selfing 49
semiotic 44; chora 43, 138; writing exercises 103–4, 106, 107, 109–13, 143
shadow 56, 125, 136; *see also* dark material
shared mental states 130
Sheets-Johnstone, Maxine 69, 80, 81
shelter imagery 54–5
shifts, attentional 74–5, 76, 107, 111
shoulds 88, 90, 111

Siegel, Daniel 74, 75, 76, 77, 78, 81, 82, 92, 93, 94, 129, 134
significant learning 164
Simon (student) xv, 29, 84, 87, 116; compliance 85; conflicts 34–5, 38, 39; fictional dialogues 30–1; group work 122; metaphor use 36–9; personas 35–6; psychodynamic theory 91, 92; reflection 137–8; space for the imagination 32–4; transformative learning challenges 152, 153; writer self 65, 86, 93, 104; writing process problems 29–30
snake imagery 51–2
social agents 77
social identity 67
social self-concepts 64, 71, 91, 93
soft structures 130, 133, 136, 161
somatic marker hypothesis 168
soul work 9
sound master model 93
space for the imagination 30–4
spatial modes of consciousness 73–4
'Speak Properly' (Megan) 105
spiritual me 71
splitting: creative 113; and learning 40–1; sub-personalities 85, 86–7; *see also* multiple self
spontaneity 15, 16, 17
Stacey (student) 20; psychodynamic theory 83, 91; reflexivity 104, 120, 123, 133
Stella (student) 18, 22, 27; psychodynamic theory 84, 91; reflexivity 104–5, 112–13; transformative learning 152, 166
Stern, Daniel 69
structure, and agency xiii, 94, 115–16, 130
stickiness 50, 59, 77, 143; *see also* hyperreflexivity
student perspectives: *see* Claire; Claudia; Harriet; Jill; Lucy; Maria; Megan; Miranda; Rhiannon; Ruth; Simon; Stacey; Stella; Susanna; Tess
stunned fog metaphor 23, 81
subconscious sources of creative writing 30, 32, 33, 34
subject-in-process 110
subjective reframing 63, 151
subjectivity, Kristeva on 43
sub-personalities 24, 85, 86–7, 89, 165

Susanna (student) xv, 50, 91, 92, 116; diaries/journals 133; disclosure 65; freewriting exercise 104; future self 53; group work 120, 122, 124, 128–30; integration 93; learning environments 100, 101; loss/illness 50–1; reanimation 51–2; reconceptualising learning 55–6; reflexivity 57; relationality 58–9; self as process 54–5; self in time 109, 111; therapeutic education 165–6; time perception 56–7; trauma 81
symbolic: Kristeva on 43; realm 138
systems theory: *see* dynamic systems theory

Taylor, Edward W. 10, 11, 64, 79, 128, 168
Taylor, Kathleen 65, 145
teaching approaches 174
temperament 83–4, 85, 86
temporality: *see* time
tension between opposites 42
Tershakovec, Andrew xii, 75, 76, 77, 81, 88, 93, 109
Tess (student) 16, 20, 21, 22, 26, 124; psychodynamic theory 83–4, 86; transformative learning 166–7
theory, literary 32; experiential grounding 43–5; Maria 46; Susanna 55
theory of mind 76
therapeutic education xii, xvi, 162, 164–5; pros and cons 168–70; and psychotherapy 165–8; and transformative learning 170–1
thinking feelings 15, 100, 137–9
thinking mode 73–4, 134–5
This is How I Shelter, When I Shelter writing exercise 54
This is What I Remember writing exercise 55–6, 124
This is Where I Risk, What I Risk writing exercise 135
This is Who I Am writing exercise 44
time: perception 56–7; self in 108–11
time-space levels 116
top-down control 112; dynamic systems theory 76–8; meaning-making 106; model of thinking 173–4; self-regulation 88, 92
Tosey, Paul 11, 134
transference 125, 156–7
transformative learning xii, xv, xvi, 9–11, 15–16, 53, 63, 64; adult learning

implications 161–2; assessment 160–1; blocks 16, 19–21; emotional opening-up 21–8, 92, 111, 151–3; feedback 158–60; liberating lost parts of the personality 24–6; loosening cognitive control 15, 16–21; managing the expanded psyche 26–7; multiple ways of knowing 141; non-learning 154–5; professional identity 27–8; theory 77; and therapeutic education 170–1; tutors 155–8
transgressions, boundaries of self-identity 41–3
transitional spaces 172; diaries/journals as 133
trauma 80–2
travel memoir, Susanna 58
trust, developing 144; group work 119–22, 127–8, 130; Simon 137
trusting core consciousness 112
turning points, Susanna 53, 58
tutors: expertise 157–8, 160; group work 127–9; transformative learning challenges 155–8, 161–2; see also Cohen Park; Moskowitz; Salway
two-tier model of consciousness 76

unconscious mind: integration 64; neuroscience of 76; prairie metaphor 33, 38, 65, 92, 116
universal sense of self 67

validation 27, 127; by others 88; self 93; Susanna 56
vicious circles 37, 88, 143, xi

virtual reality game show 114–15
visual metaphors 27
vitality affects 69
voice, writing 120; see also writer self
voicing criticism 156

water: metaphor 37–8
ways of knowing, multiple 141, 142
Web of Words writing exercise 5–6, 52, 173
website, Lapidus organisation 1
West, Linden xiv, xvii, 164
wholeness: see holism/wholeness
whole-person epistemology 141
wild prairie metaphor 33, 38, 65, 92, 116
Winnicott, Donald xi, 40, 99, 133
working memory 73
writer self: Maria 40, 46; Simon 29, 32–3, 38, 65, 86, 92–3, 104, 138
writing exercises 5–7, 103–4; Cohen Park 175–7; embodied-experiential learning 109; semiotic 103–4, 106, 107, 109–13, 143; see also Freewriting; Future Self; Imagined Reader; Proust; Self as Source; This is How I Shelter, When I Shelter; This is What I Remember; This is Where I Risk, What I Risk; This is Who I Am; Web of Words
writing metaphors 46
writing process, problems 29–30
writing voice 120; see also writer self

'Yan, Tan, Tethera, Methera, Pimp' (Harriet) 105
Yorks, Lyle xvii, 9, 141, **142**, 143, 164